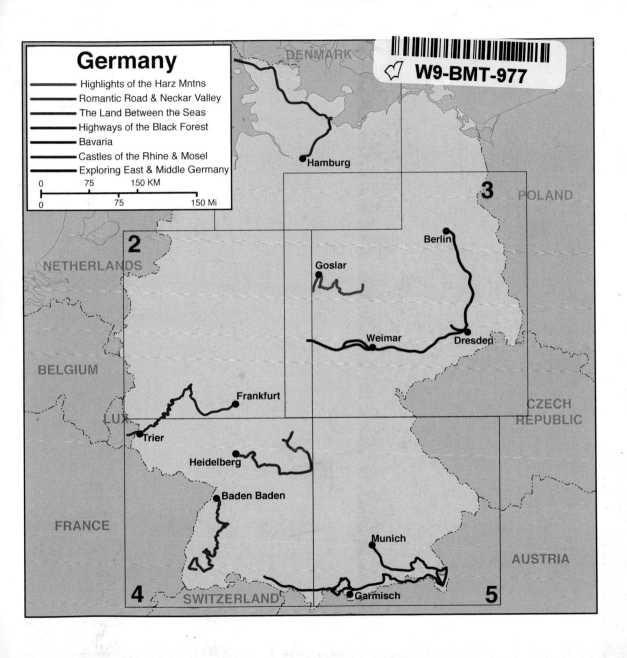

Germany

- Highlights of the Harz Mntns
- Romantic Road & Neckar Valley
- The Land Between the Seas
- Highways of the Black Forest
- Bavaria
- Castles of the Rhine & Mosel
- Exploring East & Middle Germany

| 0 | 75 | 150 KM |
| 0 | 75 | 150 Mi |

DENMARK

POLAND

Hamburg

3

2

NETHERLANDS

Goslar

Berlin

BELGIUM

Weimar

Dresden

CZECH
REPUBLIC

LUX

Frankfurt

Trier

Heidelberg

Baden Baden

Munich

AUSTRIA

FRANCE

4

SWITZERLAND

Garmisch

5

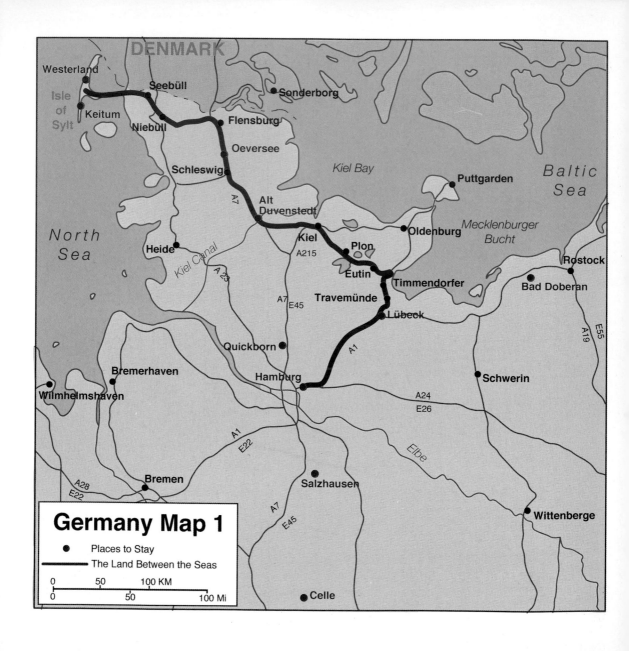

Germany Map 1

● Places to Stay

── The Land Between the Seas

0   50   100 KM
0   50   100 Mi

Germany Map 2

●   Places to Stay

────   Castles of the Rhine & Mosel

0	50	100 KM
0	50	100 Mi

Mittellandkan

Osnabruck

Hannover   E30   A2

A2   E30

Bielefeld

Weser

Münster

Ems

E34

A7 E45

Rhine

Marienthal

Lembeck

Uslar

Sababurg

Gottingen

Duisburg

Essen

Dortmund

Kettwig

Kassel

Dusseldorf

Waldeck

Spangenberg

Cologne

A4

E40   E35   A3

Siegen

Bad Hersfeld

A4

E40

Aachen

Stolberg

Bonn

Giessen

A5

E40

Fulda

E451

E45   A7

Koblenz

Braubach

A 3

A 48   Burg Eltz

St. Goar

Kloster Eberbach

Cochem

Oberwesel

Oestrich-Winkel

Wiesbaden

Frankfurt

Moselle

Beilstein

Assmannshausen

A 66

Mainz

Bernkastel-Kues

Zell

Rüdesheim

Hattenheim

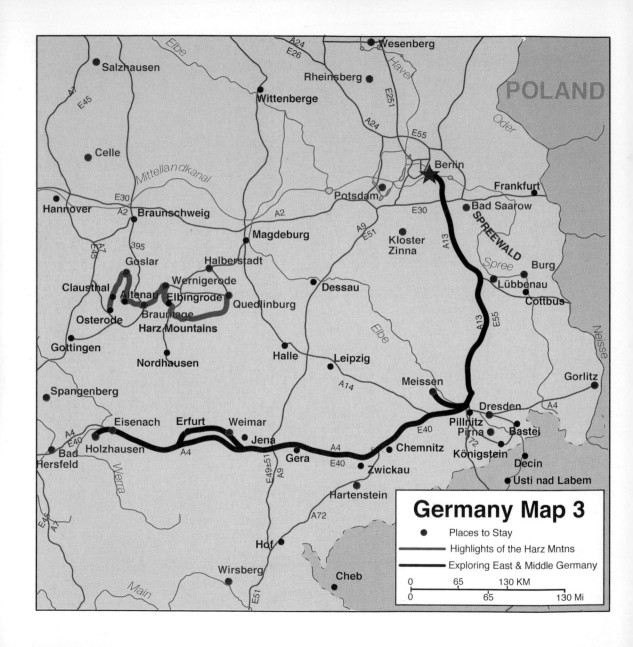

POLAND

Salzhausen

Elbe

A24
E26

Wesenberg

Rheinsberg

Wittenberge

Havel

E251

Celle

Mittellandkanal

A24

E55

Berlin

Frankfurt

Hannover

E45

A7

E30

A2

Braunschweig

Potsdam

Bad Saarow

395

A2

E30

A13

SPREEWALD

Goslar

Halberstadt

Magdeburg

A9
E51

Kloster
Zinna

Spree

Burg

Clausthal

Wernigerode

Altenau

Elbingrode

Quedlinburg

Dessau

Lübbenau

Cottbus

Osterode

Braunlage

Harz Mountains

A13

E55

Neisse

Gottingen

Halle

Elbe

Leipzig

Nordhausen

Gorlitz

Spangenberg

A14

Meissen

Dresden

A4

Eisenach

Erfurt

Weimar

Pillnitz

Bastei

A4
E40

Holzhausen

Jena

A4

E40

Pirna

Chemnitz

Königstein

Bad
Hersfeld

Werra

A4

E49±51

A9

Gera

E40

Zwickau

Decin

Usti nad Labem

E45

A7

Hartenstein

A72

Hof

Main

E51

Wirsberg

Cheb

Germany Map 3

● Places to Stay

— Highlights of the Harz Mntns

— Exploring East & Middle Germany

0   65   130 KM

0   65   130 Mi

Germany Map 4

- ● Places to Stay
- ─── Highways of the Black Forest
- ━━━ Bavaria
- ━━━ Castles of the Rhine & Mosel
- ━━━ Romantic Road & Neckar Valley

0   50   100 KM
0   50   100 Mi

Luxembourg
Trier
Horbruch
Moselle
A61
E31
A 5
Laudenbach
A3 E41
Volkach
Würzburg
Tauberbischofsheim
Iphofen
Kallstadt
A 62
Mannheim
Amorbach
Bad Mergentheim
Weikersheim
Deidesheim
Heidelberg
Schloss Guttenberg
Bad Wimpfen
A81
Creglingen
Rothenburg
Feuchtwangen
Saarbrucken
Heinsheim
Neuenstadt
Friedrichsruhe
Schwäbisch Hall
Heilbronn
Rhine
Karlsruhe
Grossbottwar
Baden-Baden
Bühl
Stuttgart
A81 E41
A8
E52
Strasbourg
Freudenstadt
Neckar
Ulm
A7 E43
FRANCE
A 5
Oberwolfach-Walke
500
Wolfach
Weitenburg
Gutach
Danube
Waldkirch
500
Triberg
Rottweil
Freiburg
Furtwangen
St. Margen
Titisee
Wangen
A7
Hinterzarten
31
Staufen
Todnau
Schluchsee
Meersburg
Mulhouse
Münstertal
Konstanz
Badenweiler
Lindau
Pfronten
Doubs
Basel
Aare
SWITZERLAND
Bodensee
Bodensee
Zurich

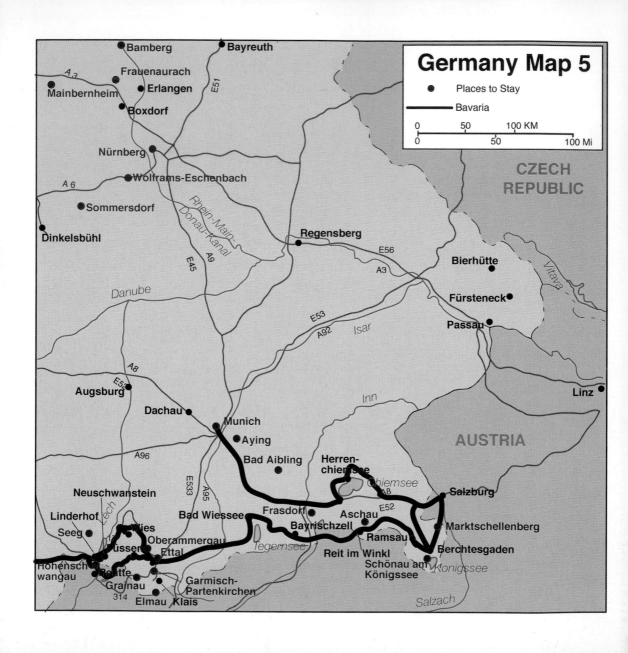

Karen Brown's
GERMANY
2006

Contents

For our dear Astrid
You will always be in our hearts
for the love you gave our children.

2006 Cover Painting: Schwäbisch Hall

Photograph front: Wolfach

Authors: Clare Brown, Karen Brown and June Eveleigh Brown.

Editors: Anthony Brown, Clare Brown, Karen Brown, June Eveleigh Brown, Kim Brown Holmsen, Michael Fiegel, Yvonne Sartain, Debbie Tokumoto.

Illustrations: Barbara Maclurcan Tapp.

Cover painting: Jann Pollard.

Maps: Michael Fiegel.

Technical support: Michael Fiegel, Gary Meisner.

Distributed by National Book Network, 15200 NBN Way, Blue Ridge Summit, PA 17214, USA. Tel: 717-794-3800 or 1-800-462-6420, Fax: 1-800-338-4500, Email: custserv@nbnbooks.com

A catalog record for this book is available from the British Library.

ISSN 1533-4651

Introduction

From the sand dunes of the North Friesian Islands to the snow-capped Alps, Germany has a great variety of destinations. To help you choose what to visit, we have designed seven driving itineraries, each highlighting the beauty of a particular region. Whether you want to explore the restored baroque city of Dresden, marvel at Ludwig of Bavaria's fantasy palaces, or go hiking in the Black Forest, we have an itinerary to suit you. To further help you in choosing where to go, we have listed outstanding sights beginning on page 14. Sightseeing that you will want to go out of your way to visit is highlighted in the itineraries with an asterisk (*). Because we believe that where you lay your head each night makes the difference between a good and a great vacation, we have included a section on wonderful *little* hotels that we enjoy throughout Germany—you'll find lots of fluffy down comforters and gargantuan breakfast buffets here.

The Brandenburg Gate

About Germany

The following pointers are given in alphabetical order, not in order of importance.

AIRFARES

Karen Brown's Guides have long recommended Auto Europe for their excellent car rental services. Their air travel division, Destination Europe, an airline broker working with major American and European carriers, offers deeply discounted coach- and business-class fares to over 200 European gateway cities. It also gives Karen Brown travelers an additional 5% discount off its already highly competitive prices (cannot be combined with any other offers or promotions). We recommend you make reservations by phone at (800) 223-5555. When phoning, be sure to use the Karen Brown ID number 99006187 to secure your discount.

BEER AND WINE

BEER: Germany's national drink, beer, is served at beer halls and taverns, particularly in the southern part of the country. Munich is the capital of beer drinking. A visit would not be complete without taking in the Hofbräuhaus beer hall and, in summer, visiting a German beer garden, such as the one in the Englischer Garten. Brewed across the nation, the beers vary from light (*helles*) to dark (*dunkles*). From bottled beer served in glasses to foaming steins filled straight from the barrel, beer is consumed in copious quantities.

WINE: Eleven different wine-growing regions producing mostly white wine stretch from Bonn south to Lake Constance, with each region's wines having a very distinctive flavor. The wine regions often have a signposted route that combines sights and wineries in such a way that you work up a proper thirst. You can sample wines by the glass in taverns—*weinstube* and *weinhaus*—while restaurants offer house wines served in pottery jugs and bottles from a wine list. However, the most appealing way to celebrate German wines is to attend one of the more than 500 wine festivals that take place in the wine regions from July to late October—the Tourist Office can give you details about festivals and tours.

When looking at German wine lists, selecting an appropriate bottle often seems a daunting task. If you can see the wine labels, your job is made much easier since the label tells you the district, producer, type of grape used, and the year it was bottled. In addition, look for labels with yellow borders or backgrounds denoting dry wine, and those with lime green denoting semi-dry. Sometimes the labels are not color coded and the word *trocken* indicates dry and *halbtrocken* semi-dry. Labels grade the wine into *tafelwein*—tablewine, *qualitätswein*—quality wine, and *qualitätswein mit prädikat*—quality wine with special attributes. Some of the wine regions also have special glasses "just for their wine" such as the green-colored wine glass of the Mosel.

CURRENCY–EURO

All pricing, including room rates, is quoted in euros, using the "€" symbol. The euro is now the official currency of most European Union (EU) countries, including Germany. As of February 2002, the euro completely replaced their national currencies. Visit our website (*www.karenbrown.com*) for an easy-to-use online currency converter.

Banking hours vary, but banks are usually open weekdays from 9 am to noon, and again from 2 to 3 pm. Currency exchange offices are located at airports and railway stations in large cities. As a service to their guests and clients, hotels and department stores will also often convert foreign currency to euros.

An increasingly popular and convenient way to obtain foreign currency is simply to use your bankcard at an ATM machine. You pay a fixed fee for this but, depending on the amount you withdraw, it is usually less than the percentage-based fee charged to exchange currency or travelers' checks. Be sure to check with your bank or credit card company about fees and appropriate pin numbers prior to departure.

EATING

Hearty appetites are catered to—you will certainly not starve.

Breakfast (*Frühstück*) consists of a lavish assortment of delicious rolls, wurst or sausages, patés, cheeses, homemade jams, country butter, and often cereals, yoghurt, and fresh cream.

Lunch (*Mittagessen*) is often the main meal in Germany. Served customarily from noon to 2 pm, it generally consists of soup, meat, and vegetables. However, when traveling, you might opt to save valuable afternoon time by stopping at a brewery (*bräuhaus*) or beer hall (*bierkeller* or *biergarten* in the parks) for simpler fare of hot sausage, sauerkraut, and fried potatoes accompanied by a glass of cold beer.

Another popular daytime dining option is the pastry shop (*konditorei*) where you can enjoy the treat of having your pastries and cakes served *mit schlag*, with a thick helping of cream that makes any regional specialty a delight (albeit a caloric one).

Dinner (*Abendessen*) is usually enjoyed between 6 and 9 pm. When served at home it is usually a light meal, but in restaurants, you will find the same types of meals as at midday. In tourist centers, the menus are printed only in German, so take your dictionary to dinner with you.

ELECTRICITY

If you are taking any electrical appliances made for use in the United States, you will need a transformer plus a two-pin adapter. A voltage of 220 AC current at 50 cycles per second is used almost countrywide, though in remote areas you may encounter 120V. The voltage is often displayed on the socket. Even though we recommend that you purchase appliances with dual-voltage options whenever possible, it will still be necessary to have the appropriate socket adapter. Also, be especially careful with expensive equipment such as computers—verify with the manufacturer the adapter/converter capabilities and requirements.

FESTIVALS AND FOLKLORE

With claim to such legends as *Snow White* and *The Pied Piper of Hamelin,* and with a colorful history, the Germans find numerous occasions for festivals and celebrations honoring everything from children saving a town from destruction to the completion of the grape harvest. Since these are staged over the course of the year, it would be impossible to experience them all when on a limited holiday, but it might prove rewarding to plan your travel dates to coincide with a particular festival. Some of the possibilities are the following, listed by town:

Bad Durkheim: Second and third Sundays in September—Germany's largest wine and sausage festival.

Bad Harzburg: April 30—*Walpurgisfeier*, the night the witches come to life for one night of merry celebration.

Bad Tolz: November 6—*Leonhardiritt*, a fun-filled parade to honor the patron saint of animals.

Dinkelsbühl: Third Monday in July—*Kinderzeche*, a reenactment of the children saving the town during the Thirty Years' War.

Hamelin: Sundays in July and August—a reenactment of the Pied Piper spiriting away the town's children.

Heidelberg: First Saturday in June, July, and September—the castle is illuminated and fireworks are fired over the river.

Koblenz–Braubach: Second Saturday in August—*The Rhine in Flames*, the Rhine valley between the towns of Koblenz and Braubach is lit by bonfires and floodlights.

Munich: Late September and early October—*Oktoberfest*, the world's biggest beer festival.

Rothenburg: One Sunday a month in summer—*Maistertruk*, a reenactment of the drinking feat that saved the town from destruction during the Thirty Years' War.

GETTING AROUND

BOATS and RIVER CRUISES: Köln-Düsseldorfer German Rhine Line (known as KD for short) operates cruises and day excursion services on the Rhine, Mosel, Main, Danube, and Elbe rivers from April to the end of October. These excursions vary in duration from several hours to a week. No reservation is needed for day ferryboat services—you buy your ticket from the pier before departure. The most popular excursions are the half-day trip through the Rhine gorge between Koblenz and Mainz; along the Mosel river between Koblenz and Cochem; and

the multi-night cruises on the Elbe River between Wittenberg (Luther's town) and Prague.

BUSES: In conjunction with the German railroad, buses make the trip along the Romantic Road between Füssen and Würzburg. Principal stops include Rothenburg and Dinkelsbühl. Additional service connects Mannheim, Heidelberg, and Rothenburg. If you have a German Flexipass or a Eurailpass, the price of the bus ticket is included and you do not need to pay a supplement. The buses operate on a seasonal basis. Schedules are available from the German Tourist Office and are published in the Thomas Cook European Timetable.

CAR RENTAL: Readers frequently ask our advice on car rental companies. We always use Auto Europe—a car rental broker that works with the major car rental companies to find the lowest possible price. They also offer motor homes and chauffeur services. Auto Europe's toll-free phone service, from every European country, connects you to their U.S.-based, 24-hour reservation center (ask for the Europe Phone Numbers Card to be mailed to you). Auto Europe offers our readers a 5% discount (cannot be combined with any other offers or promotions) and, occasionally, free upgrades. Be sure to use the Karen Brown ID number 99006187 to receive your discount and any special offers. You can make your own reservations online via our website, *www.karenbrown.com* (select *Auto Europe* from the home page), or by phone (800-223-5555).

There is a definite price advantage to reserving and pre-paying for a car rental, but remember, you will have to pay taxes and insurance locally. Also, depending on the policies and locations of a particular company, there are often surcharges for returning a car to a place other than the originating rental location. Gasoline is very expensive, so budget this as part of your trip if you are driving, and be aware that small service stations in the countryside often do not accept payment by credit card. Your local driver's license is accepted in Germany, where the minimum driving age is 18. Automatic transmission is usually available only in larger, more expensive vehicles. Lead-free fuel is *bleifrei*.

DRIVING: The German road network consists of autobahns (freeways/motorways marked with blue signs) and secondary roads (also excellent highways). Traffic moves fast on the autobahns where, unless signposted, there is no speed limit. On the secondary highways the speed limit is 100 kilometers (62 miles) per hour. The speed limit within city and town boundaries is usually 50 kilometers (31 miles) per hour. There are a few toll roads, usually over secondary mountain passes, but these are not always open. While most road signs are international symbols, a few very important ones are usually written: *einbahnstrasse*—one-way street, *links fahren*—keep left, *parken verboten*—no parking, and *umleitung*—detour.

TRAINS: From the high-speed ICE train to the local trains that stop in every little village, Germany has a rail system that is easy to use, operates on time, and embraces over 30,000 kilometers of track, enabling the tourist to crisscross the nation with ease. Trains arrive and depart with clockwork precision. The cars are marked on the outside with their destination and first or second class, and, within each, there are seating areas for smoking and no smoking. Most trains of substantial size have a dining car, while those that do not often have a vendor who sells snacks and drinks from a cart. In each train station there is usually an information desk where someone speaks English to assist you with schedules. Other services at large stations include currency exchange, accommodation information, shops, and restaurants. Baggage carts are free.

For trains within Germany you can buy point-to-point tickets or a German Flexipass, or use a Eurailpass. We highly recommend the Flexipass that permits unlimited rail travel in all of Germany for five, ten, or fifteen days within the period of one month. Travel does not have to be on consecutive days. The superhigh-speed ICE trains that link many of the major cities in Germany (such as Hamburg to Munich, Hamburg to Frankfurt, and Berlin to Munich) are covered by the Flexipass, but reservations are necessary. The Flexipass also allows free travel on buses along the Romantic Road and reductions on river steamers on the Rhine and Mosel rivers. In the USA, Flexipasses and Eurailpasses, as well as point-to-point tickets are available through DER Tours, 9501 West Devon, Suite 301, Rosemont, IL 60018. In addition to being the agent in the United States for the

German Flexipass and train tickets, DER offers several short tours that include transportation and accommodation. Rail Europe also provides detailed information on schedules, prices, and availability, *www.raileurope.com.*

You can also research schedules and fares and even purchase tickets and passes on the internet. (Note that many special fares and passes are available only if purchased in the United States.) For more information and to book tickets online, visit our website, *www.karenbrown.com.*

HISTORY

Germany has always been a country of shifting frontiers. Since Roman times the country was continually subdivided in an ever-changing mosaic of "units" of different degrees of political importance. These "units" comprised states, kingdoms, Hanseatic cities, free towns, principalities, and ecclesiastical fiefs. Held together by leagues, reichs, confederations, and empires, Germany fills vast volumes of European history. In 1871 Germany became a united country, and this unity lasted until 1945 when the country was occupied by Britain, France, America, and Russia (the Allies) at the conclusion of World War II. In 1949, the British, French, and American sectors were linked as the German Federal Republic—West Germany. The Russian sector developed into the German Democratic Republic (East Germany). In November 1989, the Berlin Wall came crashing down, astounding and inspiring the entire world. It took only until the fall of 1990 for Germany to become officially once again a single nation.

This nation has been home to some of the world's most influential leaders: Charlemagne, Frederick Barbarossa, Otto the Great, Martin Luther, Frederick the Great, Bismarck, and Adolf Hitler. Although there has been an impressive list of German leaders who have shaped world history, it is Ludwig II, King of Bavaria, who is most often remembered by tourists. Ruling Bavaria between 1864 and 1886, Ludwig II is fondly known as Mad King Ludwig. A notable patron of art and music, he idolized and subsidized the composer Richard Wagner. Lonely, eccentric, cut off from the mainstream of world politics and obsessed by the glories of the past, Ludwig sought solace in a fanciful building scheme—his Bavarian castles of Neuschwanstein, Herrenchiemsee, and Linderhof. His building extravaganzas brought Bavaria to the brink of bankruptcy and, before he could begin on further palaces, he was declared unfit to rule by reason of insanity. Within a week of his deposition, Ludwig mysteriously drowned in Lake Starnberg.

HOLIDAY ROUTES

Germany has a network of holiday routes that allow visitors to follow special-interest, scenic, and historic paths. All are signposted and indicated on most maps. A sampling of the more popular routes are:

Burgenstrasse—The Castle Highway
between Mannheim and Nürnberg.

Alpenstrasse—The German Alpine Way
between Berchtesgaden and Lindau.

Marchenstrasse—The German Fairy-Tale Route
between Hanau and Bremen.

Weinstrasse—The German Wine Road
between Schweigen and Bockenheim.

Moselweinstrasse—The Mosel River Wine Route
between Trier and Koblenz.

Romantische Strasse—The Romantic Road
between Würzburg and Füssen.

Schwarzwald Hochstrasse—The Black Forest High Road
between Baden-Baden and Freudenstadt.

The Goose Girl–Gottingen

Introduction–About Germany

INFORMATION

Within Germany, a big blue "I" denotes the location of the tourist information booths in all major towns, train stations, airports, and tourist centers. Before you go; information, maps, and brochures can be obtained from the German National Tourist Offices or by accessing their website: *www.germany-tourism.de.*

UNITED STATES

German National Tourist Office, 122 East 42nd St., 20nd Fl., Ste 2000, New York, NY 10168, USA, email: gntonyc@d-z-t.com, tel: (212) 661-7200, fax: (212) 661-7174

German National Tourist Office, 501 Santa Monica Blvd., Suite 607, Santa Monica, CA 90401 USA, email: info@gntolax.com, tel: (310) 394-2580

GREAT BRITAIN

German National Tourist Office, Post Office Box 2695, London W1A 3TN, England email: gntolon@d-z-t.com, tel: (020) 7317-0908, fax: (020) 7317-0917

GERMANY

German National Tourist Board, Beethovenstrasse 69, 60325 Frankfurt/Main, Germany email: info@d-z-t.com, fax: (069) 751903

SHOPPING

Most shops are open Monday through Friday from 9 am to 6 pm, and Saturday until noon or 2 pm. Many small shops close for an hour or two in the middle of the day, when the shopkeeper goes home for lunch. In resort areas, some of the shops are open seven days.

You will discover the same consistently high standard of products throughout Germany, with minimal price variations. Department stores are large and display a magnificent assortment of items. In the cities, some of Germany's larger department store chains to watch for are Kaufhof, Hertie, Karstadt, and Horten, as they usually have excellent souvenir departments and competitive prices.

SALES TAX: If you are not a resident of one of the EU countries, when you buy goods and have the store ship them out of the country, you will not be charged Germany's 15% Value Added Tax. If you plan to carry your purchases home with you, you can be reimbursed the tax you paid by one of two methods. The first is to show all your receipts and merchandise at the Tax Check Service at the airport as you leave the country and they will reimburse you immediately, less a small commission. The more time-consuming process involves asking for a tax refund form at the time of purchase or saving all receipts and getting forms from the customs office. When you leave the country or cross a border, be sure to have these forms stamped by the German customs official. If you are leaving by train, you must get off the train at the border and have the customs inspector stamp the form. Keep your purchases together because the customs agent will probably want to see what you have bought. After your trip, mail the forms back to the stores from which you made your purchases, and they will reimburse the tax you paid in your local currency, mailed to your home address.

TELEPHONES

Calls made from your hotel room can be exceedingly expensive due to a surcharge system. The easiest and least expensive way to call the USA is to use telephone calling cards issued by AT&T, MCI, and Sprint. With these cards, you dial a number to reach the American phone system and calls are charged to your card. Contact the particular company for international access numbers before you leave the United States.

CELLPHONES: Cellphones are wonderful to have, as some hotels do not have direct-dial phones in the guestrooms. Also, cellphones are enormously convenient when you are on the road and want to call for directions or advise of a changed arrival.

Cellphones can be rented through your car rental company, at the airport or train stations, or you can purchase an international phone once you are overseas. If you are considering taking your cellphone from home, check with your carrier to make sure that your phone even has international capability. Sometimes it is necessary to make arrangements before you depart to activate a special service. We would also recommend getting international phone access numbers and inquiring about international access charges or rates so there are no billing surprises.

WEATHER

Rainfall occurs at all times of year. Autumn is mild and long, spring chilly and late, winter, often snowy and cold; and summer can vary from cloudless and balmy through hot and muggy, to cold and wet. Bring a woolen sweater, a fold-up umbrella, and a raincoat that can be taken off as the day warms, and you will be all set to enjoy Germany, rain or shine, cold or warm.

About Itineraries

The second section of this guide outlines driving itineraries throughout Germany. At the beginning of each itinerary we suggest our recommended pacing to help you decide the amount of time to allocate to each region. Most sightseeing venues operate a summer and winter opening schedule, with the changeovers occurring around late March/early April and late October. If you happen to be visiting at the changeover times, be sure to check whether your chosen venue is open before making plans. While we try to give an accurate indication of opening times, there is every possibility that these will have changed by the time you plan your trip; so before you embark on an excursion, check the days (lots of places are closed on Mondays) and hours of opening. We indicate outstanding sightseeing spots by preceding them with an asterisk (e.g., *Burg Eltz).

HIGHLIGHTS

To help you decide where to go and what to see, here are the highlights of our itineraries.

BAVARIA

Munich, a delightful city whose major sights are: **Marienplatz**, the lively town center; **Hofbräuhaus**, a world-famous beer hall; **Englischer Garten**, a most attractive park; **Alte Pinakothek**, a great art museum; **Residenz Museum,** an outstanding museum; and in its suburbs **Dachau**, a concentration camp with the motto "Never Again."

Drive to the nearby **Königssee**, a picturesque, high Alpine lake. Tour along the **Alpenstrasse**, a narrow road that winds along just below the Alpine peaks. The most photographed place along the Alpenstrasse is **Ramsau Church**.

Garmisch-Partenkirchen, a larger, picturesque Alpine resort; perfect for hiking, walking, and sightseeing.

Linderhof, Ludwig's oh-so-fanciful home, totally over the top in design and decor. In the garden you find the **Venus Grotto**, a man-made cave complete with lake and shell-shaped boat even more fanciful than the house.

Füssen, a charming, walled town with a maze of pedestrian streets and the **Hohes Schloss**. On its outskirts, overlooking **Lake Forggen**, is the recently built **Musical Theater Neuschwanstein,** where a performance in tribute to the life of Mad King Ludwig is staged.

Neuschwanstein, Ludwig's early Disney castle, a riot of turrets with a fantasy interior set in a magnificent location.

Wieskirche, a simple countryside church with a magnificent painted interior.

Lindau, a quaint walled town on an island in the Bodensee.

Meersburg, on the banks of the Bodensee, is another quaint walled town with a castle that is fun to explore. From here, take a day trip to **Mainau,** an island in the Bodensee with magnificent subtropical gardens.

CASTLES OF THE RHINE & MOSEL

The **Rhine gorge** between Koblenz and Mainz is the most scenic section of this powerful river. Visit the castle **Burg Rheinfels**.

River Mosel, a meandering river in a steep-banked valley covered in terraced vineyards. Picturesque villages include **Beilstein**, **Zell**, and **Bernkastel-Kues**.

Burg Eltz, the most wonderful fairy-tale castle I have ever seen, is still a family home.

HIGHWAYS & BYWAYS OF THE BLACK FOREST

Take to the quieter side roads to enjoy picture-book scenery.

Schwarzwalder Freilichtermuseum, a collection of old Black-Forest farmhouses.

Baden-Baden, a resort town famous for its casino and health spas: **Friedrichsbad**, the suits-off spa, and **Caracalla Therme**, the suits-on spa.

THE ROMANTIC ROAD & THE NECKAR VALLEY

Würzburg is not a particularly interesting city, but if you enjoy baroque architecture, you will adore the magnificent **Residenz** (palace).

Creglingen, a simple village on the Romantic Road with the most superb altarpiece in its nearby church, **Herrgottskirche**.

Rothenburg, the justifiably world-famous, medieval walled town with lots of interesting sightseeing and a **nightwatchman** to point you in the right direction.

Deutsche Greifenwarte, the Raptor Research Center in Schloss Guttenberg, where the talons of eagles in flight almost brush the top of your head.

HIGHLIGHTS OF THE HARZ MOUNTAINS

The **Harz Mountains**, with their tumbling streams, green forests, and cool blue lakes.

Goslar, a quaint town at the northern foot of the mountains with lots of attractions. On the edge of the town you can tour a mine, the **Rammelsberger Bergbaumuseum**.

Wernigerode, a quaint town of half-timbered houses and an exquisite town hall. Visit the homey castle **Schloss Wernigerode** rising above the town and ride a steam train, the **Harzquerbahn**, into the mountains.

Quedlinburg, a magnificent city with a great many unrestored medieval houses—it's like taking a walk back in time, though some may find it rundown. An interesting castle and church overlook the town.

EXPLORING EAST & MIDDLE GERMANY

Eisenach, has Bach's home (**Bachhaus**) and **Wartburg Castle** on its outskirts.

Weimar has an attractive town center and Goethe's home (**Goethehaus**).

Dresden, the city of culture, was badly damaged in the closing days of World War II. Cranes dot the skyline and restoration is well under way. Stroll by the **Parade of Princes**, a porcelain mural. Spend a week museum-hopping in the **Zwinger Palace** to visit the **Gemäldegalerie Alte Meister** (European paintings) and **Porzellansammlung** (porcelain museum). In the Albertinum visit the **Grünes Gewölbe** (silver, gold and jewelry museum). Visit nearby **Meissen** where you can see the famous porcelain being produced at the **Staatliche Porzellanmanufaktur** (porcelain factory).

Spreewald, an agricultural area where you travel on quiet canals that connect traditional Sorb villages.

Potsdam, not a town with lots to see, but on its outskirts the magnificent palaces of **Sanssouci** will astound you.

Berlin, a large city perfect for city lovers. Tour the bullet-riddled **Reichstag** (parliament building). Walk beneath the **Brandenburg Gate**. Marvel in the **Pergamon Museum** at the Pergamon Altar and Babylonian Street. Be amazed at how citizens escaped across the wall at **Haus Am Checkpoint Charlie**. Visit the everlasting beauty, Nefertiti, at the **Ägyptisches Museum**. Stroll among the gardens of the Hohenzollerns' grand palace, **Schloss Charlottenburg**. View the incredible collection of art in the **Picture Gallery**.

SCHLESWIG HOLSTEIN–THE LAND BETWEEN THE SEAS

Hamburg, a lively city where a large body of water, the **Aussenalster**, stretches from the city to the suburbs.

Lübeck, an attractive, walled, red-brick town.

Sylt, the jewel of the Frisian Islands, whose capital **Keitum** is the island's prettiest village.

MAPS

Each itinerary is preceded by a map showing the route. Itinerary routings are also superimposed on the same maps that show hotel locations at the front of the book, with each itinerary highlighted in a different color. These maps are not intended to replace detailed commercial maps. For detailing itineraries we like Michelin's overview map of Germany, number 718, and use highlight pens to outline our route. We also find the orange regional Michelin maps very useful, and we indicate which Michelin 500-series map each hotel's town is found on in the hotel description. Since we ourselves often had difficulty finding all the maps we wanted from one source, for our readers' convenience we stock a full inventory of the Michelin maps referenced in our books, in addition to other Michelin products. You can easily order maps online through our website, *www.karenbrown.com*, and we will ship them out within 48 hours.

Castle above the Rhine River

Introduction–About Itineraries

About Hotels

This guide does not cover the many modern hotels in Germany with their look-alike bedrooms, televisions, and direct-dial phones. Rather, it offers a selection of personally recommended hotels, which might range from a splendid 12th-century castle crowning a mountaintop to a simple vintner's house perched on the banks of the Mosel. However, there is a common denominator—they all have charm. Therefore, if you too prefer to travel spending your nights in romantic wine houses, appealing little chalets, dramatic castles, thatched cottages, and 14th-century post stations, we are kindred souls.

For some of you, cost will not be a factor if the hotel is outstanding. For others, budget will guide your choices. The appeal of a simple, little inn with rustic, wooden furniture will beckon some, while the glamour of ornate ballrooms dressed with crystal chandeliers and gilded mirrors will appeal to others. What we have tried to do is to indicate what each hotel has to offer and describe the setting, so that you can make the choice to suit your own preferences. We feel that if you know what to expect, you will not be disappointed, so we have tried to be candid and honest in our appraisals.

Our goal is to recommend hotels that we think are outstanding. All of the hotels featured have been visited and selected solely on their merits. Our judgments are made on the charm of the hotel, its setting, cleanliness, and, above all, the warmth of welcome. However, no matter how careful we are, sometimes we misjudge a hotel's merits, or the ownership changes, or unfortunately sometimes hotels just do not maintain their standards. If you find a hotel is not as we have indicated, please let us know and accept our sincere apologies.

CREDIT CARDS

Whether or not an establishment accepts credit cards is indicated in the list of icons at the bottom of each description by the symbol 🟦. We have also specified which cards are accepted by using the following codes: none, AX–American Express, MC–MasterCard,

VS–Visa, or simply, all major. Note: Even if an inn does not accept credit card payment, it will perhaps request your account number as a guarantee of arrival.

ICONS

Icons allow us to provide additional information about our recommended properties. When using our website to supplement the guides, positioning the cursor over an icon will in many cases give you further details.

We have introduced these icons in the guidebooks and there are more on our website, *www.karenbrown.com*. ❄ Air conditioning in rooms, ⊥ Beach nearby, ● Breakfast included in room rate, 🐾 Children welcome, ♨ Cooking classes offered, 📷 Credit cards accepted, ☎ Direct-dial telephone in room, 🐕 Dogs by special request, 🛗 Elevator, 🏋 Exercise room, ⅋ Mini-refrigerator in rooms, 🚭 Some non-smoking rooms, P Parking available, 🍽 Restaurant, ✿ Spa, ≈ Swimming pool, ⊁ Tennis, 🖼 Television with English channels, 🎗 Wedding facilities, ♿ Wheelchair friendly, ⛳ Golf course nearby, 👫 Hiking trails nearby, 🏇 Horseback riding nearby, ⛷ Skiing nearby, 🏄 Water sports nearby, 🍷 Wineries nearby.

FINDING HOTELS

At the front of the book is a key map of the whole of Germany, plus five regional maps showing each recommended hotel's location. The pertinent regional map number is given at the right on the *top line* of each hotel's description. To assist you in finding towns where we recommend hotels, we give some indication of their location on the next-to-bottom line of the hotel description.

MEMBERSHIP AFFILIATIONS

A number of properties recommended in our guides also belong to private membership organizations. These associations impose their own criteria for selection and membership standards and have established a reputation for the particular type of property they include. One affiliation that is very well recognized throughout Europe is Relais &

Châteaux. A number of properties that we recommend are members of this fine organization. We are familiar with their selection process, criteria, and membership standards, and we feel comfortable in recommending these prestigious associations to our readers. If a property that we recommend is also a member of the Relais & Châteaux group, we publish the reference at the bottom of the description page.

RATES

Rates are those quoted to us for 2006 high season. Prices, in euros (€), are for two people sharing a room, including tax and service. We have indicated at the bottom of the hotel's description if breakfast is *not* included and indicate the price per person. Breakfast included is confirmed in the list of icons at the bottom of each description by the symbol 🍵. Also, assume rooms have a private bath unless otherwise specified. Be aware that throughout Germany, during festivals, conferences, or special market fairs, room prices increase. Please use the rates we give as a guideline.

RESERVATIONS

When making your reservations, be sure to identify yourself as a "Karen Brown Traveler." The hotels appreciate your visit, value their inclusion in our guide, frequently tell us they take special care of our readers, and many offer special rates to Karen Brown members (visit our website at *www.karenbrown.com*).

It is important to understand that once reservations for accommodation are confirmed, whether verbally by phone or in writing, you are under contract. This means that the proprietor is obligated to provide the accommodation that was promised and that you are obligated to pay for it. If you cannot, you are liable for a portion of the accommodation charges plus your deposit. Although some proprietors do not strictly enforce a cancellation policy, many, particularly the smaller properties in our book, simply cannot afford not to do so.

Reservations can be confining and usually must be guaranteed by a deposit. However, if you have your heart set on a particular hotel, avoid disappointment and make a reservation. Reservations should always be made in advance for the major tourist cities and resorts during the peak season of June through September, and also during certain special events such as Oktoberfest in Munich. Space in the countryside is a little easier. Note: When corresponding with Germany, be sure to spell out the month. Do not use numbers since in Europe they reverse the format used in the United States and write the day first—for example, 6/9 means September 6, not June 9. Clearly state the following: number of people in your party, how many rooms you desire, whether you want a private bathroom, date of arrival and date of departure. Ask the rate per night and if a deposit is needed. When you receive a reply, send the deposit requested and ask for a receipt, brochure, and directions. The following are several options for making hotel reservations:

EMAIL: This is our preferred way of making a reservation. All hotels featured on the Karen Brown website that have email addresses have listed them on their web pages (this information is constantly kept updated and correct). You can link directly to a property from its page on our website using its email hyperlink.

FAX: If you have access to a fax machine, this is a very quick and easy way to reach a hotel. (See section on "Telephone" below for dialing instructions.) Although most hotels can understand written English, on page 25 we have provided a reservation request letter in German and English.

TELEPHONE: If you telephone, you can have your answer immediately. If space is not available, you can then choose an alternative. To place a call from the United States: dial 011 (the international code), 49 (Germany's code), then the city number (dropping the 0 in front of the city code), then the telephone number. If you are calling WITHIN Germany, do not drop the 0 before the city code.

TRIP CANCELLATION INSURANCE

Because unexpected medical or personal emergencies—or other situations beyond our control—sometimes result in the need to alter or cancel travel plans, we strongly recommend travel insurance. Prepaid travel expenses, such as airline tickets, car rentals, and train fares, are not always refundable, and most hotels and bed & breakfasts will expect payment of some, if not all, of your booking—even in an emergency. While the owners might be sympathetic, many of the properties in our guides have relatively few rooms, so it is difficult for them to absorb the cost of a cancellation. A link on our website (*www.karenbrown.com*) will connect you to a variety of insurance policies that can be purchased online.

WEBSITE

Please supplement this book by looking at the information provided on our Karen Brown website (*www.karenbrown.com*), which serves as an added dimension to our guides. Most of our favorite hotels are featured on the site (web participation is a hotel's choice), and from their web page you can usually link to their own website for even more detailed information and directions, and also to their email, so that making a reservation is a breeze. Also featured on our site are comments: feedback, and discoveries from you, our readers; information on our latest finds; post-press updates; contest drawings for free books; special offers; unique features such as recipes and favorite destinations; and special savings offered by certain properties.

WHEELCHAIR ACCESSIBLE

If an inn has *at least* one guestroom that is accessible by wheelchair, it is noted with the symbol ♿. This is not the same as saying it meets full disability standards. In reality it can be anything from a basic ground-floor room to a fully equipped facility. Please discuss your requirements when you call your chosen place to stay to determine if they have accommodation that suits your needs and preference.

Introduction–About Hotels

RESERVATION REQUEST LETTER

HOTEL NAME & ADDRESS

Ich moechte anfragen: I would like to request:

Number of double rooms with private bath/shower
____ (No. of double rooms) *Doppelzimmer mit Bad/Dusche*

Number of single rooms with private bath/shower
____ (No. of single rooms) *Einzelzimmer mit Bad/Dusche*

Number of persons in our party
Wir sind ____ (No. of persons) *Personen*

Arrival date
Wir kommen am _____ *an* (Day/Month/Year, spell out month)

Departure date
Wir reisen am _____ *an* (Day/Month/Year, spell out month)

Please let me know as soon as possible the following:
Bitte lassen Sie mich so bald wie moeglich wissen:

Can you reserve the space requested?	Yes	No
Ob Sie die angefragten Zimmer haben?	*Ja* ____	____ *Nein*

Rate per room per night?
Der Preis pro Zimmer / Nacht?

Are meals included in your rate?	Yes	No
Sind Mahlzeiten in diesem Preis enthalten?	*Ja* ____	____ *Nein*
Do you need a deposit?	Yes	No
Benoetigen Sie eine Anzahlung?	*Ja* ____	____ *Nein*

How much deposit do you need?
Wenn ja, wie hoch ist die Anzahlung?

Thank you, and Best Regards,   *Vielen Dank im voraus. Mit freundlichen Gruessen,*

YOUR NAME & ADDRESS

Baden-Baden

Bavaria

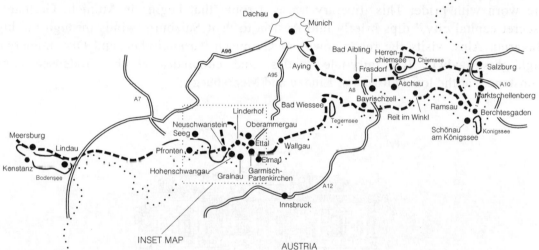

Dachau

Munich

A96

A95

A7

Bad Aibling

Herren-
chiemsee

Chiemsee

Aying

Frasdorf

Salzburg

A8

Aschau

A10

Linderhof

Bad Wiessee

Bayrischzell

Marktschellenberg

Oberammergau

Tegernsee

Ramsau

Berchtesgaden

Neuschwanstein

Reit im Winkl

Seeg

Meersburg

Ettal

Wallgau

Schönau
am Königssee

Königssee

Lindau

Pfronten

Elmau

Konstanz

Hohenschwangau

Grainau

Garmisch-
Partenkirchen

Bodensee

A12

Innsbruck

INSET MAP

AUSTRIA

- ● Orientation/Sightseeing
- —— Other roads
- ═══ Autobahn
- ▬ ▬ ▬ Itinerary route
- · · · · Borders

Bavaria

It is no wonder that Bavaria is a favorite destination for so many travelers. This southeastern corner of Germany proudly maintains the reputation of having the friendliest people, the most breathtaking mountains, the quaintest villages, the prettiest lakes, and the most famous castles in Germany. Summertime paints Bavaria's valleys and hillsides with edelweiss, Alpine roses, and orchids. Winter gently softens the landscape with a carpet of snow. This is a region where traditional dress of lederhosen and dirndls are worn with pride. This itinerary traces a route that begins in Munich, Germany's "secret capital city," dips briefly into Austria to visit Salzburg, winds through the high Bavarian Alps, visits the resort towns of Garmisch-Partenkirchen and Oberammergau, highlights Ludwig II's fairy-tale castles, and concludes at the Bodensee (Lake Constance) at the lovely towns of Lindau and Meersburg.

Linderhof

Recommended Pacing: Spend two full days in Munich, giving you time to visit one or two museums, explore the city center, experience one or two beer gardens, and make a half-day trip to Dachau. A half-day drive (including sightseeing) brings you to Berchtesgaden (we offer a hotel in Schönau am Königssee), which merits a three-day stopover (two if you do not visit Salzburg). The drive along the Alpenstrasse takes a complete day (with sightseeing and lunch). Base yourself in the Garmisch-Partenkirchen area (we suggest places to stay in Ettal, Elmau, Garmisch-Partenkirchen, Grainau, Hohenschwangau, Oberammergau, Pfronten, and Seeg, any of which make an excellent base for exploring the area). If you cover all of our sightseeing suggestions here, you will need four nights. A half-day drive will find you in Lindau or Meersburg, where we recommend a one-night stay.

*Munich, the "gateway to Bavaria," stars as one of Europe's most beautiful cities. Locals refer to Munich as "the village" because it is compact and easily explored on foot with the aid of short trips on the clean and efficient U-Bahn and S-Bahn underground railway systems. Munich, a wonderful beer-drinking, music-loving city, rivals Paris and London with its excellent shopping, museums, cultural events, and plethora of things to see and do. You do not need a car during your stay here, so if Munich is your first German destination and you are arriving by plane, leave your large pieces of luggage at the luggage office at the airport, and travel downtown via the S-Bahn, returning to pick up your car and bags as you depart. Purchase a pass for the subway system: it's a great deal and allows five adults, up to three children, and a dog unlimited U-Bahn, S-Bahn, bus, and tram travel for 24 hours.

A logical place to begin a tour is the **Hauptbahnhof** (main train station), a dynamic, lively place with tourist information, fast food, bookstore, bus terminal, and the convergence of many of the U-Bahn and S-Bahn lines. Walk out the front door of the station and head for the first square, the **Stachus**, whose official name is the Karlsplatz, after Elector Karl Theodor. The townspeople, however, had such a high regard for Foderl Stachus that they named the square after him in 1730. Leaving the Stachus, wander under **Karlstor Gate** (past McDonald's and Burger King) and into the pedestrian zone of the

Neues Rathaus Clock

old city, which is alive with fountains, fruit stands, ballad singers, and lay preachers. Off to the left, notice the Renaissance façade of **St. Michael's,** and ahead, the twin turrets (square with rounded domes) of the **Frauenkirche** (cathedral), both a landmark and symbol of the city. *****Marienplatz**, the beautiful square that serves as the heart of Munich, is just a short distance farther. Tables and chairs spill from cafés well into the square dominated by the ornate, lacy, wedding-cake, golden-sandstone exterior of the *****Neues Rathaus** (town hall). When the clock on the town hall strikes 11 am, noon, or 5 pm, colorful figures emerge from around the clock to perform a jousting tournament. Awaiting the hour is a perfect excuse to frequent one of the little cafés in the square.

Take a short walk off the square to Munich's oldest parish church, **Alter Peter**, with its impressive 11th-century interior. Climb its tower for a panoramic view, which on a clear day extends to the Alps. Close by the Alter Peter church is the **Viktualienmarkt**, a permanent marketplace/beer garden full of stalls providing excellent, inexpensive things to eat. Head back towards the Marienplatz past the **Speilzeugmuseum**, a toy museum with lots of dolls and soldiers, along with a vast array of cars, planes, and trains, and onto the Tal. Munich is famous for its beer halls, which serve well-priced food, as well as huge quantities of beer, and at Tal 7, you find **Weisses Bräuhaus** with a sophisticated, pub-like atmosphere. If you are looking for oomp-pa-pa music, singing, joviality, and fellow tourists, the famous Hofbräuhaus is just a five-minute walk away. Head down the Tal, turn left on Hochbruchstrasse, turn left again as you face the Hotel Rafael, and you arrive at the enormous barn of a building that houses the *Hofbräuhaus. Row after row of rough-hewn tables and benches surround the musicians, and in summer, the merriment spills out to the tables and chairs set beneath the trees on the large patio. (Our favorite beer garden for a warm summer evening is found in the vast park *Englischer Garten near the Chinese pagoda.)

There are three outstanding museums to visit: the Alte Pinakothek, the Residenz Museum, and the Deutsches Museum. The *Alte Pinakothek has an incredible collection of works by 14th- to 18th-century masters such as Raphael, Michelangelo, Van Dyck, Rembrandt, Brueghel, Goya, and Titian. (*Alte Pinakothek, Barer Strasse 27, U-Bahn 2; Neue Pinakothek, Barer Strasse 29, U-Bahn 2, 10 am–5 pm, closed Mondays.*) The Deutsches Museum, often referred to as "Germany's Smithsonian," has a vast array of displays where you push buttons, turn wheels, and pull levers, making the serious subject of science and technology great fun. There are over 19 kilometers of displays, so you need to be very selective. The lack of explanation in English makes it frustrating for non-German speakers, though you can purchase a guidebook in English. (*Located on its own island in the River Isar, S-Bahn to Isartorplatz, 9 am–5 pm, closed certain holidays.*) The *Residenz Museum is so huge (over 100 rooms) that different tours are offered on alternating days. This was the enormous gilded home of the Wittelsbachs, who ruled Bavaria for more than 700 years. A separate ticket admits you to the Schatzkammer, a treasure house filled with the Wittelsbachs' glittering crowns, jewelry, and knickknacks. (*Located on Max-Joseph Platz, 3 blocks from Marienplatz, 10 am–4:30 pm, closed Mondays.*)

An easily accessible half-day trip from Munich is Hitler's first concentration camp, *Dachau (1933). The barracks are gone but reconstruction gives an idea of the conditions prisoners had to endure. Around the perimeter fence the watchtowers still stand and a museum (unsuitable for children) exhibits, without compromise, what life was like here. You can view the crematorium ovens where over 31,000 people lost their lives, even though this was not primarily an extermination camp. A visit here is a very powerful experience, and the camp's motto, "Never Again," strikes home. Dachau is 45 minutes northwest of Munich. Take the S-Bahn 2 towards Peterhausen to Dachau and the 724 or 726 bus from outside the station. The driver knows where you are going and indicates when to alight. From here, it is a ten-minute walk following signposts for *Konzentrationslager*. When you leave, the bus will take you from just outside the camp gates back to Dachau's train station. (*9 am–5 pm, closed Mondays.*)

Fall, of course, translates as the **Oktoberfest** and many people from all over the world congregate in Munich to participate in the festivities. This happy, noisy celebration of sausage and hops begins in September and concludes on the first Sunday in October. The festival confines itself to a meadow in the southwestern part of Munich called the Theresienwiese.

Leave Munich on autobahn 8 in the direction of Salzburg. About an hour's drive brings you to **Prien** (just a few kilometers north of the autobahn) where you turn right for the **Chiemsee,** Bavaria's largest lake set against a backdrop of distant mountain peaks. Although not as beautiful as some of Germany's other lakes that are tucked into mountain pockets, the lake is a draw for sports enthusiasts, and has two very interesting islands: **Herreninsel**, the lake's largest island, where Ludwig II built his imitation of Versailles, **Schloss Herrenchiemsee;** and the adjacent picturesque little island **Fraueninsel**, crowded with a Benedictine convent and fishing community.

Park by the lake and buy your ferry ticket (which affords a visit to either one or both islands). A 20-minute ride across the lake brings you to Herreninsel, where after a 20-minute stroll through woodlands, you reach Schloss Herrenchiemsee, set in a clearing facing magnificent fountains with lawns running down to the lake. If you prefer, you can take a horse-drawn carriage between the dock and the front steps of the palace. **King Ludwig II** of Bavaria had two idols, Louis XIV of France and the composer Richard Wagner. Herrenchiemsee was his recreation of Versailles, complete with the magnificent hall of mirrors. While Louis XIV used Versailles to dazzle the world, Ludwig used his *Versailles* as the backdrop for his exuberant fantasies. During his numerous visits, he ordered thousands of candles to be lit at night, and he wandered the decadent rooms enacting his fantasy of absolute monarchy, secluded from the real world on his isolated island. Tours leave every 20 minutes and last half-an-hour in length—English tours are available. The **König Ludwig Museum** that occupies the ground floor of the south wing gives a summary of the king's life, and outlines his building projects: Herrenchiemsee, Neuschwanstein, and Linderhof are the only projects that were partially completed before his death at age 40 in 1886. Raised in isolation at Hohenschwangau, Ludwig began his reign with great promise at the young age of 18. Before long, though, his interest in politics diminished and, in a vain pursuit of happiness, he embarked on his monumental building spree of fairy-tale castles. The expense of the program and Ludwig's erratic behavior alarmed the government, who feared (probably justifiably) that the king might bankrupt the country with his wildly extravagant projects, so they declared him unfit to rule by reason of insanity. Four days later, Ludwig was found drowned under mysterious circumstances—supposedly suicide, but the world still wonders, "Who done it?" Whatever the truth of the matter, today the tourist benefits, as all of Ludwig's palaces are now museums. (*9 am–5 pm, April to September; 10 am–4 pm, October to March.*) Be prepared for long lines in high season.

Leaving the Chiemsee, continue east along the scenic autobahn to exit 115 at **Bad Reichenhall**, following signposts to the mountain town of **Berchtesgaden**. Set in a crescent of towering mountains, Berchtesgaden, an ancient market town, is a very popular tourist destination. Explore the **Schlossplatz** (the picturesque castle square) with its ancient granary, accounting house, and the **Residenz** that was transformed from an Augustinian monastery and is now an interesting museum full of weapons, tapestries, paintings, and porcelain. (*10 am–noon, 2–5 pm, last admission 4 pm, closed Saturdays Easter through September and only open on weekends October to Easter.*) Berchtesgaden is a lively town which is packed with visitors in summer. Confine your sightseeing (Königssee, Salzbergwerk (salt mines), and Kehlstein (Eagle's Nest)) to early mornings and spend your afternoons on the well-marked walking paths.

Located 4 kilometers south of Berchtesgaden, ***Königssee's** setting and beauty are comparable to some of the world's most magnificent fjords. Steep walls enclose this idyllically beautiful Alpine lake, which is accessible from the tip of its one small resort village. It is a popular excursion, and overhead signs direct you to the huge parking lots (paying, of course). Traffic on the lake is restricted to electric boats, which glide on a half-hour journey around the bend of the glass-like green lake, where the picturesque 18th-century chapel and settlement at **St. Bartholomae** are built on a pocket of land near the lake's edge. A backdrop of maple trees and mountains completes the idyllic scene. There are cafés, restaurants, and walking paths to explore before the return boat journey. (*Sailing every 10 to 20 minutes, 8:15 am–4:15 pm, May to September.*)

Salt was the principal source of Berchtesgaden's prosperity in the 16th century and now the ***Salzbergwerk** (salt mines) are one of the town's principal tourist attractions. Don miners' garb, sit astride a mining wagon, and travel through tunnels of gleaming salt crystal. On the hour-long tour you'll raft across an illuminated subterranean lake, slide down two long, slick, wooden banisters, and learn how they mined salt long ago. (9 *am–5 pm, May to mid-October, 12:30–3:30 pm, mid-October to May, closed Sundays, tel: 08652 60020, fax: 08652 600260.*)

Hitler's Alpine retreat **Kehlstein** (**Eagle's Nest**) is overrated and should be visited only for its view, not for its associations with Hitler who visited there only five times (go only on clear, sunny days). The road from Berchtesgaden to **Obersalzberg** winds two-thirds of the way to the summit where the parking lot is crowded in summer. A shuttle bus takes you on the narrow, winding road with its hair-raising hairpin bends over the Scharitkehlamn gorge. An elevator whisks you the last 125 meters to the foreboding, granite-walled structure. (*8 am–4 pm, May to end of October, weather permitting.*)

SIDE TRIP TO SALZBURG

The proximity of **Salzburg** (25 kilometers) makes this Austrian city made famous by *The Sound of Music* just too exciting a proposition to pass by (allow a day, and be warned that it is very crowded in summer). Cross the border at Marktschellenberg, and you know you are in Salzburg when you see McDonald's and car dealerships. As in all cities, parking is the problem—watch for a small, blue signpost "P Altstadt" (for parking), indicated to the left. Follow signposts for Altstadt Mitte, which lead you beneath the castle and through suburbs to a parking garage, carved into the rocky promontory beside the Altstadt (old town). Take your parking ticket with you as you pay at the booth before returning to your car.

Getreidegasse

Salzburg Cathedral with its three massive bronze doors was built about 1630 and modeled after St. Peter's in Rome. There are over 4,000 pipes in its organ.

You can tour the adjacent **Residenz,** the grandiose palace commissioned by Archbishop Wolf Dietrich. It's an impressive baroque edifice. You can tour only with a group and tours in English are given only in July and August. (*10 am– 3 pm daily.*)

Getreidegasse is the old town's colorful main street, famous for its many old wrought-iron signs looking much as they did in 1756, when Mozart was born at number 9. **Mozart's Birthplace (Geburthaus 1756)**, filled with portraits, musical scores, old keyboard instruments, and violins, is a popular Mozart shrine. (*9 am–5 pm in summer, shorter hours off-season.*)

The **Hohensalzburg Fortress** dominates the skyline. While it is not worth touring the interior, the basic entry fee gives you access to the view and the courtyard. The funicular from the edge of town near the cathedral, which runs every ten minutes, whisks you up to the castle. (*8 am–4 pm daily.*) Just across the pedestrian bridge from the heart of Old

Salzburg are **Schloss Mirabell and Gardens**, built by Archbishop Wolf Dietrich for his mistress Salome Alt. There is no charge to wander through the lovely terraced lawns.

Returning to Schönau am Königssee from Salzburg, follow signposts for Munich and the autobahn. When Munich signposts disappear, keep following those for the autobahn, which you take in the direction of Villach (E55). Once on the autobahn, follow signposts for Berchtesgaden (exit 160).

It's a five-hour drive from Schönau am Königssee to Garmisch-Partenkirchen, much of it along the **Alpenstrasse* (Alpine Road). Adding in time for sightseeing and lunch along the way, allow a day for the journey. Hope for sunny weather as the Alps are incredible

Ramsau Church

against a backdrop of blue sky. Mark your route on a detailed map as you often follow signposts for towns without ever going there.

From Berchtesgaden drive towards Ramsau (9 kilometers, road 305). At **Ramsau** turn left for Hintersee, which takes you into the village past the world-famous ***Ramsau Church** with the towering Alpine peaks in the distance, and brings you to a small Alpine lake, the **Hintersee**, whose crystal-clear waters reflect the hotels on its far shore. Drive around the lake and continue on the narrow road that takes you through pine forests to an Alpine meadow dotted with farmhouses. Turn left (signposted Alpenstrasse), following a country road that returns you to the 305 at the head of the pass.

Descend to **Unterjettenberg**, a cluster of houses in a green meadow with the high Alpine peaks in the background, and cross the River Saalach (signposted Traunstein). The 305 descends through woodlands and just as it opens up to a broad valley, makes a sharp, left-hand turn (signposted Reit am Winkl) and climbs the pass high above the village of Ruhpolding. Passing high Alpine lakes, isolated farms, clusters of chalets, hiking trails, and breathtaking vistas, it's a 21-kilometer drive to ***Reit im Winkl**. This attractive village provides the perfect excuse to leave your car and explore its quaint shops and restaurants. On the outskirts of Reit im Winkl, you cross the border into Austria and the 305 becomes the 172, which follows a tumbling mountain river for the 5-kilometer drive into **Kössen**.

Just 7 kilometers away lies **Walchsee**, a small lake with a beautiful setting where the pastures rise steeply from the lake to forests and the craggy, gray mountains. Pass through the town of **Durchholzen** before crossing back into Germany. Cross the busy autobahn (E45) into **Oberaudorf** and wind through the town's bustling main street following signposts for Niederaudorf (2 kilometers). Before reaching the village, turn left on a narrow country road for Bayrischzell (20 kilometers): en route the road climbs steeply to the little village of **Wall**, which clings to the hillside with spectacular, rolling valley vistas below and rocky, snow-covered peaks above. Passing through hamlets of two or three chalets, the road crests the pass and winds down to the enticing ski village of **Bayrischzell**. Detour into the village and browse through the shops and cafés around the little square that sits beside the church.

A 15-kilometer drive (on the 307) brings you to the **Schliersee** lake where **Neuhaus** nestles at one end and the town of **Schliersee** clusters at the other. The more industrial town of **Hausham** lies just 1 kilometer away and from here you follow signposts to the **Tegernsee**. At the lake turn right into the attractive town of **Gmund**, skirt the lake on its northern shore, then turn left for the resort town of **Bad Wiessee** (road 318). At the southern end of the lake turn right towards Achensee. The road soon leaves the Alpine pastures and travels through wooded forests toward the Austrian border (if you arrive at the Austrian border post, you have gone too far). Turn right at the signpost for Bad Tolz, following the 13 as it travels beside a large dam where Alpine peaks are reflected in the deep aquamarine waters. Take the first left (Wallgau) and follow the 307 to **Vordereiss** where you leave the main road and cross the river to follow a narrower toll road through rugged countryside to **Wallgau**. Between Wallgau and **Kryn** the green pastures are strewn with picture-postcard barns. From Kryn follow the E533 into Garmisch-Partenkirchen.

Our suggestion is to base yourself in the Garmisch-Partenkirchen area. We suggest hotels in Garmisch-Partenkirchen; nearby Grainau, Elmal, Ettal, Hohenschwangau, and Oberammergau; and just a little farther away in Pfronten and Seeg. Any of these towns makes an excellent hub for exploring this lovely area.

Framed by some of Germany's most dramatic, jagged peaks, ***Garmisch-Partenkirchen** is backed up against her highest—the towering Zugspitze. At one time two villages, Garmisch and Partenkirchen, merged to meet the demands of accommodating the 1936 winter Olympic Games, and the distinction between what were once two communities is still apparent. Garmisch is a bustle of activity with broader, newer streets lined by larger stores and hotels. Partenkirchen, with narrow, winding streets and timbered buildings, preserves more old-world charm.

Garmisch-Partenkirchen is a skiers' delight in winter and a walkers' paradise in summer and fall. One of the loveliest well-marked trails takes you through the **Partnachklamm Gorge** (behind the Olympic ski stadium), where you walk along a rocky ledge with a guardrail between you and the tumbling river, sometimes passing through rock tunnels and behind cascading waterfalls. You get a little wet (take a raincoat) and the gorge is chilly even in summer, but the experience is breathtaking.

Pretty walks can be by taken by riding the cable car up the **Wank** mountain and walking down to the valley floor. (*8:45 am–5 pm, May to October.*) Additional scenic views are found by taking the Osterfeldbahn to **Osterfeldkopt** (2050 meters).

For some it's a must to travel to the top of Germany's highest mountain, the **Zugspitze** (2966 meters)—remember to take warm sweaters for this excursion. The Zugspitze cog railway departs from the Zugspitzebahnhof, next to the main railway station, almost every hour on the hour (also from Grainau). The train ascends through the valley and brings you out below the summit of the Zugspitze—a cable car departs about every half-hour and whisks you the last 3 kilometers up the mountain. Enjoy the view, soak up the high Alpine sunshine, and return to the valley on the other cable car for the ten-minute descent to the **Eibsee Lake**. From here the train returns you to Garmisch or Grainau. (*Departs hourly 7:35 am–3:35 pm in summer, last return approximately 5 pm.*)

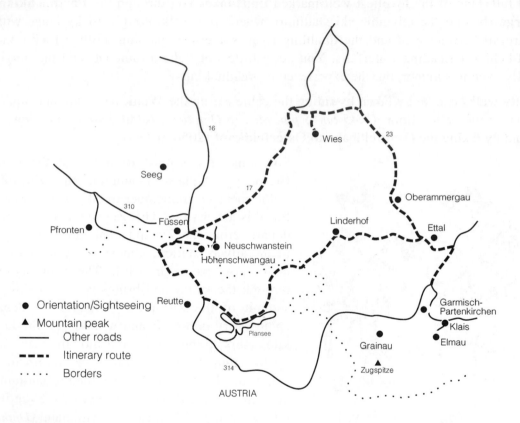

Because there is so much to see and do around Garmisch-Partenkirchen, we outline a circular tour; but be aware that there is so much sightseeing that you cannot accomplish everything in one day, especially if you plan to include the *Ludwig II* theatrical performance. Leave Garmisch-Partenkirchen in the direction of Munich for a short distance, then follow signposts for Augsburg and Oberammergau, which brings you to the little village of **Ettal**. You cannot miss your sightseeing destination here for overshadowing the village is the **Klosterkirche** (monastery) where Benedictine monks distill liqueur, although you will see not a monk nor a sign of their commercial operation. The church is an exquisite baroque riot of colorful paintings and gilded woodwork.

Klosterkirche, Ettal

Continue for a very short distance in the direction of Oberammergau and turn left on a country road that quickly brings you to ***Linderhof,** the smallest and most homey of Ludwig II's palaces. Be sure to buy an English guidebook at the entrance, as there aren't always enough English-speaking guests to warrant a guided tour in English. A ten-minute stroll through parklike grounds brings you to the squat, little palace with its fountains and Italian-style gardens. The guided tour leads you from one outrageous room to another, including the decadent state room, and the dining room where Ludwig ate solitary meals at a table which was lowered, like a dumb waiter, below the floor so that meals were served without Ludwig being disturbed by servants.

Walk up the hill to the ***Venus Grotto**. Ludwig commissioned the building of this cavernous grotto hung with stalactites and festooned with garlands where a conch-shell boat floats in the middle of an illuminated lake and the jeweled Lorelei cliff glitters with crystals. A short distance farther along the woodland path you come to the **Moorish Kiosk** where Ludwig dressed up as a Turkish sultan and smoked his hookah surrounded by young boys dressed up as palace eunuchs. Small wonder that the Bavarian government questioned his sanity! (*Allow for a wait in summer, 9 am–5:30 pm, April to September; 10 am–4 pm, October to March.*)

Continue across the Austrian border through wooded countryside on a road that quickly brings you to the **Plansee,** whose rocky shore seems to rise almost directly from the glassy lake. As the valley opens up to the rooftops of Reutte take a right-hand turn signposted Deutschland (Germany). This takes you around the town and brings you onto the road for Füssen and Königsschlösser (King's Castles).

Füssen is a charming walled town whose maze of pedestrian streets are fun to explore. There are lots of shops, outdoor cafés, and restaurants, and a wonderful indoor market. Füssen's **Hohes Schloss**, standing high above the river, is usually overlooked in favor of its more famous neighbors; but now Füssen has an attraction all its own, the **Musical Theater Neuschwanstein,** with a majestic setting right on the edge of Lake Forggen surrounded by the Alps. Here the legend of Mad King Ludwig and his fantasy-filled life is presented in the musical production *Ludwig II.* The musical, which lasts three hours, including a 45-minute intermission, is performed in a heavy Bavarian dialect: so English, Japanese, French, and Italian translations are projected above the stage to aid comprehension. A remarkable tribute to Bavaria's king, the production is as opulent as

Ludwig's own life, with a revolving stage, sleighs pulled by real horses prancing through a dramatic snowfall, and a grand finale when the king walks on the lake and the golden fountain, a replica of the one at Linderhof, rises up from the depths of the water. An enchanting performance! Tickets are available at the theatre ticket office in Neuschwanstein and conveniently at almost all the hotels in the region that proudly display the Ludwig II Musical decal. I would strongly recommend obtaining tickets through your hotel or travel agent before you leave home to enable you to schedule your trip accordingly and not waste precious travel time trying to obtain reservations. (*May to October, shows at 7:30 pm every day except Mondays, matinees at 2:30 pm, Saturdays and Sundays; November to March, shows at 7:30 pm, Sundays, matinees at 2:30 pm, Saturdays.*)

Many recognize ***Neuschwanstein**, located high above the valley atop a rocky ledge, as being the inspiration for Walt Disney's Sleeping Beauty's castles at Disneyland and Disneyworld. You begin to appreciate the effort that went into building this castle as you walk up the steep path to the fortress high above. The only way to decrease a half-hour uphill hike to a ten-minute one is to take a shuttle bus or horse-drawn wagon partway to the castle. This is one of Germany's most popular sightseeing attractions and the only way to avoid summer crowds (and long lines) is to arrive early in the morning. If you just cannot schedule the first tour of the day, our advice is to admire Neuschwanstein from afar and tour Linderhof (less crowded) to get an appreciation of Ludwig's taste in interior design. The castle's fanciful interior, designed by a theater-set designer and an eccentric king, is a romantic flight of fancy whose rooms afford spectacular views of Alpine lakes and snowy peaks. Ludwig greatly admired Richard Wagner and scenes from his operas are found throughout in the decor. At the end of the castle tour, walk up the Pollat gorge to the Marienbrucke which spans the ravine above the castle: you will be rewarded with a spectacular view. (*Allow for a long wait in summer, 9 am–5:30 pm, April to October; 10 am–4 pm, November to March.*)

Neuschwanstein

From the road at the foot of the castle, it is a short walk to King Ludwig's childhood home, **Hohenschwangau**. Though the interior is somewhat heavy, it has a homey quality to it. It was here that Ludwig met his adored Wagner, and here that the young king lived while he kept a watchful eye on the building progress at Neuschwanstein. (*9 am–5:30 pm, April to October; 10 am–4 pm, November to March.*)

Leave the castles in the direction of Augsburg and travel up the ever-broadening valley through rolling green farmland to the large village of **Steingaden** where you leave the 17 and turn right onto a country road signposted Weis and Oberammergau (29 kilometers). Detour to **Wies** to visit the ***Wieskirche**, a pilgrimage church whose simple exterior belies the most exquisitely beautiful interior. It's a popular excursion, so there are cafés and paid parking but once you step into the beautiful interior, all the surrounding commercialism is forgotten. (*8 am–5 pm, October to March; 8 am–6 pm, April to September.*)

As you drive from the Wieskirche to Oberammergau, you cross the **Echelsbacher Bridge**, which spans a deep, wooded ravine with the rushing River Ammer far below. To appreciate the fabulous view, park at one of the car parks (found at both ends of the bridge) and take a few minutes to walk along the bridge.

Detour off the main road into the famous village of **Oberammergau** where many of the homes have ornate murals and seemingly all the shops sell very expensive carvings. Every ten years the *Passion Spiel* (Passion Play), a religious play, is performed here. It was a spectacular performance for the millennium and will be staged next in 2010. All the residents in town are involved in the production and performance of this play, which celebrates the end of the misery and death associated with the Black Plague. In between plays it seems that everyone in the village carves. While it's a bustling spot during the day, in the evening it's very serene. The church has a very attractive interior. From Oberammergau a half-hour drive through Ettal returns you to Garmisch-Partenkirchen.

When it is time to leave the Garmisch-Partenkirchen area, a two- to three-hour drive will take you to the most westerly part of Bavaria, the lovely island of Lindau. Along the way there is much to see. Leave Füssen following the 310 towards Kempten. As you near **Pfronten,** study the nearby hilltops and locate the ruined medieval fortress of Schloss Falkenstein where Ludwig planned to build his next castle. His death put an end to his fanciful building program, so instead of a grandiose castle you now find several lovely hotels on the mountain.

Just as you leave the village of **Nesselwang** take a left-hand turn down a lane for Wertach, which gives you an opportunity to travel a quiet country road for a short distance. Regaining the 310 at **Wertach**, turn towards Sonthofen. The road climbs steeply to **Oberjoch**, a ski resort spread across the summit, and opens up to vistas of the valley as it winds down past **Hindelang,** where you pick up signposts for Lindau. Join a

Meersburg

dual carriageway for several kilometers at **Sonthofen** and on to **Immenstadt** whose narrow streets are clogged with traffic as you follow signposts for the 308 and Lindau. Leaving Immenstadt, you leave the soaring granite peaks of the Alps behind and travel beside a lake and along a valley bordered with green hills. The valley opens up at **Oberstaufen**, a small town that steps down the hillside where every home seems to have a fabulous view of the far side of the valley whose green pastureland is dotted with farmhouses.

Traversing rolling green hills, you arrive at the **Bodensee** (Lake Constance), the nearest thing to an inland sea in Germany. The problem with the Bodensee is that it is impossible to appreciate its beauty from the shoreline. There are not many places where you can actually get beside the lake, and the traffic-clogged road (31) that parallels its shoreline runs slightly inland. A solution to this is to tackle the 31 to reach your base in the Bodensee at Lindau, or beside the Bodensee at Meersburg and do your sightseeing by boat.

Arriving at the Bodensee, follow the well-signposted route through the suburbs to Lindau Insel. If you are not staying on the island, park your car in the large car park just before the bridge road to the island of ***Lindau**. The island's main thoroughfare, Maximilianstrasse, is bordered with lovely old houses. The **Altes Rathaus** (old town hall) on Bismarckplatz dates from the 15th century and is famous for the brightly colored frescoes that decorate its façade. The harbor is guarded by the Lion of Bavaria and the Mangturm, a tower that was once part of the town's medieval ramparts. All along the harborside promenade, restaurants and cafés spill out onto the pavement. During the summer months regular ferry service connects Lindau to Konstanz (Constance), Meersburg (2½ hours), Mainau island, Bregenz (Austria), and Rorschach (Switzerland).

Another base for explorations of the Bodensee, ***Meersburg**, lies an hour's drive (two hours' in heavy traffic) beyond the geographic bounds of Bavaria towards the other end of the lake. We include it in this itinerary because it is such an adorable little medieval town, offers charming accommodation, and is perfect for boat trips on the Bodensee. Arriving in Meersburg, follow signposts for the Altstadt. (If you cannot find parking at the top of the hill, follow signs for the ferry and park in the large car park beside the ferry terminal.) During the summer months regular ferry service connects Meersburg to nearby Konstanz (Constance) and Mainau island, and farther afield to Lindau and Bregenz (Austria).

Wander among the little narrow, cobbled streets lined with half-timbered houses along the Steigstrasse. Atop a rocky promontory overlooking the lake, the **Altes Schloss** (old castle) dates back to 628, when a longhouse and tower fortress were built by King Dagobert. The castle was enlarged over the years, and by 1510, the structure you see today, complete with drawbridge and moat, was in place. The castle was purchased in the 19th century by Baron von Lassburg as a storage place for his vast collection of books and weapons. His sister-in-law, Annette von Droste-Hülshoff, wrote some of her most famous poems here, and her little rooms are very much as they were when she lived here. (You can also visit her little house in a nearby vineyard.) The Lassburgs went bankrupt and the castle was bought by the Furstenberg family (as in the beer). They sold the books to buyers in the United States but kept much of the weaponry. Tour the castle at your own pace with the aid of a typed-sheet (in English), and enjoy the various rooms, which are furnished to illustrate what life was like in the castle's different eras. (*9 am–5 pm.*)

In 1520 the nearby town of Konstanz (Constance) became Protestant so the bishop moved from Konstanz to the castle in Meersburg. It was decided that the castle was not grand enough for a resident bishop, so the **Neues Schloss** (new castle) was built between

1750 and 1802 to suit the bishop's palatial tastes. No sooner was the bishop installed than his bishopric was moved (furniture and all) to Freiburg. Happily, they were not able to move the magnificent ceiling paintings, and the grand rooms are a perfect venue for changing art exhibits and musical concerts.

Garden lovers will not want to miss taking the boat excursion to the tiny island of ***Mainau**. Lovely, fragrant gardens bloom from March to October in the grounds of an 18th-century castle owned by a Swedish count. From Mainau you can return directly to Meersburg, or take the ferry to **Uhldingen** to tour the prehistoric lake-dwellers' village reconstruction before either taking the bus (every half hour) or walking 5 kilometers beside the lake back to Meersburg.

From Meersburg a two-hour drive takes you to Freiburg, where you can join the *Highways & Byways of the Black Forest* itinerary.

Castles of the Rhine & Mosel

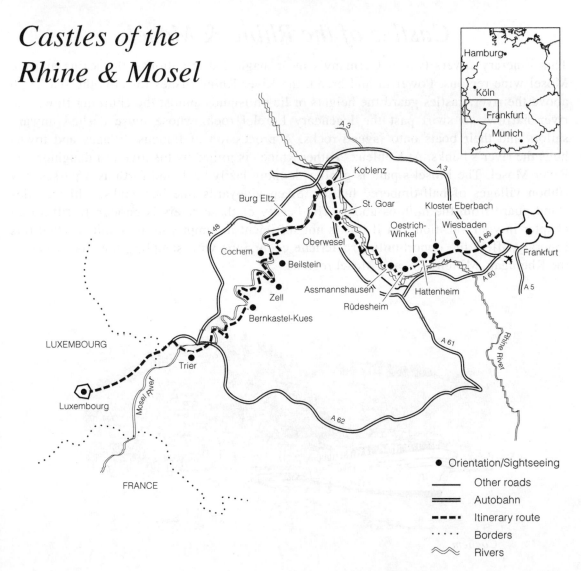

Hamburg

Köln

Frankfurt

Munich

Koblenz

Burg Eltz

St. Goar

Kloster Eberbach

Oestrich-Winkel

Wiesbaden

Oberwesel

Cochem

Beilstein

Frankfurt

Assmannshausen

Hattenheim

Zell

Rüdesheim

Bernkastel-Kues

LUXEMBOURG

Trier

Luxembourg

Mosel River

Rhine River

A 3

A 48

A 66

A 60

A 5

A 61

A 62

FRANCE

● Orientation/Sightseeing

——— Other roads

═══ Autobahn

- - - Itinerary route

· · · · Borders

〜〜〜 Rivers

Castles of the Rhine & Mosel

This itinerary covers two of Germany's most magical destinations—the Rhine and the Mosel wine regions. Powerful and broad, the River Rhine rushes towards the sea. High above the river, castles guard the heights or lie on islands amidst the churning flow. The river narrows to swirl past the legendary Lorelei rock, whose muse dashed unwary sailors and their boats onto jagged rocks. A procession of famous villages and towns hugs the river's banks. At Koblenz "Father Rhine" is joined by his loveliest daughter, the River Mosel. The Mosel's path is gentler, looping lazily back and forth as it passes tiny ribbon villages of half-timbered houses. Steep vineyards line her banks, while castles stand guard from the hilltops above. The beauty of these rivers is enough to fill a rich chapter in your vacation, but if this is not sufficient to tempt you, be reminded that this itinerary offers the opportunity to alternate excursions with sampling the fine wines of the Rheingau, Mittelrhein, and Mosel regions.

Cochem

Recommended Pacing: Spend one night along the Rhine (Hattenheim, Assmannshausen, Oestrich-Winkel, Oberwesel, St. Goar, or Braubach) and one along the Mosel (Beilstein, Bernkastel, or Horbruch). If you include Trier and Luxembourg in your sightseeing, allow two nights along the Mosel. As you travel along both the Rhine and the Mosel, know that there are a limited number of opportunities to cross back and forth between their banks. Study your map to plot your route to take advantage of the few bridges or passenger/car ferry points. The ferry crossings are frequent and inexpensive.

This itinerary begins in **Frankfurt**, conveniently reached by direct flights from cities throughout the world. If you arrive at the Frankfurt airport, you can easily begin your journey immediately by picking up a rental car at the airport and starting on your way. If you choose to visit the pleasant, modern heart of the city, be aware that a couple of historic gems have been restored. **Goethehaus**, where Johann Wolfgang von Goethe was born in 1749, is open as a museum showing how a well-to-do family lived in the 18th century and nearby you find the **Romerberg**, a square of old restored gabled buildings.

Follow the autobahn 66 west from Frankfurt through **Wiesbaden**. In a few kilometers the autobahn ends and continues as road 42: this main road and the busy intercity railway trace the river's bank. The first part of this itinerary loops back and forth from this main artery, exploring the gently sloping, vineyard-covered hillsides that line the bank of the River Rhine. Known as the **Rheingau**, this small wine area is especially famous for its Riesling wines.

A short drive brings you to the wine town of **Eltville** where in medieval times the archbishops of Mainz had their summer palaces. You then leave the busy river road and climb through the vineyards to **Kiedrich**. Drive into the little village and visit its pretty pink church with its elaborate interior before continuing up the hill to **Kloster Eberbach**. Set in a snug, little hollow at the upper reaches of the vineyards, this former Cistercian monastery enjoyed 700 years of prosperity thanks to the production of wine. The Cistercian monks led an austere, silent life of prayer and hard work, allotting only a few hours a night for sleep on hard, narrow wooden pallets. Stroll through the quiet cloisters and cool halls with their graceful fan-vaulted ceilings to the refectory, which now houses an impressive collection of enormous old wine presses. The severe architecture, plain plaster walls, and lack of embellishments mirror the austere lifestyle led by the monks. (*10 am–6 pm, April to October; 10 am–4 pm, November to March.*)

Leaving the monastery grounds, turn to the right and follow the country road as it dips down through the vineyards back to the river at **Hattenheim**. Drive through the old town center to the adjacent village of **Oestrich**. Turn left down one of the winding village streets and you emerge back on the busy Rhineside road for the short drive to **Winkel**.

Turn right in Winkel and follow the road up through the vineyards to the bright-yellow castle on the hill, the **Schloss Johannisberg**. This famous castle is the emblem of wines produced in this area and its name, Johannisberg, is synonymous with the production of Riesling wine. From April to December you can enjoy a meal at their country-style restaurant (*closed Tuesdays*) and visit the wine shop. On a fine day the castle terrace affords a panoramic view across the vineyards to the river below. The palace cellars contain century-old wines of extreme value. You can arrange for a tour of the cellars and winetasting (on weekdays only) by writing to Schloss Johannisberg, 65366 Geisenheim-Johannisberg, Germany. *(Open daily, tel: 06722 700929, www.schloss-johannisberg.com.)*

Returning to the river road, it is a short distance to the most famous wine town of this area, **Rüdesheim**. Park you car and walk by the river, bypassing the many tourist shops selling gaudy souvenirs, and turn into the narrow, cobbled **Drosselgrasse**, the town's most attractive street. Here, on what is reputed to be the jolliest street in the world, one wine tavern props up another and, even if you do not partake of the wine, it is fun to wander along this festive street. A short stroll along the river brings you to the more serious side of wine production, the **Wein Museum Brömserburg** in Brömserburg Castle. Ask for a leaflet in English that guides you from room to room, up turret stairways, to see the artifacts pertaining to the production and consumption of wine from the earliest days. (*February to November, closed Mondays.*) If the weather is agreeable, consider taking the **seilbahn** (cable car) to **Niederwald** high above the town where you find a huge statue of Germania erected to celebrate victory over the French in 1871.

Leaving Rüdesheim, the river road winds below steeply terraced vineyards as the Rhine forsakes its gently sloping banks and turns north into a rocky gorge. Passing below the ruins of **Ehrenfels Castle**, the **Mauseturm** (Mouse Tower) comes into view on an island near the opposite bank. Legend has it that Archbishop Hatto II was a cruel master who paid a terrible price for his sins: he was driven into this tower by mice who then procceded to eat him alive.

The river valley narrows as you near the town of **Assmannshausen,** and the first of the famous castles that overlook the river comes into view on the opposite bank— **Rheinstein Castle**. Take time to drive into Assmannshausen and explore its poky, narrow streets full of charming, little, old houses. The wisteria-covered terrace of the **Hotel Krone** provides you with a refreshment stop (or excellent place to stay) and lovely views of the passing river life.

As you drive north along the riverbank, as fast as one castle disappears from view, another comes into sight perched high above the rocky river valley. The Rheingau wine region ends in the little town of **Lorch**, where you take the small, chugging, car ferry which fights the strong river currents and slowly transports you across the river to **Rheindiebach**. As you enter the **Mittelrhein** wine district, you see verdant vineyards gently sloping to the river replaced by steep, river terraces occupying every southern-facing slope, where the grapes can soak up the warm summer sun. Between the vineyards, the high riverbanks are thickly wooded.

It is just a few minutes' drive from the ferry to **Bacharach**. Park your car by the river and walk into the town to discover that the plain riverfront façade conceals a picturesque village of half-timbered medieval houses around a market square. As you leave Bacharach, a much photographed castle, the **Pfalz**, comes into view marooned on an island amidst the swirling flow.

The Pfalz

As you drive into **Oberwesel,** turn left before the brick-red church, the **Liebfrauenkirche,** and pause to see its interior. Gothic in style, the church is noted for its many beautiful altarpieces, the oldest built in 1506. Follow the winding road upwards to the **Auf Schönburg** castle, perched high above Oberwesel. Park your car beneath the castle walls, cross the wooden bridge spanning the gully that isolates the Auf Schönburg on its rocky bluff, and climb the well-worn cobbles which wind you through the castle to the hotel at the summit. The façade is out of a fairytale—towers, turrets, and crumbling battlements. If you are lucky enough to be staying at the hotel, you can explore the interior of the castle. However, if you are not staying at the castle, you can enjoy the view from the terrace below the hotel.

Leaving the Auf Schönburg, glance to the river where it swirls and eddies in the rocks on the opposite bank. Legend has it that these rocks are the seven maidens of Oberwesel

Castle who were so cold-hearted towards their suitors that the river overturned their boat and turned them into stone.

Around the first river bend, the fabled **Lorelei** rock comes into view. The currents around the rock, which juts out sharply into the river, are so dangerous that the legend arose of an enchantress sitting high on top of the rock combing her golden tresses, and so entranced the sailors were with her singing that the rules of navigation were forgotten and their boats were dashed onto the rocks.

The Rhine landscape is splendid when viewed from the river; but even finer views await you from the ramparts of the castle, *****Burg Rheinfels**, located high above **Saint Goar**. Below flows the mighty Rhine dotted with chugging barges, and on the opposite bank are the whimsically named **Burg Mauz** (Mouse Castle) and the adjacent larger **Burg Katz** (Cat Castle). Built in 1245, the Rheinfels castle was reduced to the crumbling ruin you see today by the French in 1797. With map and English explanation in hand, you tour the castle, climb the ramparts, and get a feeling for what the fortress must have been like in its heyday. A model in the museum shows just what a grand edifice this was. (*9 am–5 pm, April to October.*)

Keeping the river close company, about a 20-minute drive brings you to the outskirts of **Koblenz,** where you bid the Rhine farewell and, by following signposts for Cochem (49), navigate through town to the banks of the *****River Mosel**.

The pageant of the riverbank marches steadily on, but how different the Mosel is to the Rhine. The Mosel is narrower, moving more slowly—gracefully looping back and forth. The road, too, is narrower, with thankfully less traffic and no busy adjacent railway track. The Mosel's steep banks are uniformly covered with vines—for this is wine country and every little ribbon village, with terraced vineyards rising steeply behind it, is involved in the production of wine. The villages are often no more than a cluster of houses, yet they all have their own famous brand of wine.

Pass beneath the 61 autobahn, which bridges the river valley high above you, and cross the Mosel to the village of **Lof**. A few minutes' drive brings you to the edge of

Niederfell where you turn right, signposted Burg Eltz P & R. (Look specifically for this sign: it leads you to parking that involves the least amount of uphill walking.) After several signposts Burg Eltz P & R signs become Burg Eltz and the route winds you uphill out of the river valley, through rolling farmland to the village of **Munstermaifeld**, where you turn left to arrive at the parking for ***Burg Eltz**. A 1-kilometer (15-minute) walk downhill means that you have a 1-kilometer walk uphill to return to your car. The walk is worth it for this is, in our estimation, the loveliest of castles in Europe. High upon a rocky outcrop encircled by woodland, the picturesque Burg Eltz is a fairy-tale castle of turrets and towers piled one upon the other between the 12th and 16th century. It's still the home of the Count and Countess of Eltz, and the Countess designs the lovely flower arrangements in each of the rooms. Tours are rarely given in English; but with the aid of an English fact sheet, this is not a problem. Your guide leads you from one magnificent historic room to another and you learn that, at a time when many castles contained only one fireplace and one toilet, this castle contained forty fireplaces and twenty toilets. While waiting for your tour to begin, be sure to visit the Treasury (*additional charge*) where you will be rewarded by displays of absolutely elegant china, silverware, and jewelry. (*9:30 am–5:30 pm, April to end of October.*)

Leaving the castle, take the first right-hand turn signposted Mozelkurn, which drops you back to the river and quickly brings you into **Cochem**. Park your car and explore the pedestrian center of this small town. Turn a blind eye to the souvenir shops and instead let yourself be tempted inside a coffee shop for some mouth-watering pastries and a cup of coffee. Thus fortified, wander through the narrow streets and follow the well-signposted walk to the castle (Burg), **Reichsburg Cochem**, sitting atop a hill above the town. The trek is worth it, for while the valley is beautiful when viewed from below, the view from above is even more impressive. Touring the castle is not recommended: too many gloomy rooms full of heavy, ornately carved furniture. (*9 am–5 pm, mid-March to mid-November.*)

Cross the river at Cochem (signposted Beilstein) and the prettiest stretch of the Mosel river valley opens up before you as the loops of the river almost double back on themselves. Soon *Beilstein comes into view, a little picture-postcard village hugging the riverbank below the vineyards.

Beilstein

Walk up to the tiny, cobbled square crowded by centuries-old houses. Stroll up the quiet, cobbled streets to the church and the little **castle** (*9 am–6 pm, mid-March to end of October*) and return to the square to tour the little **Weingut Museum**, which is full of winemaking artifacts, before going into the cool, deep cellars of Joachim Lipmann to sample his wines. If the weather is warm, settle on the Hotel Lipmann's terrace to watch the little ferry as it shuttles cars back and forth across the river while long river barges chug slowly by.

Winding down to Bernkastel-Kues, as you go through one small village, another appears on the opposite bank; each with little houses fronting the river, a large church, and a backdrop of steeply sloping vineyards. Among the many villages, **Zell** stands out as one of the larger ones, famous for the production of Black Cat wine: you see a black cat on murals throughout the village.

A half-hour drive brings you to *****Bernkastel-Kues**. Bernkastel-Kues is two villages: Bernkastel on one side and Kues lying just across the bridge on the other side of the river. In this wine valley, Bernkastel stands out as the most picturesque of the larger villages. You will fall in love with this quaint wine village where colorful, 400-year-old, half-timbered houses are grouped around a flower-filled marketplace and beautiful medieval houses extend for several blocks. A couple of blocks up the main street is an interesting toy and doll museum.

For a closer look at another castle overlooking the river, follow Bernkastel's main street up a narrow valley to **Berg Landshut**, the ruins of a castle set in vineyards that tumble to the river below. A restaurant has been incorporated into the ruined keep and the view is impressive.

An hour's drive brings you to **Trier**, one of Germany's oldest cities, founded by the Roman Emperor Augustus in 15 B.C. Follow signposts for Zentrum Park and make your way on foot to **Porta Nigra**, the largest fortified gateway in the Roman Empire. Still intact, it stands guard over the city 20 centuries later. This gate is like a giant wedding cake of 3½ tiers standing nearly 30 meters high. (*9 am–6 pm, April to end of October.*) The tourist office by the Porta Nigra will supply you with a city map (splurge for the larger one) showing you the historic sights of the city, all found within a few blocks of the gate. (*Walking tours of the city in English leave at 2 pm, April to October.*) With your back to the Porta Nigra, walk up the main shopping pedestrian street, the Simeonstrasse, passing the Turkish-looking **Dreilonigen-Haus**, built in 1260, to the Hauptmarkt (marketplace) where a colorfully painted fountain is surrounded by ancient timbered houses. The **Dom** (cathedral) lies just a block off the square, a surprisingly spacious, simply adorned edifice where behind the altar you can peer into an ornate shrine that is purported to contain the robe of Christ.

Retrace your steps to your car and with the aid of your detailed map, following signposts for Universitat, drive to the **Roman Amphitheater**, which was built above the town to provide up to 20,000 people with gladiatorial entertainment. After the Roman Empire fell, the site was used as a quarry, and now soft, grassy mounds have taken the place of the stone seats. (*9 am–6 pm, April to end of September.*) If walking around Roman amphitheaters is not your cup of tea, turn just beyond the amphitheater up a narrow lane and into the vineyards onto the **Weinlehrpfad**, an educational walking route through the vineyards that offers bird's-eye views of the amphitheater.

Bernkastel-Kues

When it is time to leave this lovely wine region of the Mosel, it is only a short drive to Germany's borders with Luxembourg, France, and Belgium. You can take an autobahn to join Würzburg (*The Romantic Road & the Neckar Valley*), Baden-Baden or Freiburg (*Highways & Byways of the Black Forest*), or Eisnach (*Exploring East & Middle Germany*).

The proximity of **Luxembourg**, an hour's drive from Trier, makes an excursion there too tempting an opportunity to pass up. Leave Trier across the Römerbrüke bridge signposted for Luxembourg and the autobahn. Arriving in Luxembourg, follow signposts for Zentrum and parking, and set out on foot to explore. Walk to the Place d'Armes and the tourist office where you are given maps, a walking tour brochure, and information on this cosmopolitan city atop the rocky Bock promontory. As long ago as 963 Count Siegfried built his fortress here but, in spite of it being a heavily fortified position, the Burgundians took the city in 1443. Over the next four centuries the best French, Spanish, Austrian, and German military engineers fortified the city, turning it into the "Gibraltar of the North." The most interesting part of their fortifications was a vast network of underground casemates (tunnels) that sheltered thousands of soldiers and their horses along with kitchens, bakeries, and military workshops. The Treaty of London in 1867 stipulated the dismantling of the casemates, and only a small portion of them remains today, the **Casemates Pétrusse** and **Casemates Bock**. *(Bock: 10 am–5 pm, March to October; Pétrusse: 11 am–4 pm, July to September.)*

Highways & Byways
of the Black Forest

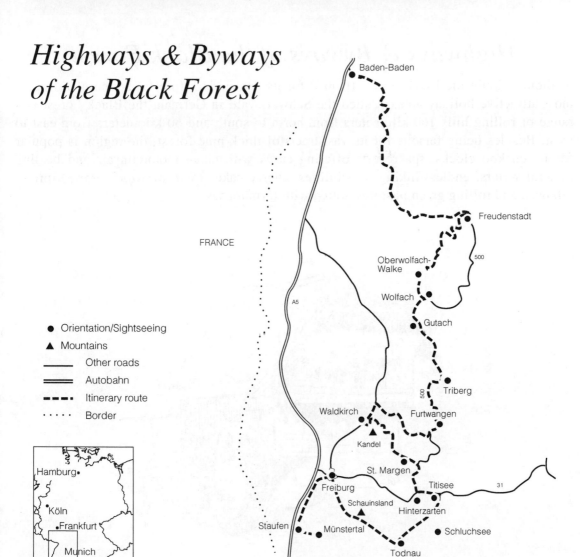

FRANCE

Baden-Baden

Freudenstadt

500

Oberwolfach-
Walke

Wolfach

A5

Gutach

● Orientation/Sightseeing

▲ Mountains

—— Other roads

══ Autobahn

━ ━ ━ Itinerary route

· · · · · Border

500

Triberg

Waldkirch

Furtwangen

Kandel

St. Margen

Freiburg

Titisee

31

Schauinsland

Hinterzarten

Hamburg

Staufen

Münstertal

Todnau

Schluchsee

Köln

Frankfurt

Munich

Highways & Byways of the Black Forest

Without a doubt the Black Forest (named for its dense, dark forests) is one of Europe's most attractive holiday areas. Called the Schwarzwald in German, the Black Forest is a range of rolling hills 160 kilometers from north to south and 60 kilometers from east to west. Besides being famous for its vast tracts of thick pine forest, the region is popular for its cuckoo clocks, spa resorts offering cures with clean mountain air and healing mineral waters, endless hiking possibilities, cherry cakes (*Schwarzwalder torte*), pretty villages, and rolling green pastures dotted with farmhouses.

Recommended Pacing: If you are driving the region, you can explore the Black Forest at leisure by spending two nights based in the south (Freiburg, Staufen, Münstertal, Badenweiler, Hinterzarten, or Schluchsee) and one night at its heart (Triberg, Wolfach, or Oberwolfach), then traveling the Hochstrasse north to Baden-Baden. Here you will need one night to simply experience the city or two nights if you plan on visiting the baths or going to Baden-Baden's beautiful new opera house.

For those whose travels originated in France, the A5 parallels the border and there are numerous crossover points from Alsace. With a gorgeous setting at the base of the mountains, **Freiburg** is the capital of the Schwarzwald and makes for an appropriate beginning to this itinerary. The dark-green forests come right down within a block or two of this large city. Full of character, the pedestrian-only old center was founded in 1120 and is laden with numerous quaint buildings. On **Münsterplatz** (main square) you find the beautiful **Münster Unserer Lieben Frau** (cathedral) whose tall spires crest all vistas. Inside the cathedral 14th-century sculptures depict sin and temptation. The nave's gorgeous 14th-century stained glass was donated by the guilds and each window shows the emblem of the guild that donated it. Three very attractive buildings are found on the south side of the Münsterplatz: the **Kaufhaus** with its steep roof and pointed turrets, the baroque **Erzbischöfliches Palais** (Archbishop's Palace), and the **Haus zum Schönen Eck**, which now houses the music academy. Here you also find the delightful **Oberkirchs Weinstuben**, a cozy wine tavern-hotel combination. Little streams run down each street between the cathedral and the Swabian gate: known as **Bächle**, these waterways are the city's trademark.

If you prefer a countryside setting, just to the south of Freiburg is a gorgeous, lush region of the Black Forest, reminiscent of the gentle foothills of Switzerland, and three towns that are convenient to Freiburg and would make an ideal base: Staufen, Münstertal, and Badenweiler. Small pedestrian bridges cross the narrow little waterways that trickle through the heart of **Staufen**. Crowned by the ruins of its castle, Staufen is a charming village whose pedestrian streets are lined with richly colored old houses.

It's a beautiful drive east from Staufen along a road that winds through a gorgeous valley to the tiny village of **Münstertal**.

Another area in the southern region of the Black Forest is just a half-hour drive traveling east from Freiburg along the scenic 31 (signposted Donauschingen). The 31 will bring you to Titisee but rather than taking the direct route, detour down scenic byways by leaving Freiburg following the white signposts depicting a gondola. Following the tram tracks to their terminus in the suburbs, the road narrows and climbs steeply as it weaves back and forth beneath the cable car that soars to the summit of the **Schauinsland** (mountain). Pause at the summit, catch your breath, and admire the view of Freiburg way below you and beyond it the plain stretching to the distant horizon. Traversing the high mountain meadow, you find the hamlet of **Horsgrund** nestled in a sheltered fold of the mountain. As you re-enter the forest, turn right (signposted Todnau) and begin a 12-kilometer descent to the valley floor passing through the villages of **Muggenbrun** and **Afterseg**.

Turn left in **Todnau** (signposted Donaueschingen) and follow this broader valley whose sides rise steeply into the dark forest. Climb through **Brandenburg** ever higher to crest the pass at the ski resort of **Feldburg** and travel down to the cool waters of the **Titisee**. Join the 31 in the direction of Freiburg and exit after Neustadt for Titisee (the resort with the same name), following signposts for parking and Ortmitte. The resort is invariably

crowded with tourists and hiring a rowboat is a pleasant way to escape the throngs of visitors.

Regain the 31 going towards Freiburg and exit on the 500 for Triburg (this is also the exit you take if you have come directly from Freiburg). Detour into the village of **Hinterzarten**, a resort noted for its clean mountain air, where pretty little houses and hotels cluster round a grassy green (for specifics on hotels, see *Hotel Descriptions*). Walking paths that lead in every direction are replaced in winter by cross-country skiing trails. The 500 is an extremely scenic road passing through wide vistas of farmland with patches of dark-green forest. If the weather is clear, consider leaving the main road to take a particularly scenic loop to Furtwangen.

Leave the 500 at **Thurner**, turning left onto a country road for St. Margen (signposted Freiburg). Travel through a broad green valley with a sky-wide landscape of rolling hills speckled with farms and patchworked with dark-green woodlands. A ten-minute drive brings you to the center of the attractive village of **St. Margen** where you turn right (signposted Glotteral). Detour into **St. Peter** to visit **Klosterkirche**, the ornate baroque church attached to the large abbey. Heading towards Waldkirch, the road twists and climbs to the summit of the **Kandel**, one of the few mountains whose summit offers a view of the surrounding countryside. Traveling through thick forest, the road twists and turns down to the small non-touristy town of **Waldkirch** and on to the adjacent town of **Glotheral** where you turn right for the much prettier village of **Simonswald** strung along the road as it winds up the narrow valley to **Obersimonswald**. You climb among the trees, high above the farms that are nestled, each in their grassy patch of pastureland, to **Güttenbach**, a small industrial town at the summit. From here the road drops steeply to Furtwangen, where you rejoin the 500.

Furtwangen is famous for its cuckoo clocks. Visit a full collection of them in the interesting **Deutsches Uhrenmuseum** (German Clock Museum), which presents the history of timekeeping. Besides the chirping birds, there are wristwatches and very modern timepieces. (*9 am–5 pm, April to November 1st.*)

Leaving Furtwangen, the 500 passes through some very pretty countryside and travels through **Schönwald,** where the cuckoo clock was born. Schönwald was the home of Franz Anton Ketterer who at the beginning of the 18th century thought of combining a clock with bellows. He incorporated a cuckoo carved in wood with a timepiece whose tiny bellows marked the hours with the notes of a cuckoo call. Records show that clocks were manufactured in the Black Forest as early as 1630, but when cuckoo clocks were invented, they became the rage. Today clockmaking remains a considerable industry for the region, and, although factories exist, the production of cuckoo clocks is sometimes still a home business with the whole family working on the intricately carved boxes and painted dials.

Triberg, located in the heart of the Black Forest just a few kilometers beyond Schönwald, is an attractive town and an ideal place to stay. The town has one main street comprised of clock shop after clock shop whose selection, variety, and competitive prices will amaze you. Just as you come into town, you find the very interesting **Schwarzwaldmuseum** (Black Forest Museum) with the bronze of a larger-than-life lady in traditional dress outside. Inside you get a good look at the costumes, carvings, clocks, and traditions of the region. (*10 am–5 pm daily; open weekends only November 15 to December 15.*) Above the town is the **Gutach waterfall**, which cascades over 160 meters (500 feet) through the forest.

Leaving Triberg, turn left at the end of town (signposted Hornburg) and follow the 33 through tunnels beside the rushing River Gutach to **Hornburg**. Continue on to **Gutach,** where just beyond the town you find the *Schwarzwalder Freilichtermuseum** (Black Forest Open-Air Museum), a complex of ancient farmhouses brought here from all over the Black Forest and set in a meadow beside the river to show what rural life was like in days gone by. All of the rustic rooms are furnished and you see not only little cottages but also grand mansions. Many of the homes are typical Black Forest *Eindachof* (one-roof farms) that come with family accommodation, bakery, granary, barn, workshops, and cattle trough all under one large thatched roof. Wander from house to lovely house and admire the rustic furnishings and old farm implements. By the entrance you find several touristy restaurants and nifty gift shops. (*8:30 am–6 pm, April to October.*)

Schwarzwalder Freilichtermuseum

Soon after leaving the museum, turn right on the 294 for the short drive to **Wolfach,** where just as you leave the main road (signposted Zentrum), you find the **Glasshütte** (glass museum) and **Kris Kringle Markt** (Christmas Market), before going through the town wall onto the town's main street. Cross the river and follow signposts for Oberwolfach which brings you onto a pretty country road leading through a narrow valley dotted with farmhouses through **Oberwolfach** to the tiny charming hamlet of **Oberwolfach-Walke.** Follow the river up the valley past sawmills with their logs and plans stacked beside the road for the half-hour drive to Freudenstadt.

At the main road turn right if you want to tour the town of **Freudenstadt**, whose market square is the largest in Europe, or turn left (signposted Strasbourg), leaving the town behind as you climb into the forest and turn right onto the **Schwarzwald Hochstrasse** (Black Forest High Road). This very aptly named road travels along the crest of the hills through dense coniferous forest, winding back and forth, up and down through the trees with only occasional clearings offering glimpses of steep valleys of dark trees. Every time you come to a clearing, you find a resort hotel (often with food and trinket booths in its car park). A 68-kilometer drive brings you to Baden-Baden where you follow signposts for Zentrum, which bring you to Lichtentalerstrasse from where it is a short distance to the three hotels recommended in our *Hotel Descriptions* section.

***Baden-Baden** was the playground of Europe's rich and famous in the middle of the 19th century. Anyone who was anyone came to soak in the curative waters and gamble at the casino. Today it is an attractive town where everywhere you want to visit is located within a 15-minute walk (park your car for the duration of your stay). Promenade yourself down the famous **Lichtentaler Allee**, strolling along a pleasant lane through the park that runs beside the river from the casino. Baden-Baden's nightlife centers on the **Kurhaus** set amidst parklike gardens beside the swiftly flowing Oosbach river. Here you find a restaurant, café, ballroom, and casino (take your passport to register: you must be over 21, must not be wearing tennis shoes, and men must wear jackets and ties). Even if you do not gamble, it is fun to tour the casino. Across the river from the casino lies the pedestrian old town full of cobbled streets lined with delightful shops.

Another great draw to this cosmopolitan city is Baden-Baden's beautiful new opera house. All of Germany takes great pride in and is quite boastful of its opera house and rightly so as it is the largest in Europe and the fourth-largest in the world. A local family, the Rademachers, who also own two of our favorite hotels, have been quite supportive of the new cultural center and have secured the best seats for every performance. Tickets are available to guests who stay at either the **Romantik Hotel Der Kleine Prinz** or the **Belle Époque**.

The highlight of a visit to Baden-Baden is taking the *kur*, partaking of the curative waters. Pluck up your courage and opt for the *****Friedrichsbad** (Roman-Irish Bath), a two-hour ritual involving a complex routine which is explained in the blue English instruction sheet that you pick up as you purchase your ticket (it's well worth the extra small charge to include the soap-and-brush massage). Up the stairs (men one side, women the other), insert your ticket to gain admission, put your clothes in the basket, put your card in the locker to get a key, walk self-consciously to the showers, grab a towel, don slippers, and follow the numbers (and English explanation) on the walls. Relax in a hot room for 20 minutes, followed by an even hotter steam room (remember to lie on your towel—it's that hot); inhale steam from the curative waters; forget your modesty as you enter the pool (station 9)—it's men and women mixed (this came as quite a surprise); enjoy an invigorating massage; suffer a cold plunge; and finish with a relaxing rest wrapped in a warm towel beneath a blanket in a dimly lit room. (*9 am–10 pm, 2–10 pm, Sunday, last entry 7 pm.*)

The adjacent **Caracalla Therme** offers a water experience with bathing suit. Pick up the English sheet as you buy your card, put the card in a locker to get a key, and set off to enjoy an indoor-outdoor water wonderland of pools, waterfalls, showers, saunas, tanning lights, cold plunges, and sunbathing. (*8 am–10 pm, last entry 8 pm.*)

Closed to traffic, Baden-Baden's Old Town, nestled below the collegiate church, is a wonderful place for shopping. The stores display their elegant wares artistically, competing with the smells from the nearby pastry shops that summon you to an afternoon tea break. Baden-Baden is also a sportsman's paradise—golf, riding, tennis, fishing, and hiking are all available in the vicinity. Race week is held each year in August when Baden-Baden becomes a sophisticated meeting place for the wealthy "horsey set." One of the town's traditional attractions is the **Merkur mountain railway**. Built in 1913, it reopened after repairs in the spring of 1979, and you can now travel up the incline and enjoy sweeping vistas from the observation tower at its summit.

Leaving Baden-Baden, you can take the autobahn to Heidelberg (to join *The Romantic Road & the Neckar Valley,* 1 hour), the Frankfurt airport (2½ hours), or join the *Castles of the Rhine & Mosel* just outside Wiesbaden (3 hours).

Highways & Byways of the Black Forest

The Romantic Road
& the Neckar Valley

Hamburg

Köln

Frankfurt

Munich

Frankfurt

Volkach

A 3

A 3

Würzburg

A 7

Iphofen

Tauberbischofsheim

Bad Mergentheim

Creglingen

Weikersheim

Rothenburg

A 5

A 81

River Neckar

Heidelberg

Schloss Guttenberg

Neuenstadt

A 6

Feuchtwangen

Bad Wimpfen

Dinkelsbühl

A 6

Heinsheim

Schwäbisch Hall

Heilbronn

Friedrichsruhe

- Orientation/Sightseeing
  Autobahn
  Other roads
- - - - Itinerary route

The Romantic Road & the Neckar Valley

The Romantic Road (or Romantische Strasse) is one of Germany's most famous tourist routes—a road that travels between the towns of Würzburg in Franconia and Füssen in the Bavarian Alps. Every bend along the way between Würzburg and Rothenburg is spectacular. However, the beauty of the scenery wanes after leaving Rothenburg, so this itinerary deviates from the traditional route. Rather than traveling the entire 340-kilometer stretch of the Romantic Road, this itinerary samples the northern highlights of Germany's most traveled route and then detours west at Rothenberg to incorporate the attractive city of Schwäbisch Hall and the picturesque university city of Heidelberg. (The southernmost portion of the Romantic Road is included in the Bavarian itinerary.)

Rothenburg

The Romantic Road & the Neckar Valley

Suggested Pacing: A full day's sightseeing takes you from Würzburg to Rothenburg — we suggest an early start after spending the night in one of our recommended hotels in the area (Mainbernheim, Amorbach, Volkach, or Iphofen). Stay two nights in Rothenburg, taking an afternoon drive to Dinkelsbühl. Make an early-morning start from Rothenburg to arrive at Schloss Guttenberg in time for the 3 pm eagles' flight before driving on to Heidelberg (if you are not a fast-paced traveler, you could overnight in Friedrichsruhe en route). One night in Heidelberg is ample, yet if your pace is leisurely, you might opt for two.

The 12th-century diplomat, Gottfried von Viterbo, described **Würzburg** as "lovely, like a rose set in deep-green foliage — sculpted into the valley like an earthly paradise." It no longer seems like a paradise but it certainly is a lovely city with two outstanding sightseeing venues: the Episcopal princes' Residenz and the Marienberg Fortress. Try to secure a parking place in the vast forecourt of the well-signposted *Residenz, one of the finest baroque palaces in Europe, constructed between 1720 and 1744. It was built as the very grandest of homes for the prince-bishop who decided that his home in the nearby Marienberg Fortress simply wasn't grand enough. Admire its architecture from the landscaped gardens and peep into the colorful **Hofkirche** (to the right near the garden) before entering the palace. If your arrival does not coincide with a tour in English, purchase the English guidebook so that you can follow along. Climb the magnificent grand staircase (it appeared on the DM 50 bill) and admire the splendid oval Imperial Hall with its magnificent frescoes, where several characters have slipped out of the frescoes to become statues. From here you join an escorted tour of the Imperial Apartments, following along in your English guidebook as you move from one lavishly decorated room to another. (*Tour in English 11 am and 2 pm; open 9 am–5 pm, April to September; 10 am–4 pm, October to March; closed Mondays.*)

Vineyards climb up to the **Festung Marienberg** (Marienberg Fortress), overlooking the town from the other bank of the River Main. The fortress has evolved over the years and now contains the **Mainnfränkisches Museum** of regional art and folklore including some old winemaking implements. The most beloved exhibits are the sculptures of

Tilman Riemenschneider who lived in Würzburg from 1483 to 1531—you will see another of his masterpieces later in the day. (*9 am–5 pm, April to October; 10 am–4 pm, November to March, closed Mondays.*)

Leave Würzburg on the autobahn traveling south towards Stuttgart (allow four hours for the 100-kilometer journey from Würzburg to Rothenburg). Exit at **Tauberbischofsheim** and travel 2 kilometers to this appealing, small medieval town. The local history museum in the castle (Schloss) is well-signposted. (*2:30–4:30 pm, Easter to October, closed Mondays.*)

Festung Marienberg

The Romantic Road & the Neckar Valley

Follow the Tauber river valley and the Romantic Road for the short drive to **Bad Mergentheim**. The old order of the Teutonic Knights left Prussia to reside here in the castle in 1525, and remained until they were disbanded in 1809. Their **Deutschordensschloss** now houses a museum that traces the knights' history from the battles of the Crusades to becoming a charitable institution (entrance under the archway). (*10 am–5 pm, closed Mondays.*)

Detour into the village of **Weikersheim**. From the ample parking lot it's just a few steps to the attractive Marktplatz and the castle. The *****Dorfmuseum** (on the market place) is well-worth the entrance fee. On the first floor are several rooms set up to show how the locals lived in years gone by with displays of country-simple antiques, among them some lovely examples of painted beds, chests, and cupboards. The second floor is full of farm implements and the floor under the eaves covers winemaking in the area. (*9 am–6 pm, April to October; 10 am–noon and 2–4 pm November to March.*) The adjacent 18th-century **Schloss Weikersheim** is filled with its original furniture, tapestries, porcelain, and gloomy family portraits. Once you are on the hour-long tour (German only), it's hard to escape as you are locked into each floor of the castle as you enter it. Skip the tour, and go instead to admire the statues in the formal garden and the view of the Tauber valley. (*9 am–6 pm, April to October; 10 am–noon and 2–4 pm, November to March.*)

Your road follows the Tauber as it weaves south, passing under the clock-tower building in **Schaffersheim** and narrowing as it goes down the main street of **Rottingen**. Leave the Romantic Road to travel through the narrow streets of **Creglingen**, a mixture of old and new houses, and follow signposts in the village for *****Herrgottskirche**, a squat little church on the edge of town. Your entrance ticket includes a pompous English brochure, which requires detailed study to glean useful information. Of the five altars in the church, the masterpiece, the Assumption of Mary (1505–1510) by Tilman Riemenschneider, is *the* reason for visiting. Study the different expressions on the faces of the disciples surrounding Mary. On the altar base Riemenschneider carved himself as the second of the three scribes. (*8 am–6 pm, April to October.*) Across the road you find a little **Fingerhut**, thimble museum. (*8 am–6 pm, April to October.*)

Leaving the church, the country road leads you up a narrow valley, across peaceful farmland, and through quiet rural villages to enter through the old city gates into ***Rothenburg**. This is truly one of Europe's most enchanting towns (you can drive and park your car within the walls only if you are staying at a hotel—they provide you with a parking permit). Walking down the cobblestoned streets of Rothenburg is rather like taking a stroll through an open-air museum: there is history in every stone.

Rothenburg's old houses, towers, and gateways that have withstood the ravages of the centuries are there for you to explore. Tourists throng the streets, but somehow the town has the ability to absorb them and not let their numbers spoil its special magic. Being such a popular tourist destination, Rothenburg has a rich choice of places to stay: our selections are covered in the *Hotel Descriptions* section.

Rothenburg has narrowly escaped destruction on several occasions. In 1945, the Allies ordered Rothenburg destroyed as part of the war reprisals but an American general, remembering the picture of Rothenburg that hung on his mother's wall, tried to spare the town. His efforts were successful and although Rothenburg was somewhat damaged, the town remained intact. During the Thirty Years' War, General Tilly's army laid siege to the town and, despite spirited resistance, breached the walls. Tilly demanded that the town be destroyed and its councilors put to death. He assembled the town councilors to pass sentence on the town and was offered a drink from the town's ceremonial tankard filled with 3½ liters of the best Franconian wine. After having drunk and passed the cup among his subordinates, Tilly then, with a touch of humor, offered to spare the town and the lives of the councilors if one of its representatives could empty the tankard in one go. Nusch, a former mayor, who seems to have been good at drinking, agreed to try. He succeeded and saved the town. Apparently he slept for three days after the feat. Several times a day (*11 am, noon, 1 pm, 2 pm, 3 pm, 6 pm, 7 pm, 8 pm, 9 pm*) in the marketplace the doors on either side of the clock open and the figures of Tilly and Nusch reenact the historic drinking feat.

For an entertaining and informative insight into the history of the town join, the
*nightwatchman on his nightly rounds. (*April to end of December, meet under the
clocktower in the market square.*) The English tour begins after the 8 pm drinking feat, and
arrives back at the square just in time for the 9 pm event. (The German tour leaves at 9:30
pm.)

The brochure *Rothenburg Worth Seeing, Worth Knowing* is carried by all hotels and the
tourist office — with this and map in hand set off to explore. Be sure to include a section

Rothenburg

of the ***city walls**: climb the
stairs to the walkway and follow
the covered ramparts, which
almost encircle the town (the
stones with names are placed in
honor of people from around the
world who have donated money
for the walls' restoration). If
you have in tow adolescents
whose delights gravitate toward
the gruesome, be sure to include
a stop at the **Mittelalterliches
Kriminalmuseum** (Museum of
Medieval Justice). Here you will
find various instruments of
torture such as the headpiece for
women who gossiped too much

and the dunking chair for bakers who did not make their loaves the correct size. (*9 am–6 pm,
April to October; 2–4 pm, November to March.*) The **Reichsstadt Museum** in the
Dominican Convent offers an English sheet that guides you through rooms full of
furniture (including the convent kitchen and chemist's shop), past lots of paintings of
Rothenburg, and encourages you to find the Meistertrunk (Kürfurstenhumpen), the cup that

is claimed to be the one used at the drinking feat. (*10 am–5 pm, April to October.*) Wander down *Herrengasse, where the merchants and patricians lived in their elegant mansions, through the old gate with its little after-curfew entrance, and glance back to see the scary mask mouth where defenders of the town poured hot tar down on their attackers. The pretty castle garden offers lovely countryside views. Rothenburg has many lovely shops and boutiques, one of the most enchanting being **Kathe Wohlfahrt's Christkindlmarkt**. Claiming to offer the world's largest selection of Christmas items, a tiny storefront near the market square opens up to a vast fairyland of decorated Christmas trees and animated Stieff animals. The town's culinary specialty is *Schneeballen*, a dessert looking like snowballs, made up of layers of thin strips of pastry rolled up, deep-fried, and then dusted with confectioner's sugar.

Consider escaping the daytime crowds that flock to Rothenburg by taking a half-day outing just a little farther down the Romantic Road to Dinkelsbühl. En route is **Feuchtwangen**, a small town whose market square is referred to as "Franconia's Festival Hall." Of interest are the **Romanesque cloisters** and the **Heimatmuseum** (Franconian Folklore Museum), which traces furnishing styles through the ages from country farms to baroque and Biedermeier.

South of Feuchtwangen is the historic, old town of **Dinkelsbühl**, a town that prospered in the 15th and 16th centuries at the junction of trade routes. Its narrow streets filled with historic houses lie behind the walls with their towers and four gateways. The most handsome houses are found on the main street, Dr Martin Luther Strasse, particularly the **Deutsches Haus** with its overhanging balconies. The **Heimatmuseum** (Folklore Museum) in the Spitalhof traces the town's history with furniture, kitchen utensils, torture instruments, and a portrait of King Adolphus of Sweden. The town's siege by Adolphus's army is reenacted every year in mid-July to commemorate the town's salvation by the village's brave children in the Thirty Years' War.

With sightseeing it will take you a full day to follow our route from Rothenburg to Heidelberg. Get a fast start on the day by taking the autobahn (about an hour's drive) to **Schwäbisch Hall**, a town that stands out by the fact that it is not very heavily visited by tourists. Built on a steep hillside sloping down to the River Kocher, the town contains many well-preserved medieval houses. The Marktplatz is one of the prettiest in Germany and always teeming with activity—a real town center with women carefully selecting their produce for the evening meal from small stalls in the square (*market days Saturday and Wednesday*) and children neatly dressed in uniforms chatting gaily on their way to school. The monumental **Fischbrunen** fountain with its statues of Samson, St. Michael, and St. George sits at the base of the 53 steps that lead up to **St. Michael's Church**. A statue of the archangel is found in the church's porch. Inside the church admire the high altar with its painted and sculpted scenes by unknown Dutch artists. Opposite the church sits the **Rathaus** (town hall), an elegant, baroque-style building. Follow the cobbles down to **Obere** and **Untere Herrengasse** with their fine, half-timbered houses.

Leave on the 14 in the direction of Stuttgart, then after 6 kilometers turn right for **Waldenburg**. A 12-kilometer drive through pretty countryside brings you to the town, which you enter along the defense wall with a sheer drop on either side. Meander beneath the castle ramparts down to the plain. Another 12-kilometer drive brings you to **Neuenstein** where, amidst the town's narrow streets, you find **Schloss Neuenstein**, which we were unable to tour because the owner's daughter was getting married that day. (*9–11 am and 1:30–5 pm, mid-March to mid-November, closed Mondays.*)

Now we drive on to **Öhringen** (6 kilometers), an industrial, workaday town, **Neuenstadt** (13 kilometers, follow signposts for the autobahn then Neuenstadt), and **Bad Friedrichsal** (8 kilometers). Cross the River Kocher and turn left to **Bad Wimpfen**. Leave the broad river valley and climb up to park near the town walls. Walk to the Marktplatz (it's a little town so you will not get lost) and obtain a town map from the tourist office in the **Rathaus** (town hall). Walk beside the town hall to the **Blamer Turm** (blue tower), whose turreted top was the home to the nightwatchman in years gone by. It is not worth the entrance fee to climb the tower (more dramatic towers await). Continuing along the wall, you have a panoramic view of the valley from the viewpoint adjacent to the **Kaiserpfalz**, which now houses the town's museum with its displays of Roman remains. (*10 am–noon and 2–4 pm, April to mid-October, Wednesdays to Mondays.*) On to the **Roter Turm** (red tower) where you can climb a small section of wall before continuing through the little cobbled streets and looping back to the market place. Leaving the town, the road zigzags down to the broad river valley, weaving through the village of **Hensheim** towards **Gudshem**. Do not turn over the river to Gudshem, but left to Schloss Guttenberg, which you see perched atop the hillside in front of you.

Schloss Guttenberg is particularly fun to visit because not only does it have an interesting museum (displays on three floors of the tower and the opportunity to walk along the ramparts and climb the tower), but it also has the *****Deutsche Greifenwarte Claus Fentzloff** (German Raptor Research Center). The aviary has some magnificent eagles, vultures, and owls from around the world. Try to time your arrival to coincide with the 3 pm flight demonstration. Claus Fentzloff, his wife Bettina, and their assistants demonstrate eagles and vultures skimming just over your head across the ramparts, then swooping beyond the castle walls to ride the updrafts. The explanation is in German but if you indicate to Claus that you do not understand German, he also offers a short explanation in English. (*9 am–6 pm, March to November, raptor flight demonstration 11 am and 3 pm.*)

Continuing along the quiet river road, you will pass the **Schloss Hornburg** on the opposite bank. Cross the river onto the 37 (signposted Heidelberg) and **Schloss Zwinger** comes into view.

For another castle experience deviate into **Hirschhorn** and visit **Schloss Hirschhorn** where all of the intact building now comprises a castle hotel. There are lovely views of the Neckar river valley from the hotel's terrace. Three little castles decorate the skyline of **Neckar Steinach** and from here a few more river bends bring you to Heidelberg.

Heidelberg receives an overrated review in most guidebooks—there are just too many tourists. Nevertheless, it cannot be denied that the crowds make this a particularly dynamic city (there are lots of young people). Surprisingly, it was the romantic operetta, *The Student Prince,* that put Heidelberg on the tourist map. Unlike so many less fortunate German cities, Heidelberg has been spared the ravages of recent wars. The streets of its old town are a maze of cozy restaurants and lively student taverns—we enjoyed our visits to **Schnookeloch** (Haspelgasse 8) and **Roter Ochsen** (Hauptstrasse 215). Above the town looms the ruin of its picture-postcard, pink-sandstone castle; you can walk up to the castle, but it is easier and more fun to take the **Bergbahn** (mountain railway) from the Kornmarkt. The **Heidelberg Schloss** (castle) is now mostly a ruin, but still great fun to explore, and offers spectacular views of the town and the river from the terrace. The **Ottheinrichsbau** (1559) with its decorative façade is a particularly lovely building. Beneath the Ottheinrichsbau lies the **Deutsches Apotheken Museum** (Apothecary Museum), tracing the history of pharmacy and displaying balances and herbal boxes. (*10 am–5 pm, daily.*) The best views of the castle and the town are from the **Philosophenweg** (Philosophers' Walk) on the northern bank of the Neckar river. Cross the Alte Brucke or Old Bridge spanning the Neckar—the Philosophers' Walk is clearly indicated by signs (lit at night).

City life centers on the pedestrian **Hauptstrasse,** where you find the town's most impressive building, the 16th-century **Romantik Hotel Zum Ritter St. Georg.**

Enjoy your sightseeing in the old-world city of Heidelberg, then when it is time to continue your journey, you have many convenient options: you can easily take the autobahn south to the Black Forest or north to the Rhine and Mosel; or, if your holidays must end, it is only an hour and a half's drive to the Frankfurt airport.

Heidelberg

The Romantic Road & the Neckar Valley

Highlights of the
Harz Mountains

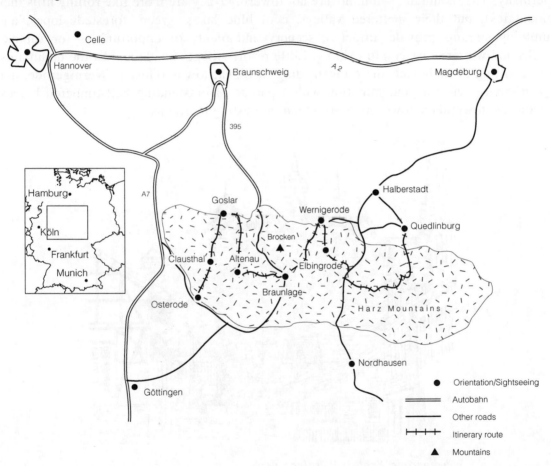

Celle

Hannover

Braunschweig

A 2

Magdeburg

395

Hamburg

Köln

Frankfurt

Munich

A7

Goslar

Wernigerode

Halberstadt

Brocken

Quedlinburg

Clausthal

Altenau

Elbingrode

Osterode

Braunlage

Harz Mountains

Nordhausen

Göttingen

● Orientation/Sightseeing

Autobahn

Other roads

┼┼┼┼ Itinerary route

▲ Mountains

Highlights of the Harz Mountains

Rising from the plains, the Harz Mountains are the tallest in northern and central Germany. The mountains' summits are not towering (they are more like rolling hills than mountains), but their sheltered valleys, cool blue lakes, green, forested slopes, and tumbling streams provide attractive scenery and plenty of opportunities for summer walks and winter cross-country skiing. Little resort villages nestle amidst the mountains; while sitting at their feet, three outstanding medieval towns (Goslar, Wernigerode, and Quedlinburg) vie for your attention with a parade of outstanding half-timbered homes, decorative town halls, towering castles, and interesting museums.

Wernigerode, Schloss Wernigerode

Recommended Pacing: Concentrate your first day's sightseeing in the charming town of Goslar and spend your first night either here, or in the resort of Braunlage. Follow this with one night in Wernigerode (two if you take the steam train into the Harz) or just visit Wernigerode and go directly on to the quaint, medieval town of Quedlinburg where—if you are not pressed for time—you can relax at the exceptionally charming Romantik Hotel am Brühl for a few days. (Note: If your journey begins from the north, consider a detour to the delightful walled town of **Celle**, just north of Hannover. Nestled in a region where horses are bred and orchids flourish, Celle is enchanting with its half-timbered, gaily painted houses and cobbled streets.)

Nestling at the foot of the Harz Mountains, **Osterode's** brightly painted half-timbered houses make exploring the historic city center an attractive proposition. (Follow signposts for Innerstadt Ring, park your car, and walk into the pedestrian precinct.) The historic **Rathaus** (town hall) was built in 1522, and beneath its ornate bay window hangs a whale rib that is supposed to protect the town from flooding and inclement weather. Continuing along the street from the town hall, you come to the **Marktkirche** (market church) on the Kornmarkt. The church dates back to the Middle Ages and until 1936 the town's nightwatchman lived in the little flat just below the spire—it was his job to sound the alarm in case of fire. Festivals and flea markets are held at the Kornmarkt along with the weekly market on Saturdays.

Leaving Osterode, follow signposts for Goslar (241): a dual carriageway takes you to the base of the mountains where a narrower, forest-lined road continues up into the mountains to the twin towns of **Clausthal** and **Zellerfeld**. At the top of the hill in Zellerfeld you find the **Bergwerkmuseum**, dedicated to mining in the Harz. Apart from displays of old-fashioned mining paraphernalia, rooms have been set up to give you a glimpse of eras long past showing how the miners lived and worked. Leaving the first museum, you cross a rustic courtyard to explore buildings full of old-fashioned wooden mine machinery and walk through a short length of underground mining tunnel. (*9 am–5 pm daily.*) The blue-painted **Marktkirche Zum Heiligen Geist** (Holy Ghost Parish

Goslar

Church) with its stubby onion domes was built between 1636 and 1642 and is the largest wooden church in Germany.

From Clausthal-Zellerfeld the 241 winds down through vast forests to *Goslar where a full day's sightseeing awaits you in this lovely city full of historic buildings. Try to park at the Kaiserplatz (signposted). Here you find the majestic 11th-century **Kaiserpfalz** (Imperial Palace), one of the largest non-church buildings in the country, now displaying military paintings in its vast hall. (*10 am–3 pm, daily.*)

Amble down the pedestrian-only cobbled streets, past timbered houses to the Marktplatz. Occupying a corner of the square, the old town merchants' guildhall is now the **Hotel Kaiserworth** (see *Hotel Descriptions*) where statues of German emperors guard the portals. Here you are only steps away from the **Rathaus** (town hall) with its Hudigungssaal (chamber of allegiance) displaying German emperors on the wall and the life of Christ on the ceiling. (*10 am–4 pm, daily.*) The different scenes on the clock on the market square represent the 1,000-year-old mining history of the region (the clock performs at 9 am, noon, 3 pm, and 6 pm). The tourist office is also located on the square.

Follow the cobbled street beside the Kaiserworth to the **Goslar Museum** with its exhibition of life in old Goslar—a geological overview of the Harz—and displays of minerals. One room contains art treasures from the cathedral and the Goslar gospel. (*10 am–4 pm, closed Mondays.*) Follow the tumbling River Gose past the **Lohmühle** (tanning-mill) with its ancient waterwheel to the **Puppen Museum** (Puppet Museum) in the basement of an antique shop on Hoher Weg. The **Barock Café** next door serves scrumptious cakes.

At Münzstrasse 11, the **Tin Figure Museum** is situated in the coach house of an inn built in 1644 and used as a stopping place for the mail coach. Here you see displays of over 1,000 little tin figures depicting historic scenes. (*10 am–4 pm, closed Mondays.*) Just round the corner on Jakobistrasse you find the **Mönchehaus Museum of Modern Art** in an imposing farmer's townhouse which dates back to 1528. It has exhibitions of modern art and works by the prize-winners of the Kaiserring, an art award given by the town of Goslar. Its garden is full of sculptures. (*10 am–1 pm and 3–5 pm, closed Mondays.*)

Leaving the town center, retrace your steps towards Clausthal-Zellerfeld for a very short distance and turn left for the brief drive to the *Rammelsberger Bergbaumuseum**. The Rammelsberg Mine on the edge of Goslar closed in 1988, the only mine in the world to have been in continuous operation for over 1,000 years (968 to 1989). Everything is the way it was on the mine's last day of operation. Don your hard hat and miner's garb and follow your tour guide (tours are given in German but several of the guides speak English and give bilingual tours) past the 10th-century waste heaps, down long, low (well-lit) tunnels to the 12th-century Rathstiefster gallery, visiting ingenious wooden water wheels used for removing water from deep underground. You emerge in a more modern tunnel to see the little yellow train that carried the miners deep underground. The tour concludes with a film (in German) showing activities at the mine. Plans are afoot to offer a tour where you not only don mining garb, but take your hammer and lamp underground to the face to mine your own rock sample. (*9:30 am–4:30 pm, daily.*)

Leave Goslar on the 82 signposted Bad Harzburg, which brings you onto the 6 (also signposted Bad Harzburg). As you go onto the dual carriageway, stay to the right as yours is the immediate first exit: the 498 to Oker. Oker is an industrial town and after passing through it you quickly regain the forests and the mountains as the 498 follows a tumbling stream up a steep grade to the **Oker Dam**. This wild valley is understandably a favorite walking spot for summer visitors and there are several parking places where you can also hike beside the tumbling stream. The road traces the dam for several kilometers to arrive in **Altenau** (an attractive resort town) where you turn left for the 17-kilometer drive to Braunlage.

Before reunification the resort town of **Braunlage** was on the border (the edge of the Harz Mountains as far as tourists from the West were concerned). Braunlage is now a central location to use as a base for explorations of the area.

The tragicomically named village of **Eland** ("misery") lies 7 kilometers from Braunlage where the well-paved road turns to cobbles. Turn left for Wernigerode, a 17-kilometer drive down **Mount Brocken**. It is said that on Walpurgisnacht, April 30, cackling witches astride their broomsticks gather on the summit of the mountain to cavort and cast their wicked spells.

Arriving at the northern foot of the mountains in *Wernigerode, secure a parking place on one of the little side streets near the pedestrian Altstadt and make your way to the Marktplatz where you find the magnificent *Rathaus (town hall) whose slender spires and intricate woodwork occupy one side of the square. The **Oberfarrkirchof** is a picturesque little nook behind the town hall. House number 13, the House Gadenstedt, dating from the 15th century, is one of the loveliest houses in the town. The nearby Kochstrasse contains the smallest house in town — its little door is only 1.7 meters high and the house is only 4.2 meters up to the eaves. Number 72 Breite Strasse was built in 1674 and you can hardly see the original half-timberwork for the amount of intricate carving that decorates it. A horse's head and horseshoes over the door of 95 Breite Strasse indicate that this was for over 300 years a blacksmith's shop, **Krell'sche Schmeide**. The museum contains a display of all things pertaining to blacksmithing and outlines the lifestyles of two families who lived here. (*1–5 pm, Wednesdays to Sundays; 10 am–3 pm, Fridays.*) The tourist office is on Nicolaiplatz. High above the town, the *Schloss Wernigerode dominates the skyline. While it is possible to walk up to the castle (a half-hour walk through the suburbs), a less strenuous approach is to take the little tractor-train from just behind the market place. A castle has been here since the 13th century but beyond the ancient portcullis what you see today is an ornate, 19th-century baroque castle-style home. Guided tours are available in German or you can tour the castle with the aid of an English brochure and walk from one beautifully furnished room to another. (*10 am–5 pm, closed Mondays except in the summer.*)

Wernigerode is the headquarters of the Harzer Schmalspurbahnen (HSB), which operates the great little trains of the Harz that give you magnificent views of the mountains. Their brochure *Great Adventures with Narrow-Gauge Steam* outlines three railway adventures, two of which leave from Wernigerode.

Rathaus (*town hall*), *Wernigerode*

The ***Harzquerbahn** leaves from the Hauptbahnhof, and steaming between houses and gardens, the little train chugs into the forest, winding its way up through the trees as it climbs into the mountains. Following a long tunnel, the track becomes steeper and steeper as the train approaches Drei-Annen-Hohne where the track divides: the Harzquerbahn continues across the Harz to Nordhausen (three hours from Wernigerode) while the **Brockenbahn** begins the climb of the Brocken mountain. From Drei-Annen-Hohne the Brockenbahn train climbs ever steeper to the summit of the Brocken, offering magnificent views of the **Hochharz National Park**. (*8 trains a day, May 28 to November 5, tel: 03943 558162, fax: 03943 32107.*)

While this itinerary's next major destination, Quedlinburg, lies just 40 kilometers away across the plains, take a more circuitous back road through the mountains. Leave Wernigerode (with the castle on your left) on the 244 for the 7-kilometer climb into the mountains to the pleasant little resort of **Elbingrode** where the **Büchenberg Mine Museum** is found just outside the town. A tour of this former tin mine gives you insight into the working life of a miner in the Harz. (*Tours: 10 am, noon, 2 pm, 3 pm—additional tours on weekends, open all year.*)

A 5-kilometer drive brings you to **Rübeland**, a mountain village set amongst limestone cliffs and noted for its caves. Park near **Baumans Höhle** and choose between a tour of this cave system or **Hernmanns Höhle**, a series of caves found just across the River Bode. We chose Baumans because of the availability of a tour and were led on a 45-minute walk through passages to caves with magnificent displays of stalagmites and stalactites (the tour was in German and information in English was not available). We understood that the tour of Hernmanns was very similar, but included a pool that contained "cave fish," blind, white, eel-like creatures that live out their lives in darkness. (*9:45 am–4:15 pm, daily.*)

Cross the River Bode and leave Rübeland past the entrance to Hernmanns Höhle towards Hasselfelde. The road travels up through the trees, into a tunnel, and emerges on a dam with a vast tract of water stretching to the right and the valley falling away steeply to the left. Turn left on the 81 (signposted Blankenburg), and after 1 kilometer, pass through **Wendefugh** (a speck of a village), go up through the trees, and turn right for Altenbrak; following the River Bode as it tumbles down the most picturesque of valleys for 4 kilometers to the village of **Altenbrak** whose houses are straddled along the road. Carry on to the few houses that comprise **Tresburg,** where you turn right up the **Bodetal**

Valley, following walking paths whose rustic little bridges span the tumbling little river, to **Aldrode**, a quiet farming community set high in the mountains. Turn right and a 5-kilometer drive across heathland takes you down to the tree-lined main street of **Friedrichsbrun** and on to **Bad Suderode** (8 kilometers), where nearly every old house (most in need of a coat of paint) has an ornate balcony.

Seven kilometers across the plain brings you to *Quedlinburg. Cross the river (following signposts for Zentrum), then secure a parking place and walk to the Marktplatz, where you find the tourist office and the sturdy stone **Rathaus** (town hall). Within the old town there are 1,500 half-timbered houses, many of them crumbling and in need of restoration, looking much as they must have in the Middle Ages. The entire town center is an architectural gem. Map in hand, explore the little streets behind the Rathaus, venturing down narrow alleyways where you can touch the leaning houses on either side of the cobbled walkways to emerge on streets with elaborate, picture-perfect façades. On a low promontory just a short walk from the Marktplatz you find the **Schloss Quedlinburg** and the **Stifskirche** (collegiate church) **of St. Servatius**, which is considered the most beautiful Romanesque church in north and central Germany. It is a surprisingly spacious, simply adorned edifice built between 1070 and 1129. The treasury chamber contains valuable religious relics, and the room next to it contains fragments of a knotted wall hanging discovered in the 19th century. The adjacent **Schlossmuseum** houses 16th- and 17th-century Flemish and Italian paintings, and gives you an impression of life at the time of the founding of the Damenstift, a religious institution run for ladies by nuns. The terrace gives you a spectacular view of the town's rooftops. (*9 am–5 pm, closed Mondays.*)

The **Klopstockhaus**, a magnificent patrician home at the foot of the castle, has been used as a museum for over 90 years. (*9 am–5 pm, closed Mondays and Tuesdays.*) The **Ständerbau** (half-timbered house, Wordgasse 3), built in the 13th century, is the oldest half-timbered building in the town and was a home until 1965. The tiny rooms with all their nooks and crannies house an exhibition on the half-timbered architecture of Quedlinburg. (*10 am–5 pm, May to September, closed Thursdays.*)

From Quedlinburg, a two-hour drive finds you in Berlin, Potsdam, or Dresden where you can join the *Exploring East & Middle Germany* itinerary, or travel north to Hamburg and *Schleswig Holstein—the Land Between the Seas*.

Quedlinburg

Exploring East & Middle Germany

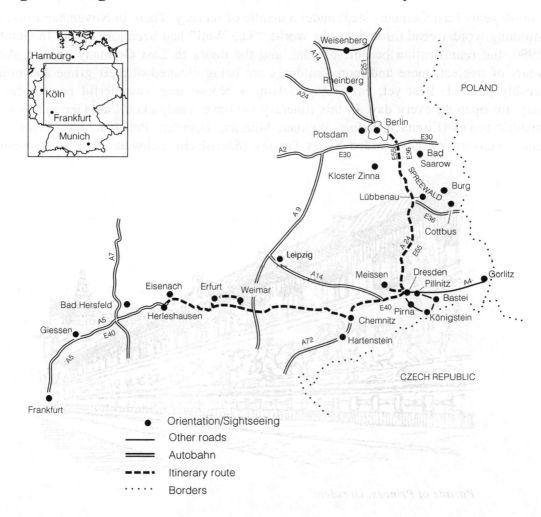

Orientation/Sightseeing
Other roads
Autobahn
Itinerary route
Borders

Exploring East & Middle Germany

For 40 years East Germany slept under a mantle of secrecy. Then, in November 1989, the stunning word spread throughout the world: "The Wall" had been torn down. In October 1990, the reunification became official, and the doors to East Germany opened. After years of neglect, more and more buildings are being cleaned of their grime and others freshly painted. Best yet, entrepreneurialism is blossoming—wonderful new places to stay are opening every day. In this itinerary we have handpicked East Germany's most historic towns (Eisenach, Erfurt, Weimar, Meissen, Dresden, Potsdam, and Berlin). For good measure we have added Swiss Saxony (Sächsische Schweiz) with its intriguing

Parade of Princes, Dresden

rock formations, and the Spreewald, where you can glide through a maze of waterways on a canoe-like wooden boat.

Recommended Pacing: If you are coming from the direction of Munich, consider the suggested side trip to Waldsassen, which is described in the following two paragraphs. Otherwise, your first sightseeing stop will be in Eisenach, where (if you have the leisure of time) you can spend the night at Hotel auf der Wartburg, next to Wartburg castle. If you are pressed for time, just stop in Eisenach for a few hours to see Wartburg castle and Bach's birthplace, and then head directly on to Weimar. We recommend two nights in Weimar to allow one full day to visit the homes of some of the world's greatest musical geniuses; three nights in Dresden to give you time to see its incredible museums plus take side trips to Meissen and Swiss Saxony; one night in the Spreewald (Lübbenau or Burg) to allow time to explore its intriguing maze of narrow waterways; and two nights in Potsdam or Berlin (three if you do extensive sightseeing in Berlin). The above pacing will give you a good overview of the cities and sights of east Germany.

If you are approaching east Germany from the south on the A7 from Munich, we cannot resist suggesting that you make a detour en route at ***Waldsassen**, conveniently close to the A7 and thus not much out of your way. This small town, snuggled right on the border of the Czech Republic, is not well known, but has a beautiful church (Stiftsbasilika) and, next to it, an incredible library (Bibliothek), which is so spectacular that it is worth making a special effort to see. As you drive into Waldsassen, follow signs to the **Stiftsbasilika**, located in the heart of town. The façade of the church looks rather sedate with square twin towers, topped by onion-like domes, framing the entrance. Inside the church (whose origin dates back to the 12th century), the mood changes completely. The interior is like an opulent wedding cake. Its white walls and ceiling are richly adorned with baroque stuccowork and its ceiling is highlighted by fine frescos. Also, notice the beautiful woodcarvings throughout the church, especially those on the choir stalls.

Bibliothek, Waldsassen

Although the Stiftsbasilika is very interesting, if you have time to see only one sight in Waldsassen, choose the **Bibliothek**, which is located near the church—you can see many splendid churches throughout Germany, but this library is one of a kind. Buy your ticket on the ground level and then take the staircase up to the library. Before you enter you are given a pair of giant slippers to put on over your shoes to protect the delicate inlaid floor. The library has a balcony that wraps around the upper level of the room. What is so astounding is not so much the beautifully bound, antique books that line the walls from floor to ceiling, but the artwork—the wood carvings, all done by local artists, are remarkable. The room is totally made of wood, and every inch is carved—from the

Exploring East & Middle Germany

shelves to the balustrades. Most extraordinary of all are the ten, life-size statues supporting the upper gallery, which depict with humor the ten guilds responsible for the production of a book—from the man who brings rags for the cloth to the smug bookseller who sells the finished product. You cannot help smiling and being enchanted by the craftsmanship and humor of this elaborate library. (*10–11:30 am and 2–4:45 pm, closed Monday mornings.*)

If you don't stop in Waldsassen, your first destination is **Eisenach**, located on the edge of the vast stretches of the Thuringia Forest. Take exit 40 from the A4, go into Eisenach, and follow the well-signposted route to your destination, ***Wartburg**, one of Europe's finest Romanesque castles, perched atop a wooded hill southwest of town. After driving through Eisenach, you will see a "Wartburg" sign indicating a narrow road to the right that weaves up through a thick forest to the parking lot, from which it is a ten-minute walk up the hill to the castle. Note: If you have reservations to spend the night at the **Hotel auf der Wartburg** (see *Hotel Descriptions* section), you can bypass the barrier at the parking lot, drive up the pedestrian walkway to the hotel, leave your luggage, and then park your car at the hotel parking area.

To visit the castle, buy your entrance ticket, cross the moat, go under the portcullis, and into the courtyard to stand in line to purchase a second ticket for the guided tour of the castle (buy a guidebook in English to help you understand this German-only tour). It was Wartburg that inspired Ludwig II to build his fanciful Bavarian castles and Richard Wagner to write his opera *Tannhäuser*. The restored castle is largely Romanesque but furnishings, artwork, and tapestries are original pieces from the medieval to the baroque eras of this castle.

One of the most interesting rooms in the castle is the Elisabeth Gallery where six large frescoed murals depict the tale of Elisabeth, a Hungarian princess who came to live at the castle in 1211. She died at the tender age of 24, but became a legend due to her work with the peasants—nursing those who were ill and helping the destitute.

Princess Elisabeth's good deeds are even more remarkable, considering that most of the nobility during this era considered the peasants a lowly class, not worthy of attention. Another room in the castle, the Elisabeth Room, has a gorgeous mosaic, consisting of more than a million pieces of glass, mother-of-pearl, and gold leaf, which also tells the story of this compassionate princess who was adored by her people.

Wartburg Castle, Eisenach

After leaving the tour, return to the courtyard and take a few minutes to visit the few simple rooms where Martin Luther hid after being excommunicated in 1521. The walls are decorated with Lucas Cranach's portraits of Luther and his wife. Luther spent his time here translating the New Testament into German—it was Luther's preaching and writing in German that established German as an important language. (*8:30 am–4:30 pm, April to October; 9 am–3:30 pm, November to March.*)

Exploring East & Middle Germany

Fortunately, Eisenach's other interesting place to visit, Johann Sebastian Bach's birthplace, ***Bachhaus**, is easy to find. After leaving Wartburg, drive back toward Eisenach. Just a few minutes before entering the main part of town, turn left on a street signposted Bachhaus and follow the road to a tree-shaded square with a statue of Bach set in a tiny park. Facing the statue is a cheerful, mustard-yellow house where Johann Sebastian Bach lived as a boy. The tour of Bach's home is not structured: follow the well-marked signs throughout the house, which is furnished in much the same style as it was when Bach was a child. The tour ends at the chamber music room where every 20 minutes a program of Bach's music, both live and taped, is cleverly woven together with a presentation about his life and work. To sit in this lovely, small music chamber dappled with sunlight filtering in from the garden while listening to Bach's music is indeed magical. After the demonstration, you may choose to walk through the flower-filled garden to another section of the house in which Bach memorabilia and sheet music are displayed. (*1:30–4:30 pm, Mondays; 9 am–4 pm, Tuesdays through Fridays; 9 am–noon and 1:30–4:30 pm, Saturdays and Sundays.*)

Leaving Eisenach, return to the A4 and continue east. It is only about 45 kilometers to exit 46, the turnoff for the road that heads north to the old university town of **Erfurt**. Don't be discouraged by the sprawling, unsightly suburbs because the heart of the historic town is extremely colorful. Head straight to the town center and park in any of the designated areas in the vast Domplatz. From there, climb the monumental staircase leading up to the triple-spired ***Dom** (cathedral). Be sure to notice its stunning entrance adorned with fine statues. Inside, look for the beautifully carved choir stalls, the exquisitely detailed stained-glass windows (1370–1420) around the altar, and the 12th-century masterpiece in the south transept, the *Wolfram,* a candelabrum in the shape of a man. The Dom also contains the tomb of the Count of Gleichen and his wives—yes, wives. According to legend, while on a crusade the count was captured, and only because the beautiful daughter of the sultan fell in love with him was he released with the stipulation he marry her. The wife at home, relieved to have her husband back, accepted the arrangement, and the two women lived happily ever after as sisters.

Adjacent to the Dom is the triple-spired **Severikirche** (church of the Augustinian monks), built between 1280 and 1400. Inside look for the splendidly carved, pink sandstone sarcophagus of Saint Severus, located in the southernmost nave.

Walk back down the enormous flight of steps to the **Domplatz**, crowded with market stalls on Wednesdays. Lining this huge plaza are gaily painted 17th- and 18th-century houses.

Cross the Domplatz and follow the narrow, pedestrian-only street, Markstrasse, in the direction of the Krämerbrücke. In a few minutes you come to the **Fischmarkt Platz** where you find more picturesque buildings, including the attractive **Gildehaus** restaurant. You might want to have lunch here or else be tempted to snack on one of the tantalizing grilled bratwurst sold by street vendors.

From the Fischmarkt Platz continue on foot to the amazing **Krämerbrücke** (Kramer Bridge). You hardly realize that you are crossing over the river because the narrow bridge (lined by little shops and galleries housed in quaint, two-story, half-timbered buildings) looks like just a continuation of the street.

After seeing Krämerbrücke, retrace your steps to the Domplatz to pick up your car. Return to the A4, continue east, and take exit 49 to Weimar. The traffic crawls through the sprawling suburbs but take heart, since after you park your car you are treated to an extremely picturesque city. As you near the town center, follow signposts for the Hotel Elephant—this route brings you to the pedestrian Marktplatz, where you find the tourist information office and the **Hotel Elephant** (you can drive into the square to drop your luggage if you are staying at the hotel). **Weimar's** status as a cultural capital led to Germany's democrats putting the town's name on the new republic in 1919. Over the years the town's princes nurtured those with artistic and musical talents, including Lucas Cranach, Franz Liszt, and Johann Sebastian Bach. Similarly, the court nurtured Germany's leading writers: Goethe, Schiller, Wieland, and Herder. Goethe spent over 50 years here. He moved into *Goethehaus in 1782 and lived here until his death in 1832 (from the market square take Frauentorstrasse to Frauenplan). His home is, by and large, the way it was when he lived here: you see the study where he worked, manuscripts and all, and his bedroom with the armchair in which he died. (*9 am–4 pm, closed Mondays.*) Goethe frequently dined in the adjacent **Zum Weissen Schwan** and housed his overflow of visitors here. The Swan has two delightful, cozy dining rooms, an excellent choice for an upmarket place to eat.

A few streets away lies the **Schillerhaus**, Schillerstrasse 12, where Schiller came to live for three years prior to Goethe's death. It was here that he wrote *Wilhelm Tell*. Behind the house an interesting museum depicts the writer's life and work. (*9 am–4 pm, closed Mondays.*) Goethe and Schiller were great friends and a large statue of them together stands outside the **Deutsches Nationaltheater** on Theaterplatz.

The exterior of the **Stadtschloss** (castle) has been restored, and the wing facing the park is now open as an art gallery that houses, among other things, an important collection of paintings by Lucas Cranach. (*9 am–5 pm, closed Mondays.*) Cross the river Ilm (on the bridge behind the museum) and stroll though the woodlands and lawns, following the river to **Goethe's Gartenhaus** (garden house) which he received as a present from August the Strong in 1776. He liked it so much that he lived there till 1782 and it always remained his favorite retreat. The country-simple furnishings in the garden house are very different from the ornate decor in his later home. (*Closed Mondays.*)

On a sadder note, just 11 kilometers northwest of Weimar lies **Buchenwald.** Drive through the woodlands to the buildings at the end of the road, where you find a bookshop and an auditorium where a film is shown. Narrated in German, this jerky, old-fashioned movie is somehow more poignant than if it were a slick, commercial production (don't worry—although it is in German, you can't miss the story line). The images generated by this concentration camp are horrific, but a part of history that should never be forgotten. The camp installations are gone and a monument pays tribute to the 65,000 victims who died here. (*8:45 am–4:45 pm, closed Mondays.*)

Depending upon road conditions, it is about a two- to three-hour drive from Weimar to Dresden, a distance of 200 kilometers. The drive takes you through pretty, rolling farmland, pasture, forest, and low-lying hills. ****Dresden**, a large, sprawling city, is not as well signposted as you would wish, so it is handy to have a city map in hand to navigate to the Altstadt (old city). Follow signs to the heart of the old city center.

Dresden, the city with a great past, is well on its way to a great future. The famous skyline of palace domes and majestic church steeples on a bend of the Elbe River was razed by Allied bombers on February 13, 1945, and it is only since reunification that the city has experienced a rebirth. Many buildings have been cleaned, renovated, and restored to their former glory. An example of painstaking renovation is Taschenbergpalais (the Taschenberg Palace), a magnificent home commissioned in 1706 by August the Strong for his mistress, the Countess Cosel. Today, behind a painstakingly restored façade, the palace has been converted into an elegant, splendidly located hotel, the Kempinski Hotel Taschenbergpalais.

Begin your Dresden sightseeing at the Catholic cathedral, **Hofkirche**, whose lacy spire faces Augustusbrücke. Just beside the cathedral is the **Brühlsche Terrace**, praised as the "balcony of Europe"—only members of the nobility were allowed to enjoy this riverside view until 1814, when the broad flight of stairs was built to allow everyone to enjoy it. If you wish to know why the city's hero, August the Strong, was given his name, study the cast-iron railing of the terrace and find what is supposedly his thumb mark—a bit hard to believe since the rail was installed ten years after his death! Facing onto Brühlsche Terrace, which overlooks the river is the ****Albertinum**, an old arsenal that was converted into a museum in the 19th century. Inside, you will find the **New Gallery** (Gemäldegalerie Neuer Meister), a museum of 19th- and 20th-century painters, and the **Green Vault Collection** (Grünes Gewölbe). Of the two, be sure not to miss the Green Vault Collection with its breathtaking precious gems and treasures that belonged to the incredibly rich kings of Saxony. *(10 am–6 pm, closed Thursdays.)*

After visiting the Albertinum, descend from the terrace in front and go back one block from the river to Auguststrasse, then follow the ****Parade of Princes** (Fürstenzug), a mural made up of 24,000 Meissen porcelain tiles. The mural, which depicts a procession of 35 kings and princes on horseback, accompanied by their knights, stretches for almost a block on the wall of the building that used to house the stables. Nearby, you will see a monumental project under way—the reconstruction of the **Frauenkirche** (Church of Our Lady), which will take many years to complete. Originally the church was to be left in ruins as a sad testimonial to the Allied bombing of 1945, but now the plan has changed and the building that was once considered the most beautiful Protestant church in Europe is rising slowly from the ashes. Next, turn behind the **Residenzschloss** (castle) and walk behind the Catholic cathedral to the beautiful **Semperoper** (Semper Opera House), where statues on the façade portray Shakespeare and Sophocles, and Goethe and Schiller flank the entrance.

Saving the very best for last, enter Dresden's greatest treasure, the ***Zwinger Palace**, where you will concentrate much of your sightseeing. Just to walk into the enormous courtyard, which seems the size of multiple football fields, is awesome. Surrounding this lovely garden courtyard is the palace, which contains a mind-boggling assortment of museums. The ***Gemäldegalerie Alte Meister** (Old Masters Gallery), full of magnificent paintings by Canaletto, Raphael, Rubens, Rembrandt, Van Dyck, and many other famous artists, is world renowned. (*10 am–6 pm, closed Mondays.*) Your gallery ticket gives you entrance to the adjacent **Rüstkammer Museum** with its displays of ancient military hardware. (*10 am–6 pm, closed Mondays.*) The **Porzellansammlung** (Porcelain Museum—entrance on Sophienstrasse) houses an important collection of Meissen, Japanese, and Chinese porcelain. (*10 am–6 pm, closed Thursdays.*) The **Wallpavillion** houses the **Mathematisch-Physikalischer Salon** (Salon of Mathematics and Physics) with its collection of mathematical and measuring instruments (it has lots of barometers, thermometers, and clocks). (*9:30 am–5 pm, closed Thursdays.*)

The **Elbe River** runs through the heart of Dresden and makes for a fun excursion that doesn't take much energy. Steamer trips depart from the Terrassenufer, underneath the Brühlsche Terrasse. A 90-minute boat trip takes you upstream to Loschwitz and Blasewitz where the boat turns around and returns you to the city center. (*Operates April to mid-November*.) A longer trip takes you upstream past the Elbe palaces of Albrechtsburg, Lingner, and Eckberg to Pillnitz Palace, where you can leave the steamer and visit the park and palace before returning to the city center two hours later. (*Operates all year, reduced rate program October to April. Sächsische Dampfschiffahrts, Hertha-Lindner-Str. 10, 01067 Dresden, tel: 0351 866090, fax: 0351 8660988, www.saechsische-dampfschiffahrt.de*.) There are also steamer trips to Meissen, but because this is quite a long river trip, it is usually best to take a boat one way and the train the other to give you ample time for sightseeing. At the Terrassenufer boat dock in Dresden, or at the Dresden tourist office, you can pick up a schedule that shows the dates and departure times for all the various steamers.

Zwinger Palace, Dresden

Exploring East & Middle Germany

There are two side excursions from Dresden that we highly recommend. The first is to the 1,000-year-old town of Meissen, which is only a 25-kilometer drive north from Dresden following the Elbe River. (Note: If time is short, you could stop in Meissen on the day you leave Dresden, heading north toward Berlin.) The second side trip is to Swiss Saxony, an intriguing, lovely area south of Dresden. Both places can be visited by car, on a package tour from Dresden, or in the summertime by boat. Details of both suggested side excursions follow.

Our first suggested side excursion is to ***Meissen,** a historic town on a knoll overlooking the Elbe River with a splendid cathedral and medieval castle. However, its main claim to fame is the production of fine porcelain, which has been known the world over for many generations. (Some of you might remember your grandmother speak of the "Dresden" doll that she played with as a child—made of porcelain with a finely painted face.) To reach the porcelain factory, follow the sign of the crossed blue swords (the hallmark of Dresden china) through the old town at the base of the castle, which leads you directly to the ***Staatliche Porzellanmanufaktur** (porcelain factory) at 9 Leninstrasse. Parking is limited and there are a great many buses. Upon entering the building, buy two tickets, one for the museum and one for the work demonstration. While the tour through the work area is in several languages, it is helpful to have the English booklet describing the making of this world-famous china which dates back to 1708, when Johann Friedrich Böttger, working for August the Strong, discovered the secret of making "white gold" (porcelain china). August founded an isolated factory at Albrechtsburg castle, keeping the workers almost prisoners to protect the secret. In 1865 the factory was transferred to its present site. After the tour, visit the museum in the same building. Here you see incredible examples of Meissen china dramatically displayed in the regal setting of these lovely old rooms. Most of the pieces you see date from the 1700s and are extremely ornate: clocks, figurines, dinnerware, candelabra, statuettes—almost anything you can name has been duplicated in this fine white china. The style might not be your taste—much is a bit flamboyant, to be sure—but you cannot help appreciating the incredible craftsmanship involved in the making of each piece of art. A shop sells china and there is a pleasant little café just by the front door. (*8:30 am–3:30 pm, closed Mondays.*) The understandable popularity of the china factory means that Meissen's other tourist attractions are, unfortunately, often overlooked: the **Dom** (cathedral) and **Albrechtsburg Castle**, high above the town and visible from afar, are masterpieces of Gothic architecture. (*1–6 pm, Mondays to Saturdays; 10 am–3 pm, Sundays.*)

Our second suggested excursion from Dresden is to ***Swiss Saxony** (Sächsische Schweiz). Contrary to its name, this region that stretches southeast from Dresden to the border of the Czech Republic does not look at all like Switzerland, but is beautiful and fascinating in its own right. To see all the places we mention, you will need to get an early start. If you are driving, go to the Albert Platz and take Bautzner Strasse (also marked road number 6), following signs to Pillnitz, which is located on the Elbe River about 15 kilometers southeast of Dresden.

Pillnitz is worth a brief stop to visit its castle, which has two parts: the Bergpalais, which has a museum displaying decorative art, and the Wasserpalais, which houses a museum of arts and crafts. (*Bergpalais: May to November, 9:30 am–5:30 pm, closed Mondays. Wasserpalais: May to November, 9:30 am–5:30 pm, closed Tuesdays.*) Don't miss the reproduction of a Chinese pavilion in Pillnitz's English-style gardens. Note: In summer, it is popular to visit Pillnitz on a steamer trip from Dresden.

After visiting Pillnitz, continue east following signs to Hohnstein. Before Hohnstein, there is a turnoff to the right to ***Bastei**. The road leads to a park where an intriguing wonder of nature magically appears. The road to Bastei seems to be over a relatively flat plateau, but after you park your car, the landscape changes incredibly. What looked like flat terrain suddenly changes to a mysterious area with giant outcrops of reddish rock jutting into the sky. There is a small fee to follow the narrow footpath that twists above deep canyons to a stunning arched stone bridge, which spans the soaring rock formations and ends up at a strategic viewpoint. From here, there is a sweeping view that embraces the River Elbe as it loops through the lush valley, more than 200 meters below your perch.

Bastei, Swiss Saxony

From Bastei, follow signs toward Bad Schandau. The road leads gently down to the Elbe at which point you cross the bridge and follow signs on 172 in the direction of Dresden. Soon you come to the town of Königstein. After leaving the town, continue on 172 as it climbs the hill, then turn left at a sign for **Königstein Fortress**. Drive your car as far as possible and you end up at a parking area. From there you can either walk or take a shuttle tram to the base of the fortress that looms high above, crowning the hilltop. Buy your ticket and take the elevator (built into the rocks) that ascends to the dramatic portal. From there, you walk farther up the well-worn road to the summit.

The fortress is actually a walled town built on the top of a flat mountain. Many of the old buildings are open to view, but they are not of remarkable interest. What is really special is to walk the perimeter of the castle walls, which drop straight down to the valley far below. Poke into a few of the museums along the way as the mood suits you. If you haven't had lunch, or even if you have, stop for refreshment at the simple snack stand that is tucked along the top of the wall—the view is incredible. (*9 am–8 pm May to September; 9 am–6 pm October, 9 am–5 pm, November to April.*) After seeing the fortress, return to 172 and follow the road all the way back to Dresden.

Leaving Dresden, follow the signs to autobahn A13 heading north toward Cottbus and Berlin. The road is well maintained and the countryside quite flat so, unless there is a lot of traffic, it is an easy drive. You pass large farms of cultivated fields and drive through some pretty pastoral countryside. Watch your map carefully: when highway A13 joins the A15 to Berlin, you turn right on A15 toward **Cottbus** and then almost immediately after take exit 2 and follow signs to **Lübbenau**, which offers the largest selection of departures for the boat excursions that explore the water alleys of the **Spreewald*. Follow the road into town (signposted Häfen with a little boat and waves) and continue to the boat landing (you cannot miss it—there is a small plaza where many boats are tied up along docks lining the River Spree). As you walk along the docks you see a large selection of boats, each with a sign posted with the price and the length of the trip offered. Tours last from two to six hours and boats leave when they are full of passengers.

The Spreewald is an enormous maze where the Spree divides into tiny fingers, creating a lacy pattern of canal-like waterways, which wind lazily in every direction under a canopy of trees. For many centuries the Spreewald has been home to the Sorbs who have their own language and folk customs. Along the banks of the river the Sorbs have built small houses which vary in style but which are all simple wooden structures with high-pitched roofs crowned on each corner with a carved snake wearing a crown.

You can experience the magic of this area only by taking one of the boat excursions. First choose your boat: the two-hour tour is excellent, giving you a good sample of the area and also time to stop at **Lehde**, a Sorb village where you can have a cup of tea and visit the museum made up of a cluster of typical wooden homes furnished with old, country-style furniture. Each canoe is almost identical: a blackened wooden shell—sort of a cross between an Indian dugout canoe and a Venetian gondola. Benches are set in rows down the length of the canoe and your "gondolier" stands at the back and poles you through the shallow waters. As the boat left the dock, I was reminded of the jungle cruise at Disneyland. The boats pass under many humped bridges from which paths disappear mysteriously into the forest. Your gondolier makes a "pickle stop," for the Spreewald is famous for its pickles and merchants sell these spicy wares along the riverbanks. As the canoe glides through the water you are surrounded by constant activity: boats pass piled high with hay or carrying laughing children on their way to school or the postman delivering his mail—all attesting to the fact that there are few roads into this world of yesteryear.

When it is time to leave the Spreewald, get an early start because we suggest you stop along the way in Potsdam. It is an easy drive of about 125 kilometers along the well-marked autobahn A13 to Berlin, but instead of continuing directly on to the center of the city, we suggest you loop to the southwest of Berlin on A10 and take the turnoff north to **Potsdam**. Not only do we recommend a charming place to stay here, the Schlosshotel Cecilienhof (more details further on), but Potsdam also offers one of Germany's star attractions: the palaces and gardens of **Sanssouci*.

Frederick II chose Potsdam instead of Berlin as his permanent residence because he wanted a place where he could escape the pressures of being a ruler, and pursue his interests in philosophy and the arts without care—*sans souci*. He had the Sanssouci Palace built to his own design between 1745 and 1747, but this was just the beginning of an entire series of palaces set in vast, landscaped grounds. Be sure to wear sturdy shoes because it is almost a half-hour's walk between some of the buildings.

Map in hand, explore the tantalizing paths (strategically highlighted with sculptures) which weave through forests and glens as they connect one palace to another. If you have the stamina, you can easily spend a full day exploring the gardens and palaces. Important stops are: ***Sanssouci Palace** with its elaborate rooms in the rococo style, which you can tour with a German-speaking guide; the even larger **Neues Palais** (New Palace), where you don felt overshoes—do not miss the grotto made from shells and semi-precious stones; the **Orangerie**, an enormous building used to grow plants and house guests in sumptuous apartments; the **Grosse Bildergalerie** (Art Gallery), an ornate gallery displaying paintings by Caravaggio, Reni, Rubens, Van Dyck, and others; and the

Exploring East & Middle Germany

Chinesisches Teehaus (Chinese Tea House), a fanciful pavilion with gilded palms for columns and an ornate green-and-gold pagoda-style roof—Chinese porcelain is displayed inside. Other attractions include **Neptune's Grotto**, the **Obelisk Portal**, the **Trellis Pavilion**, the **Dragon House**, the **Sicilian Gardens**, **Charlottenhof Palace**, the **Temple of Friendship**—and on and on.

There is a staggering amount to see and do. Obtain a map and guidebook (in English) from the information booth beside the car park and set off to explore. Even if you do not tour the interiors, just walking through the vast, parklike grounds makes this a very worthwhile visit. The Sanssouci Palace is a real highlight: tickets go on sale at 9 am and tours are often sold out by early afternoon, so buy your ticket as soon you arrive and visit the other sights before returning at your allotted time. (*Sanssouci: 9 am–5 pm mid-May to mid-October; to 4 pm in February, March, and late October; to 3 pm November to January, closed 1st and 3rd Mondays. Neues Palais: same hours as palace but closed Fridays. Grosse Bildergalerie: 9 am–noon, 12:45 pm–5 pm, mid-May to mid-October.*)

Your other stop in Potsdam is at the **Schlosshotel Cecilienhof**. Looking for all the world like an English country manor, the Schlosshotel Cecilienhof was built by Kaiser Wilhelm in 1916, and became the royal residence of the Crown Prince Hohenzollern. The mansion, which is now both a delightful hotel and a museum, is surrounded by a large park graced with lakes, trees, green lawns, and forest. The manor house is especially important because it was here that Churchill, Truman, and Stalin met in 1945 to work out the details for the Potsdam Treaty, which proposed the economic and political destiny for the defeated Germany. Although a fire destroyed some of the rooms of historical interest, you can still see where the various delegates lived and worked while they planned the treaty, and there are many interesting photographs depicting the historical event. The parklike grounds surrounding Cecilienhof are also open to the public, but it is only a lucky few who stay on to spend the night in the lovely hotel rooms occupying several of the wings. (*9 am–5 pm, closed 2nd and 4th Mondays.*)

In sharp contrast to Potsdam, **Berlin** is dynamic and vigorous. Europe's largest city can be somewhat overwhelming in size for those who have been touring the countryside, but while the major sights are quite spread out, the public transportation system enables you to get around easily. If you are staying in Potsdam, you can take a train into Berlin.

Your first stop in Berlin should be one of the tourist offices. One is at the Europa Center on Budapester Strasse 45, and another is at the Brandenburg Gate (south wing) at Pariser Platz. Here you can pick up maps of the city and the public transportation system, get data on what special events are going on in the city, and obtain information on sightseeing tours ranging from 90 minutes to half a day (the tours leave from the adjacent Kaiser Wilhelm Memorial Church). Your hotel should also have a lot of information and be able to answer many of your questions.

We do not suggest driving in Berlin—it is not easy to find your way around (even with a good map) and parking is difficult. However, there are several other ways to see the main sights. If money doesn't matter, the concierge at your hotel can arrange for a private guide with car and driver; or you can take a taxi from point to point; or take a package tour. But, more adventuresome, less expensive, and lots of fun, is to take public transportation. If this is your choice, buy a 24-hour transportation pass, which is available from a self-service machine at all the subway stations (the machine is a bit tricky, but there are basic instructions in English on how to use it). This pass is an excellent value and allows you to hop on and off buses and subway trains to your heart's content within a 24-hour period.

A good place to start your sightseeing by public transport is outside the **Bahnhof Zoo** (Zoo station) at the **BVG transportation kiosk,** where you can purchase your 24-hour transportation pass and pick up maps before boarding the number 100 bus in front of the Zoo station (runs every 10 minutes). The bus proceeds down the Kurfürstendammstrasse (before the tunnel), passing on the right the **Europa Center**, a modern building with a large Mercedes sign on top, **Gedächtniskirche** (Kaiser Wilhelm Memorial Church) whose burnt, blackened, bombed-out shell stands as a memorial to the dead of two world wars, and on the left the two majestic stone elephants that guard the entrance to the **Berlin Zoo**. As the bus turns left into **Tiergarten** (Berlin's premier park), the 67-meter-high **Siegessaül** (a huge column surmounted by a statue of Victory) comes into view. Immediately on the left comes **Schloss Bellevue**, official residence of the President of the Republic (if the flag's flying, he's at home). The arch-shaped building on your left is the **Kongresshalle** (House of Culture) with sculpture by Henry Moore floating on its lake. Approaching the **Reichstag**, notice its bullet-riddled, patched-up façade. The German parliament met here for the first time in 1990, marking the end of almost four decades of political separation. (*10 am–5 pm, closed Mondays.*) Just round the corner you go under the 200-year-old **Brandenburg Gate* (*Brandenburger Tor*) whose majestic columns support the goddess of peace upon her horse-drawn chariot. During the years when Berlin was divided, the Brandenburg Gate became a symbol of oppression instead of the symbol of peace that it was originally conceived to be. Continuing on up **Unter der Linden**, the famous avenue "under the lime trees," you pass the much-photographed statue of Frederick the Great high atop his horse. Behind the statue is **Humboldt University,** which was attended by Marx and Lenin and next to it sits a Greek temple-like façade, a memorial for the Germans who died in the world wars.

Cross the river onto "Museum Island" and alight to tour the Pergamon Museum, a highlight of any visit to Berlin. The second neoclassical building, which contains the **Pergamon Museum*, is named for its most prized possession, the enormous Pergamon Altar. This beautifully preserved altar, dating from the 2nd century B.C., was brought from the west coast of Turkey and erected in an enormous hall. Pay the small extra cost for the half-hour tape-recorded tour that gives you a real perspective on this masterpiece of Hellenistic art. Almost as impressive is the adjacent Babylonian Processional Street where lions stride along the street's walls to the soaring blue-and-ochre tiles of the Ishtar Gate (604–562 B.C.). (*10 am–5 pm, closed Mondays.*)

Leaving the Pergamon to the right, turn left before the railway lines on Georgestrasse for the short walk to the Friedrichstrasse U-Bahn station, where you take the U6 in the direction of Alt Mariendorf beyond Stadtmitte to Kochstrasse. A vast office complex now occupies the site of Checkpoint Charlie, but the adjacent ***Haus Am Checkpoint Charlie** is an unsophisticated yet poignant museum that tells the story of the wall with its many ingenious escape attempts, and shows the struggle for freedom throughout the world. Exhibitions, photos, and videos take you up and down stairs and through 15 little rooms to conclude in the Checkpoint Charlie Café. Some of the displays seem a bit slanted toward political propaganda, but then how can you ever overemphasize oppression? (*9 am–10 pm, daily.*)

Back in the underground, take the U6 towards Alt Mariendorf for one stop to Hallesches where you change to the U1 (in the direction of Ruhleben) across town to Sophie Charlotte Platz. A ten-minute walk up Schlossstrasse brings you to Charlottenburg Palace. At number 70 Schlossstrasse (opposite the palace) visit ***Ägyptisches Museum** (Egyptian Museum), worth a visit if for no other reason than to gaze into the eyes of Nefertiti, an incredible bust over 3,000 years old yet depicting a woman as beautiful as any modern movie star. (*10 am–5 pm, closed Mondays.*) Across the street from the Ägyptisches Museum is the fabulous ***Picasso Museum**, a private collection of Pablo Picasso's works, which opened in 1997. (*9 am–5 pm, Tuesday through Friday; 10 am–5 pm Saturday and Sunday, closed Mondays.*)

Schloss Charlottenburg (Charlottenburg Palace) is one of those palaces that is more impressive outside than in. Rather than taking the guided tour (in German), go around the building and stroll along the inviting paths that lead you through elaborate, sculptured gardens to woodlands and lakes. If you want to take a peek inside, visit the **Galerie der Romantik** in the Knöbelsdorf wing, a gallery containing works by 19th-century Romantic painters. (*10 am–5 pm, closed Mondays.*) Leaving the palace, take the number 109 bus, which runs from just beside the palace down Kaiser Frederich Strasse and along the **Kurfürstendamm** (nicknamed *Ku'Damm*), a boulevard lined with chic boutiques, outdoor cafés, and grand hotels, and returns you to your starting point, the Bahnhof Zoo.

One of Berlin's highlights, the **Picture Gallery** (Gemäldegalerie), takes too long to see to try to squeeze it into the previous self-guided tour. Our suggestion would be to combine a visit to this vast museum with a stroll through Berlin's beautiful park, the Tiergarten, which is within easy walking distance. The **Kulturforum** is a large complex housing several museums, but the one that you must not miss is the stunning ***Picture Gallery** (Gemäldegalerie), which opened in 1998. This museum (with a seemingly endless number of large, well-lit rooms) houses an incredible collection of art. The enormous number of over 2,700 paintings (many of them on huge canvases) will boggle your mind. The exhibit includes works of art from the German painters of the 13th to 16th centuries, Dutch painters of the 15th and 16th centuries, Flemish painters of the 17th century, English, French, and German painters of the 18th century, miniatures of the 16th to 19th centuries, and Italian painters of the 16th to 19th centuries. So many famous names appear that you almost become numb to what genius you are seeing: Rembrandt, Fouquet, Gainsborough, Rubens, Reynolds, Van Dyck, and Botticelli—to mention just a few. (*10 am–6 pm, Tuesday through Friday; 11 am–6 pm, Saturday and Sunday, closed Mondays; public transportation: Potsdamer Platz.*)

If you have the luxury of time to linger in Berlin, another pleasurable outing is to enjoy Berlin leisurely by boat. The Spree River loops through the center of the city, and in the summer, various boat companies offer tours. Ask at the tourist office for further details.

If you are traveling with little ones, don't miss Berlin's **Teddy Bear Museum**, located at 206 Kurfürstendamm. Here you will see not only some of the earliest "Teddy" bears (named after Teddy Roosevelt), but also your other childhood friends such as Paddington and Winnie the Pooh.

It would be a shame to leave Berlin without experiencing Europe's biggest department store, **Kaufhaus des Westens (KaDeWe)** (U-Bahn 1 Wittenburgplatz). With over 2,400 employees, KaDeWe offers a vast array of goods for sale from souvenirs to sweaters. Choose from 1,800 kinds of cheese in the food hall or just take the glass elevator to the self-service café with its impressive views. (*9:30 am–6:30 pm, Saturdays until 2 pm; Thursdays until 8 pm, closed Sundays.*)

From Berlin you can go northwest to Hamburg to follow *Schleswig Holstein—the Land Between the Seas,* or southwest to Quedlinburg to join *Highlights of the Harz Mountains.*

Exploring East & Middle Germany

Schleswig Holstein
the Land Between the Seas

DENMARK

SYLT
ISLAND

Seebüll

Westerland

Niebüll

Flensburg

Oeversee

Keitum

BALTIC SEA

A 7

Schleswig

Oldenburg

Alt
Duvenstedt

Kiel

Plon

Eutin

Heide

A 23

Timmendorfer

NORTH SEA

A 7

Travemünde

Lübeck

A 1

Quickborn

Hamburg

●   Orientation/Sightseeing

─────   Other roads

═════   Autobahn

– – – –   Itinerary route

· · · · ·   Border

++++++   Rail route

Hamburg

Köln

Frankfurt

Munich

Schleswig Holstein–the Land Between the Seas

Schleswig Holstein is Germany's most northerly province. With Denmark at its tip, this broad finger of land divides the placid Baltic from the wild North Sea. Along the North Sea shore, dikes protect the sky-wide landscape from being claimed by the sea's crashing waves. Safe behind dikes, sheep and cattle graze while crops grow in serene pastures. Offshore, dune-fringed islands brave the sea. Any visit to Schleswig Holstein would not be complete without a trip to one of the islands, so this itinerary takes you and your car on top of a train for a rocking ride across the Hindenburgdamm to Sylt. This island boasts an impressive landscape of sand dunes and exposed, steep cliffs sheltering quaint little thatched villages from bracing sea breezes. In sharp contrast, the Baltic coast is hilly, with long, graceful fjords extending far inland from the gently lapping ocean. Here kilometer after kilometer of white-sand beaches provide a holiday haven for northern Europeans who brave the chilly waters and relax in gaily colored, canopied beach chairs while their children decorate sand castles with sea shells. Between these two seas lies Holsteinische Schweiz (Swiss District), a confusing name as there are no mountain peaks, just a lovely area of wooded, rolling hills sprinkled with sparkling lakes.

Recommended Pacing: Spend two nights in Hamburg to appreciate the flavor of this large city, then an early-morning start will enable you to be on Sylt by nightfall. The expense of the train to Sylt discourages you from spending only one night here. Try to include a visit to the Nolde Museum in Seebüll on your way to or from the island.

Northern weather tends to be cool and rainy, so pack your warm sweaters and rain gear. But be prepared to be surprised—the weather is unpredictable, so with a bit of luck you will have balmy, cloudless days as you explore this lovely region far from the beaten tourist paths.

Hamburg is a mighty trading and industrial center on the banks of the Elbe River. Understandably, Hamburg was a target for World War II bombings—by the end of the war the town was little more than a heap of rubble. But with great determination, much of the city has been rebuilt in the old style, so that today it has the mellow feel of an older age. Hamburg's sights are spread around a large area, so the most efficient way to get from place to place is on the U-Bahn, or subway system, whose stations are marked on the city's tourist map. Hamburg has some excellent hotels—see the *Hotel Descriptions* section.

The ****Aussenalster** is a beautiful body of water stretching from the city into the suburbs. Promenade the **Jungferstieg**—the most popular spot is the terrace of the **Alsterpavilion**— along its tributary, the **Binnenalster**. Take a ferry from the **Alterrundfahrt** around the Aussenalster. (*10 am–6 pm, every half hour, April to end of October.*)

In the city center, include the following on your sightseeing agenda: **St. Mickaelis-Kirche** (Hamburg's symbol), which offers a great view of the port and city from atop its 449 stairs, and the palatial **Rathaus** (town hall), built at the end of the 19th century, at the center of the popular shopping district. Its square, **Rathhausmarkt**, is the site of summer beer and wine festivals.

A boat trip around the port gives you an idea of the enormous size of the port complex. Boat trips leave from landing stage number 2, St. Pauli-Landungsbrücken. (*8 am–6 pm, April to September.*) If you are in Hamburg on a Sunday morning, plan on visiting the

Altona Fischmarkt, an open-air market at the water's edge offering everything — fruit, flowers, rabbits, socks, antiques, and, of course, fish. The show starts at six, but plan on arriving before nine. No need to eat before you arrive: there are plenty of food stands selling everything from delicious hot grilled sausages to crunchy rolls filled with smoked eel or pickled herring. Just a short walk for sailors from their ships, Hamburg's notorious red-light district has grown up along the **Reeperbahn** and surrounding streets, where erotic entertainment knows no bounds. This raunchy area, just west of the city center, is an anomaly in what is otherwise a very straight-laced city. (Reeperbahn 136 is where the Beatles launched their career.)

After a few days of city adventures, you will be ready for a change — something quiet and relaxed, a complete change of pace from the bustling city. Drive into the downtown area and follow signs for the autobahn 1 to Lübeck. *Lübeck** was the leading city of the Hanseatic League, a group of towns who banded together for trade advantages during the 13th to 16th centuries. About an hour's drive finds you beside the canal skirting the town's medieval fortifications. Follow the walls to the north and enter the town through the **Burgtor**, a gate built in 1444, into Grosse Burgstrasse, whose tall, red-brick buildings have impressive façades. On the left the **Heiligen-Geist-Hospital**, three red-brick gables each separated by slim, pointed turrets, now serves as a home for the elderly. Turn right opposite the hospital, and on Breite Strasse you find the seamen's tavern, now a restaurant, **Haus der Scheffergesellcraft** with its long wooden tables set beneath brass lanterns hanging from ancient beams. Farther down Breite Strasse you see the tall, slender, twin steeples of the **Marienkirche**, St. Mary's church, rise above the town. In the nearby Marktplatz you find tourist information and the **Rathaus**, Lübeck's impressive town hall, covering two sides of the square. Holenstrasse leads from the market square to the imposing **Holstentor Gate**, a squat fortress crowned by twin towers shaped like enormous witches' hats. The gate houses the town history museum, which displays a model of the city in the 17th century, weapons, model ships, and instruments of torture. (*10 am–4 pm, closed Mondays.*)

Holstentor Gate, Lübeck

Leaving the old town of Lübeck, drive to the north for 15 minutes to the popular Baltic resort of **Travemünde**. It is fun to drive along its river-front road seeing the boats and ferries on one side and the crowded little seaside shops on the other, and then to drive along its wide, sandy beach fringed by modern hotels.

As you leave Travemünde, follow road 76, which parallels the coastline going north. If the weather is sunny and warm, you may want to get into the German holiday spirit and join the crowds on the beaches at the coastal resorts of **Timmendorfer Strand** or **Scharbeutz-Haffkrug**. In pleasant weather, sun worshipers soak up the sun from the shelter of their canopied beach chairs, while offshore the Baltic waters come alive with the sails of gaily colored sailing boats and wind surfers.

Follow the 76 as it turns inland at Scharbeutz-Haffkrug. Leaving the flat coastal landscape behind, you enter a region of gently undulating farmland sprinkled with lakes both large and small. Narrow threads of land often separate one lake from another. The region is known as **Holsteinische Schweiz** (Swiss District) not because of its Alpine peaks, of which there are none, but because it shares a similar rock formation with Switzerland. About a half-hour's drive brings you to the lakeside town of **Eutin**. This is a colorful medieval town with a quaint, central pedestrian square. Park by the old moated castle and meander down to the lakefront through a gorgeous forested park, following the promenade that leads you along the shores of the lake, the **Eutiner See**.

Farther on, lovely lake vistas are provided by the drive around the **Keller See** to Malente-Gremsmühlen. Take the road along the northern shore through **Sielbeck** for the prettiest views. **Malente-Gremsmühlen** is the departure point for motor-boat tours of the beautiful five lakes to the west of town. The frustration of catching only glimpses of the lakes through the trees is removed when you glide along them on a boat.

Just a short distance to the west is **Plon**, positioned atop a small hill overlooking the region's largest lake, the **Grosser Plonnersee**. Drive through the town to the quaint, cobbled marketplace near the church. Park your car and walk up the narrow, cobblestoned alley to the castle terrace, where you have a lovely view of the lake below.

Leaving Plon, you follow road 76 for the half-hour's drive to the outskirts of **Kiel**. Unless you are interested in busy freight and yacht harbors, do not go into the city but take road 404 to the 4 and on to the suburban town of **Molfsee**. Here you will find the **Freilichtmuseum**, Schleswig-Holstein's Open-Air Museum, a collection of rustic farms and country homes dating from the 16th through the 19th centuries that have been brought here and reassembled. It is great fun to watch the local craftsmen operating the old smithy, potter's shop, mill, and bakehouse. You can explore the old houses and barns and retire to the timbered inn for welcome refreshments. (*9 am–6 pm, Tuesday through Sunday, April to October; and daily July to mid-September.*)

Make your way to the autobahn A7 going north (Schleswig and Flensburg) and exit at the ancient Viking stronghold of Schleswig. Soon after you leave the autobahn (before you reach the main town), watch for signs to the road going to the left to the baroque **Schloss Gottorf**. The **Archäologisches Landes-Museum** (archaeological museum) displays Viking artifacts, such as dishes and fishing nets. Their prize exhibit is the 4th-century Viking ship, the **Nydam-Schiff**, a long and slender 36-oarsman boat that was preserved in the marshes. (*9 am–5 pm, daily March to October; 9:30 am–4 pm, November to February, closed Mondays.*)

Schleswig's old town (Altstadt) hugs the northern bank of the Schlei inlet. Its Gothic brick Dom (cathedral) dates from the 12th century and is noted for its handsome carved altar (1521) in the chancel. Admire the 14th-century cloisters with the floral motif on their vaults. Also in Schleswig (around Friedhofplatz) is the picturesque fishermen's quarter called **Holm**. Don't miss this tiny, but ever-so-special hamlet—it is truly picture-perfect. Explore its quaint lanes, follow the circular road that wraps around the park and toy-like church, and stroll down to see the fishing boats at the water's edge.

Continue north on the A7 taking to the exit for Niebüll. Do not go into the town, but follow the well-posted signs of a car atop a railway car for the train to Sylt. On your way to or from the island make a little side trip from the car station to the north to visit the **Nolde Museum**, the home of Emiler Nolde the painter, in **Seebüll**. His house is a 12-kilometer drive north via Neukirchen. Over 200 paintings, watercolors, and drawings are displayed and his studio shows his religious paintings. The Nazis condemned him as a painter (ironically he was a die-hard racist and a member of the Nazi party) and it's touching to see the vast collection of miniature watercolors (*Ungemalte Bilder*) that he painted between 1941 and 1945 when the Nazis forbade him to paint. (*10 am–6 pm Monday to Friday, March to October; 10 am–5 pm, November to April.*)

Train to Sylt

You cannot drive your car to the island of ***Sylt**, but can take it on top of a railway carriage along the causeway that connects the island to the mainland. There is no need to make advance reservations—purchase your round-trip ticket as you drive into the railway yard. Do not worry about catching a particular train for there are between 11 and 16 departures each day. The car-train trip seems excessively expensive for such a short journey, so plan to stay awhile on the island.

Leaving the ticket office, you drive your car onto the train and sit in it for the 50-minute bumping ride past fields of sheep and Holstein cows towards the shoals that lead to the Hindenburg Levee, which connects the island to the mainland. From your lofty perch atop the train you can appreciate the centuries-long battle to keep the sea from flooding this flat, low-lying land. A series of dikes protects the land from the water and the farms are built on earthen banks, which become islands if the dikes fail. Crossing the sea dike, the train arrives in the island capital, **Westerland**, a town of elegant boutiques, sophisticated nightspots, and a casino.

The island is lovely—a long, narrow strip, much of it sand dunes—facing the North Sea. Dikes, sand dunes, and cliffs protect the island from North Sea storms. Forty kilometers of white sand attract summer sun worshipers (bathing suits are as welcome as none) and canopied beach chairs provide snug shelter from the wind. Hardy Germans enjoy swimming in the chill North Sea waves, but you will probably find the wave pool in Westerland (or your hotel pool) more to your liking.

*Keitum is the island's prettiest village, an old Friesian settlement of squat, thatched cottages, lilac bushes, and tree-lined streets. Keitum's low-slung houses are topped by thick roofs of reeds gathered from the tidal marshes, just the kind of house from which you would expect Hansel and Gretel to emerge. High garden walls protect against storm, flood, tides, and winds. On Museumweg, you can visit the **Old Friesian House**. Built in 1739 by a sailing captain, the red-brick old Friesian farmhouse passed into the hands of a 19th-century historian who assembled a history of the island. The house and the furnishings are such that a Friesian of two centuries ago would feel immediately at home. Next door the **Sylter Heimatmuseum** (folklore museum) contains collections of island seafaring memorabilia and coins, porcelain, and costumes dating back hundreds of years. Inspired perhaps by their forefathers, modern artisans have set up their shops in nearby houses. (*10 am–noon and 2–5 pm, April to October, closed Tuesdays.*)

As you explore farther afield, you pass Keitum's **St. Severin church**, a landmark for seafarers since it was built seven centuries ago. The island's days as an important maritime center are long past, yet once a year, on the eve of February 22, the islanders pile straw, reeds, and wood into a huge bonfire as a symbolic send-off for the island's sailors.

Devote a day to exploring the island and its villages huddled behind the sand dunes, then use the remainder of your stay for relaxation—hike to the **Rotes Kliff** and see the water turning red as it erodes the cliff. Behind the cliffs climb the 53-meter **Uwe Dune**, a vantage point for seeing the North Sea to the west and the mud flats to the east. Bird watchers head for **Vogelkoje** bird sanctuary.

When your island holiday is over, if your destination is Denmark, you can take a ferry to Havenby, or retrace your steps to **Niebüll** for the short drive to the Danish border. For those who are returning to Hamburg, follow the road south across the flat polder lands that have been reclaimed from the sea. The waters offshore are shallow: sea dikes keep them at bay, protecting the lush, green pasture and farmlands behind.

Schleswig Holstein–the Land Between the Seas

Hotel Descriptions

If you are looking for an isolated hideaway far from the often-trod tourist paths, the Seehotel Töpferhaus fits the bill. Hugging the shores of the tranquil Bistensee and surrounded by manicured gardens, the Seehotel Töpferhaus commands a serene setting. On our first visit, the Töpferhaus was a small hotel with guestrooms in a simple, whitewashed farmhouse. This original part of the inn remains but a new section has been built, adding 20 deluxe guestrooms and a restaurant with a view of the Bistensee gently lapping at the lawn in front of the hotel. As a result of the expansion, the hotel has gained a sophisticated elegance, but happily there is no jarring, commercial feeling to spoil the mood. The setting remains superbly pastoral, the warmth of welcome sincere, and the furnishings throughout extremely tasteful. All the guestrooms are appealing, but I especially love numbers 11 to 13—on the ground floor with French doors opening out to the garden. The Töpferhaus is not the kind of hotel for an overnight stop, but rather an enchanting place to stay for at least several days to enjoy the unspoiled solitude of the countryside. *Directions:* 100 km north of Hamburg. Take the A7 north from Hamburg and exit at Rendsburg. Go east on 203 (towards Eckernforde). After 2 km you see a sign for the hotel, turn left and the narrow road brings you to the hotel. Do not go to Alt Duvenstedt—it is on the other side of the autobahn.

SEEHOTEL TÖPFERHAUS
Manager: Martin Brandenburg
27491 Alt Duvenstedt am Bistensee, Germany
Tel: (04338) 99710, Fax: (04338) 997171
46 Rooms, Double: €120–€175
Open: all year, Credit cards: all major
Region: Schleswig-Holstein, Michelin Map: 541
www.karenbrown.com/topferhaus.html

Der Schafhof, one of Germany's loveliest hotels, sits on a hillside dotted with grazing sheep near the town of Amorbach. Built in 1721, the main building originally belonged to the estate of the Amorbach Benedictine Abbey and is now owned by the Ullrich family who in years gone by were titled millers hereabouts. Der Schafhof is still an operating farm with all the farming paraphernalia of barns, tractors, ducks, and geese next to the hotel. Just inside the front door is a snug lounge warmed on cool evenings by a blazing log fire. Here you find a gourmet restaurant (with a prestigious Michelin star) serving sumptuous cuisine and fine wines, while more casual dining is offered in the Benedictine Room in the adjacent barn, which dates back to 1524. While there are lovely bedrooms in the main house, those in the barn are especially delightful. In fact, the decor is consistently beautiful in all of the bedrooms, whether you choose the spaciousness of a suite or the coziness of a beamed bedroom tucked under the eaves. For relaxation enjoy spa treatments, walks across farmland, a game of tennis, the sauna, solarium, or simply soaking up the countryside view from the terrace. *Directions:* Located 80 km southeast of Frankfurt, 67 km northeast of Heidelberg. From Amorbach take the B47 towards Michelstadt for about 1 km and you find signposts directing you for the 3-km drive to Der Schafhof.

DER SCHAFHOF
Owners: Vera & Herbert Ullrich
Otterbachtal, 63916 Amorbach, Germany
Tel: (09373) 97330, Fax: (09373) 4120
24 Rooms, Double: €130–€275
Open: all year, Credit cards: all major
Region: Bayern, Michelin Map: 545
www.karenbrown.com/schafhof.html

The Residenz Heinz Winkler, conveniently located in the quaint village of Aschau, is a real charmer. The hotel is easy to find—as you drive into Aschau you will see a small hill rising from the town. Perched on this hill is a picturesque church with twin onion domes, and right next to the church is the Residenz Heinz Winkler. This stately hotel was once an annex of the 15th-century Hohenaschau Castle. From the moment you enter, the mood of sophisticated elegance is set: light streams through large plate-glass windows into a spacious lobby with a marble floor enhanced by a handsome Oriental carpet. The hotel has several sophisticated dining rooms and on warm summer days you have the option to have lunch outside on a protected terrace that affords a sweeping view of the mountains. If you appreciate truly fine cuisine, you will be pleased to note the restaurant has three Michelin stars. The mood of subdued grandeur continues in the bedrooms, which are all elegantly appointed with fine furniture and lovely fabrics. We prefer the bedrooms in the old section of the hotel to the more contemporary wing where the rooms have a small sitting room downstairs and a bedroom upstairs. Relax in the spa complex complete with sauna, steam rooms, and a swimming pool where you swim against the current. *Directions:* Aschau is almost midway between Munich and Salzburg, just three minutes off the autobahn. At Frasdorf turn south on the 175 to Aschau.

RESIDENZ HEINZ WINKLER
Owner: Heinz Winkler
Kirchplatz 1, 83229 Aschau, Germany
Tel: (08052) 17990, Fax: (08052) 179966
32 Rooms, Double: €180–€270*
*Breakfast not included: €20
Open: all year, Credit cards: all major
Relais & Chateaux
Region: Bayern, Michelin Map: 546
www.karenbrown.com/winkler.html

The tiny wine village of Assmannshausen sits at a slight widening of the narrow Rhine River gorge and, limited by its location and unspoiled by modern development, remains a cramped cluster of old houses overlooking the river. Fronting the Rhine, the Hotel Krone has been providing hospitality to weary travelers since 1541. The hotel's wisteria-covered terrace and raised restaurant provide lovely places for dining while watching the busy river life glide by. Much of the building dates from the turn of the century and has an interior perfectly in keeping with the exterior, with large, rather heavy pieces of lovingly polished furniture set against dark paneled walls. Some of the bedrooms are in the main building while others are located in the adjacent annex—all have been beautifully refurbished and are decorator-perfect, styled after the age of the building (a bit dark), each accompanied by a luxurious marble bathroom. All the rooms are attractive but the spacious junior suites are especially appealing. The rooms in the front are choice since these offer the added advantage of a view of the Rhine: I particularly liked rooms 83 and 90 (double rooms), each with a seating area tucked into the tower. River steamers dock just a two-minute walk away: if you arrive by boat, the hotel will send someone to meet you and tend to your luggage. *Directions:* Assmannshausen is on the B42, 30 km west of Wiesbaden, on the north side of the Rhine.

HOTEL KRONE
Owner: Heinz Diehl
Rüdesheim, 65385 Assmannshausen, Germany
Tel: (06722) 4030, Fax: (06722) 3049
65 Rooms, Double: €160–€650*
*Breakfast not included: €15
Open: all year, Credit cards: all major
Region: Hessen, Michelin Map: 543
www.karenbrown.com/hotelkrone.html

The Brauerei-Gasthof-Hotel Aying is a famous brewery, restaurant, and hotel, all rolled into one wonderful Bavarian package. Aying is a delightful pastoral village to the south of Munich and has the advantage of being on the S-Bahn, so a half-hour train journey finds you at the Marienplatz in the heart of historic Munich. You can sightsee to your heart's content and return to the peace and quiet of the countryside in the evening. The hotel's ivy-covered façade is easily spotted thanks to a giant, blue-striped maypole marking the entrance. Franz Inselkammer is the sixth generation of his family to be Aying's brewer and after you have toured his brewery you can enjoy a delicious candlelit dinner with a menu offering lots of scrumptious Bavarian specialties and, of course, all varieties of the famous Ayinger beer. If you prefer more casual fare and a little nightlife, then step across the square to the traditional beer garden where in fine weather you can dine on the tree-lined patio. The delightful bedrooms, which come in all shapes and sizes, are decorated in the most lovely traditional Bavarian style and each is accompanied by a state-of-the-art bath or shower room. *Directions:* Leave Munich to the south on the A8 (Munich to Salzburg autobahn). After 14 km turn west at exit 96 and follow signposts for the 7-km drive to Aying.

BRAUEREI-GASTHOF-HOTEL AYING
Owners: Angela & Franz Inselkammer
Zornedinger Strasse 2, 85653 Aying, Germany
Tel: (08095) 90650, Fax: (08095) 906566
34 Rooms, Double: €135–€180
Open: all year, Credit cards: all major
Region: Bayern, Michelin Map: 546
www.karenbrown.com/brauereigasthofhotelaying.html

The façade of the Romantik Hotel Lindner is picturesque—a pretty, cream-colored building with a stepped roof and red geraniums accenting windows framed by gray-and-white-striped shutters. You would never guess that it began life as a sturdy fortification! The entrance to the hotel is in the rear where a terrace set with tables and chairs connects the original castle to a new wing overlooking a lovely expanse of lawn and garden, which reflects a similar architectural style. The Hotel Lindner has been in the same family for over 150 years and today is run by Gabi Lindner-Jung and her mother, Erna Lindner. It is very obvious that this is a family-owned and -operated hotel: great attention is paid to every detail throughout. The ambiance is one of Bavarian allure leaning more towards sophisticated elegance than quaint rustic charm. There is a fresh, uncluttered look, with modern traditional furnishings accented by country antiques, such as dowry chests and painted armoires. The guestrooms are all very tastefully decorated with the finest-quality furnishings and handsome fabrics. This is a hotel of style and class—a direct reflection of its owners. *Directions:* Bad Aibling is 62 km southeast of Munich, just a five-minute drive from the A8, Munich to Salzburg autobahn. Turn north off the A8 at exit 100 and travel 5 km to Bad Aibling. Entering town, turn right at a traffic light onto Spielstrasse to the Romantik Hotel Lindner.

ROMANTIK HOTEL LINDNER
Owners: Erna Lindner & Gabi Lindner-Jung
Marienplatz 5, 83043 Bad Aibling, Germany
Tel: (08061) 90630, Fax: (08061) 30535
26 Rooms, Double: €120–€160
Open: all year, Credit cards: all major
Region: Bayern, Michelin Map: 546
www.karenbrown.com/lindner.html

The Hotel Friedrich Franz Palais was built by Herzog Friedrich Franz von Mecklenburg in 1793 as a holiday retreat where he would come to the Baltic Sea for his health. Thus started the concept in Germany of a spa holiday, a trend that continues to be extremely popular today. The hotel has its own style combining the fresh, clean, uncluttered look of Scandinavian design with lovely, traditional English fabrics. The mood of understated elegance is set as you enter the reception hall where classical music is playing. Soft white predominates throughout, with bouquets of freshly cut flowers and pretty slip-covered chairs in handsome English stripes adding just the right dash of color. There are two main dining rooms: each is traditional in feel, with Biedermeier-style chairs, handsome draperies, pastel colors, and fresh flowers. The guest bedrooms continue the country-manor look with English fabrics in color schemes of soft yellows or pretty greens. The hotel is located in the center of town facing a small park. *Directions:* Located 210 km north of Berlin on the north coast by the Ostsee. From Rostock travel 18 km west on B105/A20 to Bad Doberan.

HOTEL FRIEDRICH FRANZ PALAIS
Owner: Kross-Jonsson Family
Am Kamp, Heiligendamm
18209 Bad Doberan, Germany
Tel: (038203) 63036, Fax: (038203) 62126
51 Rooms, Double: €100–€140
Open: all year, Credit cards: all major
Region: Mecklenburg-Vorpommern, Michelin Map: 542
www.karenbrown.com/friedrichfranz.html

Bad Hersfeld is a handsome North German town with, at its heart, a large market square lined with old burghers' houses, part of which has been turned into a pedestrian mall. It is in this pedestrian zone, with its tables and chairs spilling over onto the square, that you find the Romantik Hotel Zum Stern. Bustling and welcoming, the inn has been offering hospitality to weary travelers for over 500 years. In recent years, as the volume of trade has grown, the hotel has expanded back from the square so that accommodations are provided both in the old section and a modern extension. Try to secure one of the darling rooms in the original hostelry. With their blackened beams, creaking floorboards, and antique furniture, they are a real prize. I especially liked room 101 with its view of the market square. A new wing of rooms has been opened in a little house across the courtyard and these are furnished with most attractive country-pine reproduction furniture. A small indoor swimming pool and sauna are found at the rear of the building overlooking a little garden. Regional specialties highlight the menu in the country-style dining room. Ines and Achim Kniese are the fifth generation of the Kniese family to operate this hotel. *Directions:* Located 130 km northeast of Frankfurt, 50 km west of Eisenach. To find the hotel follow directions to "Stadtmitte" from the "Stadtring" then turn left behind the Parkhaus onto Webergasse to the hotel.

ROMANTIK HOTEL ZUM STERN
Owner: Kniese Family
Lingg Platz 11, 36251 Bad Hersfeld, Germany
Tel: (06621) 1890, Fax: (06621) 189260
45 Rooms, Double: €97–€144
Open: all year, Credit cards: all major
Region: Hessen, Michelin Map: 541
www.karenbrown.com/romantikhotelzumstern.html

While strolling along the promenade that traces the edge of Lake Scharmützeisee, the Runges noticed a villa nestled on a gentle hill overlooking the lake. The enchanting home immediately captured their hearts so they purchased it in 1997, pouring their love into total renovations, and opened Germany's smallest first-class hotel. This tiny white villa, with mansard-style red-tile roof accented by cute gables, exudes a whimsical, fairly-tale quality. Villa Contessa, in the heart of Bad Saarow (a charming upscale thermal spa town) overlooks one of Germany's most idyllic lakes. In front, shade trees with lacy foliage frame the house and a stone fountain embellishes the garden. Behind the hotel, a lush lawn slopes down to the romantic promenade and to the lake. Within, the villa is like a wedding cake with ornate, empire-style white furniture trimmed in gold, knickknacks, crystal chandeliers, silk flower bouquets, satin upholstery, and opulent tie-back drapes. Eight guestrooms (four singles and four doubles) display the same style décor. There is an intimate dining room (specializing in Mediterranean dining) and a lavish small parlor, both opening onto a terrace with white wrought-iron tables and chairs. This adorable villa is totally a family-run affair with Marina and Bernd Runge at the helm, ably assisted by their son, their daughter, and son-in-law. *Directions:* From the A12, take exit 4 to Bad Saarow. From the train station, signs lead to the hotel.

VILLA CONTESSA   New
Owners: Marina & Bernd Runge
Seestrasse 18, Bad Saarow, Germany
Tel: (033631) 58018, Fax: (033631) 58919
8 Rooms, Double: €118–€188
Restaurant closed on Mon
Open: all year, Credit cards: MC,VS
Region: Sachsen, Michelin Map: 544
www.karenbrown.com/villacontessa.html

Facing onto a pretty cobbled square, the Hotel Am Markt is an excellent choice for a moderately-priced place to stay in the historic heart of Baden-Baden. Although the room rates are amazingly low, the quality throughout the hotel is exceptional. The entrance is modest—just a simple hallway with a reception desk where you will probably be greeted by either Doris or Andrea, two gracious sisters who own and constantly upgrade this property. It is not until you go upstairs that the merits of the hotel are revealed. The guestrooms are tastefully decorated in a pleasing, uncluttered, modern style. One of our favorites, room 2, is especially spacious and has an excellent bathroom that outshines some found in deluxe hotels. Room 21 is also a real winner with windows that capture an appealing view of the rooftops of Baden-Baden. The high-ceilinged guestrooms on the first two floors are larger than those tucked under the eaves. There is an old-world charm in the dining room with its Windsor chairs arranged round little tables beneath the paneled ceiling, and the day's newspapers hung on reading poles for guests to browse through. A few of the least expensive guestrooms do not have en suite bathrooms, so be sure to indicate your preference when making a reservation. *Directions:* Follow the blue hotel signs in Baden-Baden to the Hotel Am Markt located directly behind the Friedrichsbad. The hotel has parking on the square and in a nearby garage.

HOTEL AM MARKT
Owner: Bogner Family
Marktplatz 18, 76530 Baden-Baden, Germany
Tel: (07221) 27040, Fax: (07221) 270444
25 Rooms, Double: €80–€85*
*€2.50 spa tax per person per day
Restaurant closed Sun & Wed
Open: all year, Credit cards: all major
Region: Baden-Württemberg, Michelin Map: 545
www.karenbrown.com/ammarkt.html

I felt privileged to be present a few years ago to share the excitement and news with the Rademacher family when they had just closed the deal on a gorgeous home with plans to turn it into a second wonderful hotel. They even shared with me their decision on a name for this beautiful three-story, stately home set behind handsome gates and surrounded by its own expanse of garden—the Hotel Belle Epoque. The name seems appropriate as the building and its residential setting typify the glory and beauty of the 19th century. The Belle Epoque is conveniently set just around the corner from its sister hotel, Der Kleine Prinz. Frau Rademacher has cleverly decorated each guestroom with antiques and a theme of the different time periods of the Belle Epoque, i.e., Empire, Art Nouveau, Biedermeier, Louis XVI, but all are equipped for the new millennium in terms of modern comfort and luxury. Although the hotel has no restaurant, it is an easy stroll to Der Kleine Prinz which has a wonderful restaurant and bar. The hotel does offer a full breakfast buffet and room service, as well as complimentary high tea in the afternoon. We have enjoyed being able to recommend the Rademachers' Der Kleine Prinz and it is without hesitation that I recommend the Belle Epoque. *Directions:* From the A5 follow the "Congress" signs. Take the first exit in the tunnel, still following signs to "Congress" and then signs for the hotel.

HOTEL BELLE EPOQUE
Owners: Melissa & Andreas Rademacher
Maria-Victoria Strasse 2c
76530 Baden-Baden, Germany
Tel: (07221) 300660, Fax: (07221) 300666
16 Rooms, Double: €199–€495*
*€2.50 spa tax per person per day
Open: all year, Credit cards: all major
Region: Baden-Württemberg, Michelin Map: 545
www.karenbrown.com/hotelbelleepoque.html

Romantik Hotel Der Kleine Prinz (The Little Prince) is a most appealing luxury hotel, conveniently located close to shopping, parks, the elegant casino, and spa facilities in the popular resort town of Baden-Baden. The owners, Edeltraud and Norbert Rademacher, are often at the reception to greet guests personally. Norbert worked in hotels in the United States for many years and is very attuned to American tastes. Edeltraud is responsible for the decor of the lovely rooms. She loves English and French antiques and has taken great care in choosing fabrics, carpet, and bathroom decor to complement the lovely furniture, so you find the Louis XVI room very different from the English Victorian room. Their gracious son, Andreas, has joined the family entourage, and his presence only serves to enhance the level of professionalism and courtesy. Many of the bedrooms are suites with separate sitting areas—all have every luxurious appointment and a great many have whirlpool tubs. As a whimsical touch, The Little Prince, the irresistible hero from St. Exupéry's heartwarming fable, is painted grandly on the exterior, features in a large mural in the dining room, and appears as some memento in each guestroom. The Rademachers have secured the best seats for their hotel guests at the opera house—the largest in Europe. *Directions:* From the A5 follow the "Congress" signs, take the first exit in the tunnel, and then follow signs for the hotel.

ROMANTIK HOTEL DER KLEINE PRINZ
Owners: Edeltraud & Norbert Rademacher
Lichtentaler Strasse 36
76530 Baden-Baden, Germany
Tel: (07221) 346600, Fax: (07221) 38264
40 Rooms, Double: €180–€495*
*€2.50 spa tax per person per day
Open: all year, Credit cards: all major
Region: Baden-Württemberg, Michelin Map: 545
www.karenbrown.com/romantikhotelderkleineprinz.html

Badenweiler is an old spa town where the architecture is predominantly heavy Victorian and the clientele come for the curative powers of the water. Set in a quaint older section of town, the Sonne is the oldest guesthouse in Badenweiler and is ably run by the Esposito family. Vittorio hails from Italy and, although he speaks no English, his warm Italian welcome crosses all language barriers. Son Michael is happy to help with translating. The focus of the antique-filled living room is an old blue-and-white-tile stove with an inviting bench on which you can snuggle up and enjoy its warmth. Many guests stay for a week or longer so there is a large dining room for pension guests and two cozy restaurants for shorter-stay guests. Bedrooms come in all shapes and sizes and are found in the main building, a modern annex in the garden, and an old house across the street. If you are traveling with family, there are several apartments available with bedrooms and separate living rooms. The southern reaches of the Black Forest are around you — spectacular walks and drives abound. *Directions:* Badenweiler is located 35 km south of Freiburg, 40 km north of Basel. Turn into Luisenstrasse, opposite the Cassiopeia Therme (a large, modern complex by the park), and you arrive in the hotel's courtyard.

ROMANTIK HOTEL ZUR SONNE
Owner: Vittorio Esposito
Moltkestrasse 4, 79410 Badenweiler, Germany
Tel: (07632) 75080, Fax: (07632) 750865
34 Rooms, Double: €109–€158
€2.50 spa tax per person per day
Open: all year, Credit cards: all major
Region: Baden-Württemberg, Michelin Map: 545
www.karenbrown.com/zursonne.html

Bamberg is an absolute delight, a medieval city exuding the appeal of yesteryear. Just a few minutes' walk from the picturesque Rathaus, which is perched on a tiny island and marvelously positioned fronting the River Regnitz, you find the Hotel Brudermühle, originally a mill dating from the early 14th century. It is built within an exceptionally attractive, three-story building with green shutters and dormer windows peeking out from under the steeply pitched red roof. The gracious owners, Erna and Georg Vogler, have increased the hotel's charm in the public rooms with a few well-chosen antiques. Just off the lobby is an attractive restaurant where good home cooking of regional specialties is served. Guests also tend to linger at tables set on the entry patio enjoying both the relaxed setting and prime people watching. The guestrooms in the original mill are sweet but simple: choice rooms are number 5 (overlooking the river) or number 1 (view of the river and the Rathaus). However, our favorite accommodations are the four outstanding guestrooms in a house just across the street—ask for one of these overlooking the stream with the sound of the gushing waterfall just below your window. *Directions:* Bamberg is 61 km north of Nürnberg. Take the Bamberg/Gartenstadt exit and follow signs to Altstadt/Zentrum. Drive along Memmelsdorfer Strasse, cross the Europabrücke, turn left on Schweinfurter Strasse, and continue to Schranne. The hotel is on the square.

HOTEL BRUDERMÜHLE
Owners: Erna & Georg Vogler
Schranne 1, 96049 Bamberg, Germany
Tel: (0951) 955220, Fax: (0951) 9552255
20 Rooms, Double: €110–€130
Restaurant closed Mon
Open: all year, Credit cards: MC, VS
Region: Bayern, Michelin Map: 546
www.karenbrown.com/hotelbrudermuhle.html

Bamberg is a beautiful town and a destination that deserves more attention than given in travel literature. At its center, it is a complex of quaint, cobbled, pedestrian streets, outdoor cafés, bridges, and enchanting houses gracing and lining the waterfront. Not more than a few blocks from the old section of town, on a corner of one of the main streets into town, is a simple hotel with a wonderful restaurant—the Romantik Hotel Weinhaus Messerschmitt. With its pretty soft-yellow façade, the hotel is easy to spot, and its charming, well-known, Franconian-style restaurant (in the Messerschmitt family since 1832) is quite popular and always includes local specialties on the menu. Popular with both businessmen and restaurant patrons, the hotel is often full. The bedrooms are found up a marvelous wooden, handcarved stairway and are identified from other offices and private rooms by numbered wine bottles which hang over each door. The bedrooms are simple but sweet in decor. Down comforters deck the beds, and the bathroom facilities are modern but enhanced by lovely old fixtures. At night it is difficult to shut out the street noise, but a welcome sherry left by the management might be all you need to sleep. *Directions:* When the A22 becomes the Münchner Ring Road, on the west side of the Heinrichsbrücke, turn towards the city center on Friedrichstrasse, which becomes Lange Strasse just past Schönleinsplatz. The hotel is on the right.

ROMANTIK WEINHAUS MESSERSCHMITT
Owners: Ursula Medenwald & Otto Pschorn
Lange Strasse 41, 96047 Bamberg, Germany
Tel: (0951) 297 800, Fax: (0951) 297 8029
17 rooms, Double: €120–€160
Open: all year, Credit cards: all major
Region: Bayern, Michelin Map: 546
www.karenbrown.com/messerschmitt.html

The Altes Zollhaus sits at the river's edge in one of the Mosel's most charming villages at the foot of the region's vineyards. A soft-yellow-wash building with rust-colored timbers and a slate roof topping its third-floor dormer windows—the entrance is through its dining room. Before inquiring about a room, consider a meal as the food is quite good, well presented, and reasonable. The best accompanying wines are those of the proprietor himself. The eight guestrooms, with simple stenciling decorating whitewashed walls, are found up a basic staircase. The comfortable beds are topped with down comforters and rooms benefit from views of the Mosel. Although there is a real charm to the Zollhaus, which dates from 1634, if you prefer absolute quiet to the waterfront setting, ask Madame about their additional accommodation offered at Hotel Haus Lipmann, 150 meters up the hill. This newly constructed, attractive timbered inn has sixteen bedrooms, most enjoying the expanse of front deck, while two rooms back onto the hillside. Guestrooms at the Hotel Haus Lipmann are a little larger than those at the Altes Zollhaus and the bathrooms are new and modern. Guests at Hotel Haus Lipmann have the use of the house's own breakfast and sitting rooms. *Directions:* 60 km southwest of Koblenz. Follow the 49 along the river past Cochem, at Ernst cross to the other side of the river and Beilstein is a little way farther to the south.

ALTES ZOLLHAUS
Owner: Lipmann Family
56814 Beilstein, Germany
Tel: (02673) 1850, Fax: (02673) 1287
8 Rooms, Double: €60–€80
Open: Apr to Nov, Credit cards: none
Region: Rheinland-Pfalz, Michelin Map: 543
www.karenbrown.com/alteszollhaus.html

The Hotel Haus Lipmann has been in the same family since 1795 and Marion Thölen Lipmann, your gracious hostess, is always on hand to see that her guests are well looked after. This quaint little hotel is especially appealing because it is located at the heart of one of the prettiest villages along the Mosel — with its picturesque medieval buildings, church, and ruined castle, Beilstein is a gem. The dining rooms are just as attractive as the exterior: you may find yourself in a small farmhouse-style room before an old fireplace, in the warm, paneled main dining room, or feasting in the knights' hall surrounded by collections of old weapons. When weather permits, you can move outdoors to the wisteria-covered terrace and watch the life on the gentle River Mosel glide by as you sip a glass of excellent Mosel wine produced from the Lipmanns' own grapes. Upstairs are five charming, nicely decorated guestrooms, all located at the front of the house with an antique bed and a splendid river view. Brother Joachim offers tasting in his cellar across the square and runs the town's little wine museum. Beilstein's wine festival takes place during the first weekend in September. The Haus Lipmann makes an excellent base for exploring the Mosel. *Directions:* Beilstein is approximately 60 km southwest of Koblenz. Follow the 49 along the river and a few kilometers past Cochem, at Ernst, cross the river and Beilstein is a little farther to the south.

HOTEL HAUS LIPMANN
Owner: Marion Thölen Lipmann
Marktplatz 3, 56814 Beilstein, Germany
Tel: (02673) 1573, Fax: (02673) 1521
5 Rooms, Double: €85–€95
Open: Apr to Oct, Credit cards: none
Region: Rheinland-Pfalz, Michelin Map: 543
www.karenbrown.com/hotelhauslipmann.html

If you are looking for a small, deluxe hotel in the heart of Berlin, the Brandenburger Hof is ideal. None can surpass its warmth of welcome, understated elegance, genteel refinement, and outstanding quality. The family-run Brandenburger Hof faces onto a quiet, cobbled street edged by lacy trees. Built originally as a private mansion, the hotel is a charming, five-story, creamy-white building, with tall windows, graceful wrought-iron balconies, and a mansard roof studded with gables. You enter into a spacious lobby bathed in natural light with a soaring ceiling supported by elegant columns, modern chrome-and-leather chairs, and bouquets of fresh flowers. A stone portal leads into the enchanting Wintergarten conservatory. Guests love to dine in this beautiful oasis as well as in Die Quadriga, which has earned a celebrated Michelin star. The mood of the guestrooms is one of restful, sophisticated simplicity, with modern furnishings and white walls accented by signed drawings by leading artists. There are also eight beautiful suites with the theme and decor of the operas for which they are named and a handsome library boasting a collection of antique and modern books. *Directions:* From the A100 Berlin Ring Road, take the Wilmersdorf and then the Kurfürstendamm exits. At the first light turn left on Kurfürstendamm, go 4 km to Gedächtniskirche and turn right onto Rankestrasse. The second left is Eislebener Strasse.

BRANDENBURGER HOF BERLIN
Owner: Daniela Sauter
Eislebener Strasse 14
10789 Berlin, Germany
Tel: (030) 214050, Fax: (030) 21405100
72 Rooms, Double: €245–€515
Open: all year, Credit cards: all major
Region: Berlin, Michelin Map: 542
www.karenbrown.com/brandenburger.html

Louisa's Place is a haven within the vibrant, ever-active city of Berlin. Many guests come for a month or more to this unique property that offers huge, one to three bedroom suites complete with kitchens, for a price that is often less than a standard double room at Berlin's deluxe hotels. But the size of the accommodations fades in importance to the hotel's other qualities once you experience its charm. When planning their hotel, the owner's top priority was to create an environment where guests are treasured. The mood is set from the moment you arrive and find the front door is not left open for just anyone off the street. A bell discreetly announces your arrival and you are quickly brought inside where one of the gracious staff will welcome and assist you to your room. Not only the warmth of the all the personnel, but also the splendid furnishings, makes the hotel very appealing. The stunning library, with its antique paneled walls, glorious parquet floor, cozy fireplace, crystal chandeliers, and handsomely upholstered furniture, looks like a room in a country manor. There is also a delightful breakfast room decorated in creamy tones of white. Within the hotel is an outstanding restaurant, Wolters, owned by the talented Rainer Wolter, one of Europe's most famous chefs, at the helm. Another plus is a splendid indoor swimming pool with walls highlighted by romantic murals. *Directions:* On the Kurfürstendamm, a block west of Adenaur Platz.

LOUISA'S PLACE   *New*
Director: Sabine Deeken
Owner: Sven Schimank
Kurfürstendamm 160, 10709 Berlin, Germany
Tel: (03063) 103500, Fax: (03063) 103100
47 Rooms, Double: €130–€490*
*Breakfast not included: €18
Open: all year, Credit cards: all major
Region: Berlin, Michelin Map: 542
www.karenbrown.com/louisasplace.html

If you are looking for a moderately priced hotel in the heart of Berlin, the Hotel Residenz is a great value. Its location—on a quiet, tree-lined street just off the Kurfürstendamm—just couldn't be better at any price. The five-story building, built around 1900 as a private residence, is immediately appealing. It has a nostalgic, old-fashioned look, with ornate plaster designs on its cream-colored façade, tall windows, romantic balconies edged by flowerboxes, and a huge tree shading the entrance. You step inside to a fancy hallway with a black-and-white marble floor, mirrored walls, and a vaulted ceiling accented by pastel-colored flowers in a stucco design. At the end of the hall you turn into the lobby of the hotel where you are warmly greeted at an attractive reception counter that looks as if it was made out of a handsome, carved-wood, fine antique table. Doors from the reception lead to the cozy bar and dining room. Although the hotel offers some suites with kitchenettes, the regular guestrooms are extremely spacious and nicely furnished with a traditional flair, with dark wooden furniture, attractive, pastel-colored fabrics, and pretty lace curtains. Many of the rooms face onto the courtyard, assuring privacy. I especially liked room 317, a spacious room with a bay window. *Directions:* From the Berlin Ring Road exit at Kurfürstendamm. Meinekestrasse is off Kurfürstendamm just down from the Kaiser-Wilhelm Gedächtniskirche.

HOTEL RESIDENZ
Manager: Ralph Alsdorf
Meinekestrasse 9, 10719 Berlin, Germany
Tel: (030) 884430, Fax: (030) 8824726
81 Rooms, Double: €122–€295*
*Breakfast not included: €13
Open: all year, Credit cards: all major
Region: Berlin, Michelin Map: 542
www.karenbrown.com/residenz.html

The attractive Gasthaus Burkard is located on a cobbled street that climbs above the river at the heart of Bernkastel. This charming, three-story building painted in shades of salmon, with contrasting white trim and pretty pink hanging geraniums at each window, caught my eye, and the smell of apfelkuchen wafting from the front door definitely tempted my hungry stomach. The restaurant has been in the family for over a hundred years, but it is only the recent generation who has converted rooms upstairs to accommodate overnight guests. For dining, tables are set both on the cobbled courtyard in front of the inn, and also just inside the front door in a small, cozy dining room. Guestrooms are reached through the restaurant and up a simple back staircase. The first floor is the family quarters and the six bedrooms for paying guests are all off the second-floor corridor. The rooms are very simple in their decor, with plain pine bedframes and crisply folded down comforters. Lighting is good, with lamps at each side of the bed, as well as one overhead. The bathrooms are also simple—small but modern. The price of a room is very reasonable and includes breakfast. After a stay of three nights you can also opt for the half-pension rate. This is a family operation—they are ever-present and featured proudly in the hotel brochure. *Directions:* Bernkastel-Kues is located between Koblenz and Trier. The hotel is at the heart of the old town.

GASTHAUS BURKARD
Owner: Burkard Family
Burgstrasse, 54470 Bernkastel-Kues, Germany
Tel: (06531) 2380, Fax: (06531) 1758
6 Rooms, Double: €50–€70
Restaurant closed Wed
Open: Jan 10 to Dec 18, Credit cards: none
Region: Mosel, Michelin Map: 543
www.karenbrown.com/burkard.html

The façade of this charming, two-story hotel is easy to spot on a narrow cobbled street at the heart of the village. It has soft-pink washed walls, windows and doors in a dark, wide band of orange and green lanterns, and a dark roof with a row of small dormer windows. You enter into the hotel either through its cozy, intimate weinstube restaurant or its lovely interior-courtyard garden restaurant. The 32 guestrooms are found up a stairway accessed off the back courtyard. Rooms, quiet and comfortable but simply appointed, are described as having either old or new decor—"old" is a dark Danish modern with darker prints for the spreads and drapes, while "new" consists of light reproduction pine furniture with white down comforters topping the beds. We were able to see the largest (number 14) of the three new light-pine rooms—a two-room suite with a living room and separate bedroom; number 30, an older room with a double bed and a sitting area; and number 31, a room with the old decor whose twin beds stretch the length of the room and are curtained off by individual drapes. Hallway carpets and curtains are in a castle red and doors are a handsome green. The restaurant, charming in its rustic decor, is quite popular and can accommodate many daytime travelers. The cozy cellar bar is a popular place for dancing as live music is offered on weekends. *Directions:* Bernkastel-Kues is located between Koblenz and Trier. The hotel is at the heart of the old town.

HOTEL-RESTAURANT DOCTOR WEINSTUBE
Owner: Nau Family
Hebegasse 5, 54470 Bernkastel-Kues, Germany
Tel: (06531) 96650, Fax: (06531) 6296
32 Rooms, Double: €71–€129
Open: all year, Credit cards: all major
Region: Mosel, Michelin Map: 543
www.karenbrown.com/doctorweinstube.html

Bernkastel is actually one of twin towns (the other is Kues) on either side of the River Mosel. This picture-book wine village is famous for its oh-so-pretty half-timbered houses and cute wine cellars on the streets that surround the town hall. The Hotel Zur Post, a popular roadside hotel, is very professionally run by owners Jochen and Elke Rössling. True hôteliers, the Rösslings do a superb job and are always striving to improve their property. Located on the main road through town, slightly away from the center of town and just steps from the banks of the Mosel, the Zur Post has a mustard-colored façade complemented by dark-green shutters and windowboxes of red geraniums. The oldest part of the Zur Post dates from 1827 but in more recent decades wings of rooms have been added in a similar, old-world style. The bedrooms are all very alike in decor, having modern fitted furniture complete with TV, phone, and mini-bar. All are large enough to have sitting areas and everything is meticulously maintained. Offering food to roadside travelers for more than a century and a half, the Post has three restaurants, one of which is quite delightful with walls and ceilings entirely of carved pine complemented by dried-flower arrangements and bright tablecloths. *Directions:* Located approximately 75 km southwest of Koblenz and 48 km northeast of Trier at the junction of the 53 and 50.

HOTEL ZUR POST
Owners: Jochen & Elke Rössling
Gestade 17, 54470 Bernkastel-Kues, Germany
Tel: (06531) 96700, Fax: (06531) 967050
43 Rooms, Double: €92–€139
Closed: Jan, Credit cards: MC, VS
Region: Mosel, Michelin Map: 543
www.karenbrown.com/hotelzurpost.html

The little town of Braubach lies on the Rhine almost opposite Koblenz. In among a mixture of modern and old houses you find the Zum Weissen Schwanen leaning against the old city wall where the large tower extends into the street. Step behind the half-timbered façade and you enter a gem of an unpretentious, rustic tavern with warm pine paneling, bottle-glass dimpled windows hung with hand-crocheted curtains, and simple pine tables and carved chairs. Your genial hosts, Erich and Gerhild Kunz, will probably be there to welcome you. Although their English is limited, warm smiles and exuberant gestures overcome any language barrier. Several lovely bedrooms are found in the inn itself, all with spotless modern shower rooms and country antique furniture. Additional rooms with fitted furniture are found in the stable block behind the inn, while more delightful rooms with rustic handicrafts surrounding old pine beds topped with plump pillows and comforters lie in a nearby watermill. Room 12, Mägdestube, is an especially appealing bedroom with lovely Craftsman-style furniture. Many of the bedrooms contain two single beds with footboards that make them cramped for tall people. The Kunz family has a restaurant in the mill where a huge wooden waterwheel turns slowly at the building's center. *Directions:* 13 km southeast of Koblenz. Traveling south on A3, exit for Montabaur, from the north exit for Koblenz and travel roads 49 and 42 to Braubach.

HOTEL ZUM WEISSEN SCHWANEN
Owner: Family Kunz
Brunnenstrasse 4, 56338 Braubach, Germany
Tel: (02627) 9820, Fax: (02627) 8802
20 Rooms, Double: €85–€105
Restaurant closed Wed
Open: all year, Credit cards: all major
Region: Rheinland-Pfalz, Michelin Map: 543
www.karenbrown.com/schwanen.html

The Romantik Hotel Zur Tanne, a charming, dark-wood building graced by geranium-filled windowboxes, is on the main street of Braunlage, marked only by a discreet sign. The staff's warm welcome, excellent English, and concern for their guests' comfort add to an enjoyable stay. From a tiny entrance the hotel opens up to reveal a lovely dining room. This is the center of activity, for the hotel has gained a well-deserved reputation for excellent meals and impeccable service. Up the winding front staircase you find a few country-cozy bedrooms. A wing of modern rooms, decorated in shades of green, stretches out from the rear of the old inn, while a newer wing houses eight double rooms and three suites as well as a fitness center and small conference facility. The hotel's most rustic room is its cheery bar where guests gather for after-dinner drinks. Braunlage is in the heart of the Harz Mountains. In summer delightful trails in the forests beckon, while winter offers the opportunity for cross-country skiing. The Harz region presents for exploration an appealing ring of quaint medieval towns such as Goslar, Wernigerode, and Quedlinburg. Last, but not least, don't miss the nostalgic steam-engine train ride through the mountains. *Directions:* Braunlage is located approximately 44 km southeast of Hannover. From Braunschweig take the A35 south to Bad Harzburg where it becomes the A4. Continue another 23 km to the Braunlage exit.

ROMANTIK HOTEL ZUR TANNE
Owner: Susanne Herbst
Herzog-Wilhelm Strasse 8
38700 Braunlage, Germany
Tel: (05520) 93120, Fax: (05520) 9312444
22 Rooms, Double: €80–€199
Open: all year, Credit cards: all major
Region: Niedersachsen, Michelin Maps: 542, 544
www.karenbrown.com/zurtanne.html

If you are traveling on a budget and want to include the fascinating Spreewald in your itinerary, the simple Gasthaus Kolonieschänke makes an excellent choice. It would help if you speak a little German, since no English is spoken at this small, remote inn; but it is not vital because the employees are very gracious and eager to please. The hotel is a cute, red-brick, two-story building accented by a charming wooden porch stretching across the front. Inside you find a cozy bar and several small, casual dining rooms. The attractive, spacious bedrooms upstairs have a nostalgic ambiance with quaint, old-fashioned wallpaper and light wooden furniture. Although these guestrooms are very nice, I especially liked those in the new annex, a pretty two-story, brick building constructed in the same style as the main house. My favorites were the bedrooms on the ground level, which seem more spacious than those on the upper floor. All of the bedrooms are meticulously kept, spotlessly clean, and very attractive, with blond-wood furniture, pretty curtains, and bedspreads. In the courtyard sits a pond surrounded by a wood-and-brick terrace where tables are set for eating in warm weather. *Directions:* Burg is midway between Berlin and Dresden. From Berlin, take the A13 south and at the junction south of Lübbenau take the A15. Travel 12 km, take exit 3, and drive 9 km north to Burg. Burg Kolonies is a tiny hamlet west of Burg.

GASTHAUS KOLONIESCHÄNKE
Owner: Olaf Schòpe
Ringechaussee 136, Spreewald
03096 Burg, Germany
Tel: (035603) 6850, Fax: (035603) 68544
16 Rooms, Double: €75
Open: all year, Credit cards: none
Region: Brandenburg, Michelin Map: 543
www.karenbrown.com/kolonieschanke.html

The Hotel Zur Bleiche is located in the flat countryside just a few minutes' drive from Burg, one of the departure points for boats exploring the Spreewald. However, you don't even need to go to Burg because the Zur Bleiche is right on one of the tiny canals and has its own selection of boats for hire. The hotel, a rambling, three-story white stucco-and-wood building with a steep roof punctuated with gables, sits in the center of a level meadow. There are several buildings dotting the property, the largest housing the guestrooms, which are spacious, extremely comfortable, and very attractively decorated—many with four-poster beds and pretty fabric as wallpaper. The restaurant is in a separate building across the lawn from the hotel. A hallway connects a selection of attractive dining rooms, which become more rustic in mood as you progress down the corridor. The first is elegantly sophisticated with a color scheme of rich blue and gold. The final choice, the Fischerstube, absolutely oozes cozy, romantic charm. It is built within an old house with thick, square-cut log walls, and inside has a low wooden ceiling supported by hand-hewn beams, hanging bouquets of dried flowers, rustic carved wooden chairs, and an enormous open fireplace. *Directions:* Burg is located midway between Berlin and Dresden. From Berlin, take the A13 south and at the junction just south of Lübbenau take the A15. Travel 12 km, take exit 3, and drive 9 km north to Burg.

HOTEL ZUR BLEICHE RESORT & SPA
Owner: Clausing Family
Bleichestrasse 16, Spreewald
03096 Burg, Germany
Tel: (035603) 620, Fax: (035603) 60292
90 Rooms, Double: €240–€340*
*Includes breakfast & dinner
Open: all year, Credit cards: none
Region: Brandenburg, Michelin Map: 542
www.karenbrown.com/bleiche.html

If your taste is for more formal, sophisticated decor, the hotel for you in Celle should be the Fürstenhof Celle. Whereas most of the buildings in Celle are quaint timbered houses, the Fürstenhof is a stately mix of modern and old: a 17th-century, peach-colored palace reflecting the influence of its famous Italian architect, Stechinelli. For many years the estate belonged to one of Europe's well-known aristocratic families, the Hardenbergs, and in 1970 Count Christian-Ludwig von Hardenberg took over the property and converted it into a luxury hotel. Two timbered buildings stretch out in front of the two-story palace forming a courtyard where tables are set in the shade of 300-year-old chestnut trees. Inside, the hotel is ornately glamorous—especially the grand salon where Grecian columns support a mirror-paneled ceiling and comfortable leather chairs form intimate groups for afternoon tea. From the salon, a dramatic staircase leads up to the only four bedrooms located in the original building. Be sure to ask for one of these spacious, antique-filled rooms (all of the others are located in a modern, hotel-like wing). There are three places to dine: an elegant, gourmet restaurant, a charming Italian restaurant, as well as a Bistro with local delicacies. *Directions:* Celle is located approximately 45 km northeast of Hannover along the N3, which becomes Hannoversche Strasse once in the city of Celle. The hotel is on the left just before the castle.

FÜRSTENHOF CELLE
Owner: Count von Hardenberg
Hannoversche Strasse 55
29221 Celle, Germany
Tel: (05141) 2010, Fax: (05141) 201120
63 Rooms, Double: €150–€285
Open: all year, Credit cards: all major
Relais & Chateaux
Region: Niedersachsen, Michelin Map: 541
www.karenbrown.com/furstenhofcelle.html

Just a ten-minute walk from the cathedral or main train station and a block from the river promenade, the Hotel Buchholz offers a quiet haven away from the crowds and bustle of downtown Köln. The hotel is easy to spot, as the surrounding buildings are unadorned, so the soft-peach façade with its white awnings definitely stands out. The entry is simple but the welcome is warm and very genuine in this family-run hotel. Just off the reception there are a few ground-level rooms, still priced for those on a budget, that share a toilet and shower. Number 15 on the first level does have its own shower, private toilet, and lovely twin beds. Down the hallway you find a bar and a pretty breakfast room with country light-pine tables and a hutch set against soft-yellow-washed walls where a very scrumptious breakfast buffet is served. When the weather permits, a few breakfast tables are set in the interior courtyard. The upstairs rooms are all attractive—simple and pretty in their uncluttered decor, with fans provided in the heat of the summer. Room 19 is beautiful, with a large king bed, shower, sitting area within the room, and a wonderful outside balcony. Junior suites and large bedrooms are priced the same, but I preferred the spaciousness of the latter. *Directions:* When the main road that follows the Rhine takes on the name of Konrad Adenaeuer, turn left on Machabäer Strasse and then immediately right on Kunibertsgasse.

BUCHHOLZ DOWNTOWN HOTEL
Owners: Sascha & Carole Ann Buchholz
Kunibertsgasse 5, 50668 Cologne, Germany
Tel: (0221) 160830, Fax: (0221) 1608341
18 Rooms, Double: €89–€189
Light snacks available
Closed: Christmas, Credit cards: all major
Region: Nordrhein-Westfalen, Michelin Map: 543
www.karenbrown.com/hotelbuchholz.html

The Hotel Lyskirchen is an excellent choice for a moderately priced hotel in Cologne. The hotel occupies a side street just off the River Rhine in the historical part of the city. From the pier, only a short distance from the hotel, steamers depart for the popular Rhine day trip from Cologne to Mainz. A ten-minute stroll through the old town brings you to the cathedral, just far enough away from the hotel that you can hear the distant echo of its bells. The Hotel Lyskirchen is more modern in style than we usually prefer, but the location can't be beat. The hotel has a clean, comfortable lobby and displays of modern art lead you to the stark, modern breakfast room where you partake of a sumptuous, buffet-style breakfast. There is no restaurant at the hotel. A large, indoor swimming pool, sauna, tanning beds, and underground parking are added bonuses. Cologne hosts conventions during January, February, March, April, September, and October. If you plan to visit during these times, book well in advance. *Directions:* Exit the A555 at Köln (Cologne) Süd on B51. After passing the second bridge (Severinsbrücke), turn left on Filzengraben.

HOTEL LYSKIRCHEN
Manager: Michael Schirgewohn
Filzengraben 26-32, 50676 Cologne, Germany
Tel: (0221) 20970, Fax: (0221) 2097718
103 Rooms, Double: €112–€240
Closed: Christmas, Credit cards: all major
Region: Nordrhein-Westfalen, Michelin Map: 543
www.karenbrown.com/lyskirchen.html

Deidesheim is a particularly nice village on Die Deutsche Weinstrasse, the German Wine Road. Occupying a corner of the village square, the Hotel Deidesheimer Hof has a formal appearance, for this was once a bishop's residence but is now a sophisticated Relais & Châteaux hotel. Sampling wines is an obligatory pastime, and there is no more pleasant a spot for the task than the flower-filled terrace that spills onto the village square. Beyond the lobby, you find two delightful, country-style restaurants offering German cuisine. The kitchen is supervised by Stefan Neugebauer who has received a Michelin star for the gourmet food he serves in his cavernous, more formal, cellar restaurant. Upstairs you find the sunny breakfast room with its bright, royal-blue chairs set against white walls accented with yellow-and-blue draperies. The bedrooms are furnished in a very sophisticated modern decor as befits a Relais & Châteaux hotel. Deidesheim's wine festival takes place during the second and third week of August. *Directions:* Located 31 km southwest of Mannheim. From Mannheim take the A6 west for approximately 20 km to exit 19 and then travel another 20 km south to Deidesheim.

HOTEL DEIDESHEIMER HOF
Owner: Anita Hahn
67146 Deidesheim, Germany
Tel: (06326) 96870, Fax: (06326) 7685
28 Rooms, Double: €125–€275*
*Breakfast not included: €14
Closed: first week of Jan, Credit cards: all major
Relais & Chateaux
Region: Rheinland-Pfalz, Michelin Map: 543
www.karenbrown.com/deidesheimer.html

In our estimation, the Hotel Bülow Residenz, a small luxury hotel, is the finest in Dresden. Found on a quiet side street of old houses, the hotel is in the Neustadt just across the river from the heart of town. This baroque building with its façade dating back to 1730 has been restored, keeping the elegant exterior and adding a traditional-modern interior. At the heart of the hotel is a vine-covered courtyard set with tables and chairs for enjoying breakfast or afternoon coffee outdoors. While we enjoyed casual fare in the Italian restaurant across the street, the hotel has a formal restaurant serving more elegant food in hushed surroundings. The barrel-vaulted wine cellars are now a cozy piano bar. Found on four floors, the spacious bedrooms are each accompanied by a luxurious bath- or shower-room. A two-minute walk brings you to the golden statue of August the Strong sitting atop his horse gazing across the Augustusbrücke, which spans the Elbe to the historic heart of Dresden. Here you find the Zwinger (museums), a monumental palace that August the Strong used as a background for sumptuous festivals and housing his vast art collection. *Directions:* To find the hotel locate the Albertplatz in the Neustadt (a circular traffic island with roads spoking out) and take Königstrasse, then turn left on Obergraben to Rähnitzgasse. The hotel is located across the river from the city center.

HOTEL BÜLOW RESIDENZ
Owner: Horst Bülow
Rähnitzgasse 19, 01097 Dresden, Germany
Tel: (0351) 80030, Fax: (0351) 8003100
30 Rooms, Double: €110–€240*
*Breakfast not included: €19
Open: all year, Credit cards: all major
Relais & Chateaux
Region: Sachsen, Michelin Map: 544
www.karenbrown.com/bulowresidenz.html

The Martha Hospiz, dating back to 1899, is the oldest hotel in Dresden. It has a good location—an easy, 15-minute walk to the Augustusbrücke (the bridge to the historic city center) and only a few minutes from the Bahnhof Neustadt, one of the city's two major rail stations. When we first came to Dresden immediately after the Berlin Wall came down, this neighborhood called Neustadt looked hopelessly dilapidated. Now it's undergoing a magical transformation—block by block the houses are being repainted, buildings renovated, and stylish new cafés opening. The Martha Hospiz makes a very good choice if you are looking for a friendly, well managed, and reasonably priced place to stay within walking distance of the heart of the city. The interior is exceptionally nice. Stretching along a hallway next to the reception area is a glass-enclosed sunroom, which overlooks a small rear garden. Adjacent to this is a pretty breakfast room that exudes a pleasing, traditional look with Biedermeier-style decor. The meticulously maintained bedrooms also show the popular Biedermeier ambiance. The hotel has a cozy restaurant in the basement featuring potato-based recipes. *Directions:* Take the ring road around the heart of Dresden and on the north side Nieritzstrasse is located between the Königstrasse and Theresienstrasse, two roads that spoke off Albertplatz. The hotel is across the river from the city center.

HOTEL MARTHA HOSPIZ
Manager: Winfrid Tilp
Nieritzstrasse 11, 01097 Dresden, Germany
Tel: (0351) 81760, Fax: (0351) 8176222
50 Rooms, Double: €103–€118
Closed: Dec 22 to 27, Credit cards: all major
Region: Sachsen, Michelin Map: 544
www.karenbrown.com/marthahospiz.html

We first stayed at the Hotel auf der Wartburg, located in what was formerly East Germany, in 1990 (only a few days after the reunification of Germany). On our second visit a few years later, we were astounded at the miraculous changes. Bathless guestrooms with outdated, dreary decor had emerged like butterflies from their cocoons into some of the best-looking rooms in all of Germany. Each of the bedrooms is individual in decor, yet all have the same refined, English-country-manor look with beautiful fabrics used in the color-coordinated draperies and upholstered chairs. One of my favorites, number 104 (a deluxe corner room decorated in rich greens and yellows) looks out to the forest. Less expensive room 102 (overlooking the front courtyard) is also a charmer in tones of reds and golds. Some of the most romantic rooms are tucked up under the eaves with tiny garret windows capturing miniature views of the wooded hills. Just steps from the hotel is the museum section of Wartburg Castle, one of Germany's real gems. *Directions:* Leave the A4 at Eisenach-Ost and follow signs to Wartburg Castle. As you near the castle, take the small signposted lane that winds uphill through the forest to the castle. There is a parking area at the top with a barricade. Continue about 500 meters past the parking to the courtyard in front of the hotel.

HOTEL AUF DER WARTBURG
Manager: Hans-Lorenz Beck
99817 Eisenach, Germany
Tel: (03691) 797223, Fax: (03691) 797200
35 Rooms, Double: €240–€320
Open: all year, Credit cards: all major
Region: Thüringen, Michelin Map: 543
www.karenbrown.com/wartburg.html

Although we made what we thought was a real discovery, we were humbled to learn that all of Europe already seems familiar with Schloss Elmau and its cultural and artistic programs! Just down the lane from the castle sits a cozy farmhouse, the Alpengut Elmau, with the soothing sounds of a rippling stream in the background. Bikers and hikers in summer and cross-country skiers in winter find this a wonderful resting spot offering fine food and drink. For those lucky enough to spend the night here, the inn has simple, clean, and comfortable guestrooms furnished with light-pine dressers, closets, and beds. Rooms are not overly large or luxurious, but I especially liked number 7, a twin back corner room, and number 24, another twin with a private balcony. Both overlook the back garden and a pasture with a darling stable for the horses. Guests at the inn are invited to take part in any event at Schloss Elmau and use its facilites—but it also has its own claim to fame: King Ludwig would stay here to break his journey to one of his lesser-known hunting lodges, the Schachen Schloss. Today the lodge can be reached only by a hike of 3½ hours each way. Although this weathered chalet is surprisingly nondescript on the outside, the extreme interior decor definitely reflects the mad king's eccentricity! *Directions:* From Garmisch Partenkirchen take Route 2 towards Innsbruck. Exit 12 km later at Klais and travel to Elmau (€3 fee to enter park).

ALPENGUT ELMAU
Innkeepers: Barbara & John Brooke
82493 Elmau, Germany
Tel: (08823) 9180, Fax: (08823) 3437
25 Rooms, Double: €120–€180*
*Includes breakfast & dinner
Closed: beg Nov to Dec 20, Credit cards: MC, VS
Region: Bayern, Michelin Map: 546
www.karenbrown.com/elmau.html

As dramatic as the Klosterkirche is, you still cannot help noticing the charming little inn tucked just around the corner, the Hotel Zur Post, with its gabled roof and arched entry centered under balconies heavily laden with overflowing geraniums. Stenciling so typical of the region dresses the exterior and pine shutters look handsome against white stucco. We saw bedrooms both up the circular staircase in the main house and in the annex at the back. The rooms are all similar in their comfortable style and appointments, with pine beds topped by white duvets, pine armoires, and comfortable seating arrangements. Rooms at the back, looking out to the fields, are especially quiet. The cozy, pine-paneled dining room has pine chairs and tables set in front of benches built against the walls. The chef, Andreas Fischer, is justifiably proud of the fact that he is the chef for Germany's Olympic ski team—look for the adorable bread ornament of the chef with his skis that hangs on the dining-room wall. Luckily, we are not a team in training, so we were able to sample some of his delicious dishes. Those who overindulge can make use of the fitness room, sauna, and steam bath in the basement of the inn where there is also underground parking (for a nominal charge). *Directions:* Located about halfway between Oberammergau to the north and Garmisch to the south. As you travel east through Ettal, the hotel is on the south side of the main road, past the monastery.

HOTEL ZUR POST
Owner: Fischer Family
Kaiser-Ludwig Platz 18
82488 Ettal, Germany
Tel & Fax: (08822) 6971
21 Rooms, Double: €64–€96
Open: all year, Credit cards: all major
Region: Bayern, Michelin Map: 546
www.karenbrown.com/zurpost.html

Four generations of the Lorentz family have perfected a tradition of welcome and quality that is ever-present in their attractive hotel located on the Romantik Road, 23 kilometers south of Rothenburg. Referenced in local records as early as 1369, the Greifen Post now offers very modern comforts and facilities. The inn has a number of cozy rooms that serve as restaurants. The main restaurant is very elegant, with heavy beams and hand-painted scenes staging an attractive atmosphere. Downstairs is a more casual bar overlooking the indoor swimming pool through stone arched windows. Here tapestry-covered, high-back chairs are set around a large open fireplace used to grill steaks and cutlets. Upstairs you find a sunny breakfast room decorated in shades of yellow where a generous buffet breakfast is artfully displayed. The Greifen Post's bedrooms can be grouped by decor: Romantik (in the flamboyant French style of Louis XV), Biedermeier (with Biedermeier antiques), Himmelbett (with charming four-poster beds), and Laura Ashley (with English-style fabrics). I could not decide what style of room I liked best—all are beautiful. The entire hotel shows the touch of owners who strive to have every detail of their inn perfect. Bicycles are available for exploring the nearby countryside. *Directions:* From Rothenburg travel the A7 23 km south to exit 111 and drive 4 km east to Feuchtwangen. The hotel is at the heart of the old town.

ROMANTIK HOTEL GREIFEN POST
Owner: Eduard Lorentz
Manager: Birgt Becker-Plaha
Marktplatz 8, 91555 Feuchtwangen, Germany
Tel: (09852) 6800, Fax: (09852) 68068
35 Rooms, Double: €100–€150
Closed: Jan 4 to Jan 9, Credit cards: all major
Region: Bayern, Michelin Map: 545
www.karenbrown.com/greifen.html

We thought that our kind of little hotel could not exist in the heart of Frankfurt where most of the buildings are new and without charm but, happily, we were proved wrong. The Hotel Westend is splendidly located in a very nice neighborhood, only three blocks from the train station and within easy walking distance of shopping and sightseeing. Your heart will be won at first glance of the Hotel Westend—a pretty, pastel-pink house, reminiscent of a small villa. There is a small front lawn and steps leading up the side of the house to a long, marble-floored entry accented by Persian carpets. Three intimate little parlors are at guests' disposal, each prettily decorated with antique furniture, bouquets of fresh flowers, Oriental carpets, crystal chandeliers, handsome mirrors, and oil paintings. The overall effect is one of quiet elegance, somewhat formal, yet welcoming and homelike. Guestrooms are located upstairs and all have an old-world ambiance created by pretty, pastel color schemes, white curtains at the windows, and liberal use of authentic antiques. All double rooms have private bathrooms. An added bonus is a secluded back garden where breakfast is served during the summer. Hotel Westend is truly an oasis in the busy city of Frankfurt, but you need to book far in advance for this very special hotel. *Directions:* Just a few blocks from the railway station—take Karl Strasse to Mainzerland Strasse to Erlenstrasse and Westend Strasse.

HOTEL WESTEND
Owner: Carl-Ludwig Mayer
Westend Strasse 15
60325 Frankfurt, Germany
Tel: (069) 78988180, Fax: (069) 745396
20 Rooms, Double: €120–€240
Open: all year, Credit cards: all major
Region: Hessen, Michelin Map: 543
www.karenbrown.com/hotelwestend.html

The location of the Landgasthof Karner is very good—in a small village about midway between Munich and Salzburg and just a few minutes from the A8 autobahn, which links the two cities. However, this charming small hotel has far more to commend it than just a convenient site. Originally a 17th-century farmhouse, the building is white with pretty blue shutters. On each side of the front door there is a large painting—on one side a lady, on the other a man, both dressed in Bavarian costume. Upon entering, your first impression is one of genuine, old-fashioned hospitality and informality—nothing seems contrived or stiffly decorator-perfect. Instead, the decor is very homelike, with country-style antiques and knickknacks abounding. There is a series of restaurants, all as cozy as can be, with a rustic Alpine flavor and pretty waitresses in Bavarian dirndls. When the weather is warm, guests enjoy eating outside in the garden. The bedrooms each have their own personality, but all are large and extremely attractive, with light-pine furniture and very pretty floral fabrics. Room 103 is an especially lovely large front corner room, and 112 a spacious back corner room enjoys the quiet of the garden. *Directions:* Frasdorf is 78 km southeast of Munich, 64 km west of Salzburg. Arriving in Frasdorf, go straight through town. When you see fields in front of you, turn left on Westerdorfer. The hotel is on your left.

LANDGASTHOF KARNER
Owner: Christel Karner
Nussbaumstrasse 6, 83112 Frasdorf, Germany
Tel: (08052) 4071, Fax: (08052) 4711
26 Rooms, Double: €95–€165
Open: all year, Credit cards: all major
Region: Bayern, Michelin Map: 546
www.karenbrown.com/landgasthofkarner.html

The Schwarzer Adler, located in the cute village of Frauenaurach, exudes country charm even though it is located near the large cities of Nürnberg and Erlangen. The hotel's façade is prettily laced with intricate timbering and has green-shuttered windows above windowboxes enhanced in summer by bright-red geraniums. Inside, the inn is outstandingly decorated in a cozy style perfectly suited to its picturesque façade. A charming restaurant is on the ground floor. An antique wooden spiral staircase winds up from the lobby to the guestrooms. Two especially romantic choices (31 and 32) are on the top floor, tucked into cozy dormers. All of the accommodations are very appealing, decorated with tasteful, light-pine furniture, fluffy down comforters with crisp, white coverings, and white crocheted curtains at the windows. There is an annex just behind the main house, separated by a pretty garden. The guestrooms here are simpler and less expensive. Christiane Müller-Kinzel has renovated this historical Franconian framework house with such loving care and passionate attention to detail that the Schwarzer Adler has won several awards. *Directions:* Erlangen is located 15 km north of Nürnberg. From the A3, take the Frauenaurach exit and turn right under the A3 on Herzog-Frauenaurach. Go left on Herzogenauracher Strasse, go under the freeway, right on Brückerstrasse when the road splits, then right on Wallenrodstrasse to the square and hotel.

HOTEL SCHWARZER ADLER
Owner: Christiane Müller-Kinzel
Herdegenplatz 1, Erlangen
91056 Frauenaurach, Germany
Tel: (09131) 992051, Fax: (09131) 993195
14 Rooms, Double: €95–€105
Restaurant closed Sat & Sun
Closed: Mid-Aug to mid-Sep, Credit cards: all major
Region: Bayern, Michelin Map: 546
www.karenbrown.com/hotelschwarzeradler.html

How fortunate that driving rain drove us into Oberkirchs Weinstuben for a fortifying drink, for we discovered that it is also a darling inn. Oberkirchs Weinstuben is actually located in two buildings: the principal building sits on Munsterplatz in the shadow of Freiburg's impressive cathedral, the other just a short cobblestoned block away. The Weinstuben serves a very satisfying lunch or dinner in a congenial, cozy atmosphere. Beamed ceilings, wooden tables, white linen, and contented chatter set the mood for the charming restaurant. It is a popular place to dine in the marvelous medieval town of Freiburg and understandably so. In addition to the restaurant, there are 26 guestrooms, found either directly above the weinstube or in the neighboring building. All have been refurbished and are very attractive. The nine rooms above the weinstube are slightly more expensive. My favorite rooms are those with the romantic view out over the square to the cathedral. Freiburg is one of the most attractive walled cities in the Black Forest region of Germany, and the Oberkirchs Weinstuben makes an excellent choice for overnight accommodation. *Directions:* Freiburg is close to the French border, 60 km north of Basel. Follow signs to "Schwabentor" and drive into the pedestrian zone to the hotel. It is somewhat difficult to maneuver by auto through the pedestrian district, but the hotel provides a map and directions for parking.

OBERKIRCHS WEINSTUBEN
Owner: Doris Hunn
Munsterplatz 22, 79098 Freiburg, Germany
Tel: (0761) 2026868, Fax: (0761) 2026869
26 Rooms, Double: €138–€163
Restaurant closed Sun and Jan
Open: all year, Credit cards: all major
Region: Baden-Württemberg, Michelin Map: 545
www.karenbrown.com/oberkirchsweinstuben.html

Wald & Schlosshotel sits in manicured, parklike grounds at the edge of the village. A complex of very different buildings comprises the hotel: the 1712 hunting castle, the adjacent timbered Torhaus, a modern complex, and the beauty complex where guests can enjoy massages and skin treatments. The modern core of the hotel houses the reception area (where service is somewhat impersonal and aloof), a wing of modern bedrooms renovated in 1996, indoor and outdoor swimming pools, and the restaurants. One of the main reasons guests come here is to dine, for manager and chef Lothar Eiermann holds one Michelin star for the gourmet cuisine served in the elegant restaurant. Gourmet cuisine or more ordinary fare can be enjoyed in the informal Jagerstube where country tables and chairs are set around an old stove beneath hunting trophies. Bedrooms in the hunting castle are elegantly traditional as are those in the Torhaus and garden house. The owner, Fürst Kraft-Hohenlohe-Oehringen, lives nearby in Neuenstein Castle and you can obtain details on when the castle and gardens are open to visitors from the reception desk. *Directions:* From the A6, take the Öhringen exit. Go through town and continue for 6 km, following signs for Friedrichsruhe. Friedrichsruhe is so small it does not appear on most maps.

WALD & SCHLOSSHOTEL
Manager: Lothar Eiermann
74639 Friedrichsruhe, Germany
Tel: (07941) 60870, Fax: (07941) 61468
43 Rooms, Double: €173–€256
Open: all year, Credit cards: all major
Relais & Chateaux
Region: Baden-Württemberg, Michelin Map: 545
www.karenbrown.com/schlosshotel.html

The popular villages of Garmisch and Partenkirchen, nestling up against dramatic, towering Alpine peaks, offer a wide choice of places to stay. We were thrilled to find the truly exceptional Hotel Zugspitze, a lovely, first-class hotel "with heart" looking up to Germany's highest peak. It has a definite Tyrolean feel, from the balconies laden with overflowing geraniums to the beautiful pines and soft colors used to decorate the interior. Off the entry, a lovely salon with intimate sitting areas and a crackling fire looks out to a garden where tables are set in warm weather and tucked just off the salon is a very inviting library bar. The breakfast room is light and airy in soft colors of yellow and green, and the cozy restaurant offers excellent regional specialties. Amenities include a beautiful pool and three saunas. The guestrooms, many with balconies, are absolutely lovely with pine furniture, and fabrics and wallpaper friezes in soft colors. I loved our room, 103, looking up to the Zugspitze, which had its own balcony, a desk, and a seating area with sofa bed and chairs in front of a TV. All the suites and apartments are located on the third floor, under the eaves. Although all the rooms are charming, ask for one in the Stammhaus, where they are just a little more spacious. *Directions:* Located on a side street just up from the main road that separates Garmisch and Partenkirchen.

HOTEL ZUGSPITZE
Owners: Renate & Bernard Kauffmann
Klammstrasse 19
82467 Garmisch-Partenkirchen, Germany
Tel: (08821) 9010, Fax: (08821) 901333
48 Rooms, Double: €102–€160
Open: all year, Credit cards: all major
Region: Bayern, Michelin Map: 546
www.karenbrown.com/zugspitze.html

Without a doubt one of the prettiest walled towns in the region—Goslar oozes old-world charm. Time has been kind, and wandering along the narrow cobbled streets is like taking a walk into a history book. With a prime location overlooking the large pedestrian market square, the Kaiserworth was built in 1494 as the guild house of the cloth workers. The stunning façade, with carvings of emperors beneath the eaves, was completed in the 17th century. The Oberhuber family purchased the hotel several years ago and have meticulously restored and repainted the exterior to perfection. In summer the restaurant is bustling, as the Kaiserworth is a favorite spot to enjoy a good meal and watch all the activity in the square. You enter into an intimate reception area with wood paneling lightly accented with green, which is repeated in the green carpet. There is a small sitting area with Biedermeier-look furniture. We were not able to see any of the bedrooms on our latest visit because they were all occupied. Since the hotel is being redecorated, our suggestion would be to request one of the most recently renovated guestrooms. Step outside your hotel at six in the evening and watch the concert of the city clock, whose four different scenes represent the thousand-year-old mining history of the region. *Directions:* Goslar is located 90 km southeast of Hannover. Travel the A7 south, take exit 66, and then drive east to Goslar.

HOTEL KAISERWORTH
Owner: Karin Oberhuber
Markt 3, 38640 Goslar, Germany
Tel: (05321) 7090, Fax: (05321) 709345
66 Rooms, Double: €117–€171
Open: all year, Credit cards: all major
Region: Niedersachsen, Michelin Map: 541
www.karenbrown.com/hotelkaiserworth.html

It is always a real delight to discover a modern hotel that offers all the up-to-date comforts without sacrificing old-world ambiance. A fine example is the Hotel Alpenhof, with its romantic mood of Bavarian country charm. Soaring mountain peaks form the backdrop for this modern, chalet-style hotel with balconies front and back, accented by windowboxes filled with red geraniums. You enter into a cheerful reception area opening onto a cozy yet sophisticated bar. From the bar, steps lead down to the paneled dining room divided into several eating areas. My favorite is an intimate, wood-paneled room adorned with pewter trays, antique mugs, brass lamps, and an antique tiled oven. When the weather is warm, meals are also served outside in a pretty rear garden. This is a deluxe hotel with many amenities, including a modern wellness area with a magnificent indoor pool and arched windows looking out to the trees. The bedrooms continue the standard of excellence: the furnishings are new, but traditional in style and of superb quality. Splurge and request one of the more expensive back bedrooms with a balcony capturing the view of the majestic, soaring granite peaks of the Zugspitze. *Directions:* From Munich, turn right off the E533 (A9) just before Garmisch (signposted Reutte), and after several kilometers turn left for Grainau. Turn left down the main street and take the first left into Alpspitzstrasse. The hotel is at the end of the road.

HOTEL ALPENHOF
Owners: Manfred & Gerlinde Rosenstock
Alpspitzstrasse 34, 82491 Grainau, Germany
Tel: (08821) 9870, Fax: (08821) 98777
36 Rooms, Double: €108–€210
Open: all year, Credit cards: MC, VS
Region: Bayern, Michelin Map: 546
www.karenbrown.com/alpenhof.html

This dear, family-run hotel has guestrooms that enjoy unobstructed views of the mountains. From your bed in one of the mountain-view rooms you will have a perfect view of green meadows stretching up the hillside to the soaring, granite peaks of the Zugspitze. The 300-year-old Hotel Post is very simple—not for those expecting luxury or quaint accommodation. The guestrooms are basic, fresh, and clean and the beds made with crisp cotton sheets. The most dramatic view rooms are 1, 2, and 3, while rooms 18, 19, 20, and 21 have views plus the bonus of balconies. Full of history and charm, the breakfast rooms, with beamed ceilings, provincial-print tie-back curtains, attractive wooden chairs, tables set with linen cloths, and oil paintings and copper pots adorning fresh, whitewashed walls, are charming and one is set in what was the town's original post office. The exceptionally gracious Seufferth family has been running the Post since 1890 and now the fourth generation, the charming young Ander, who apprenticed at a hotel in Aspen, is delightfully in place. Ilse's natural talent for making guests feel very welcome has quite obviously been passed on to her son! The hotel also has ten simply furnished apartments that rent on a weekly basis. *Directions:* Driving from Munich, turn right off the E533 (A9) just before Garmisch (signposted Reutte) and turn left for Grainau. Go left down the main street—the hotel is past the church.

HOTEL POST
Owner: Hannes Seufferth Family
Postgasse 10, 82491 Grainau, Germany
Tel: (08821) 8853, Fax: (08821) 8873
20 Rooms, Double: €64–€85
Closed: Nov 1 to Dec 15, Credit cards: all major
Region: Bayern, Michelin Map: 546
www.karenbrown.com/hotelpost.html

Strategically located on the banks of the River Neisse that forms the natural border between Germany and Poland, Görlitz was once an extremely prosperous trading center with a population of 80,000. Its significance can be witnessed today in the number of historic monuments, colorful squares, and fine old buildings throughout this charming city. One, the Romantik Hotel Tuchmacher, is a splendid Renaissance manor house built for Franz Schneider, a wealthy businessman. It is located in the heart of the historic town, just a half block from beautiful St. Peter's Church (Peterskirche). The Vits family meticulously restored the derelict mansion, opening it in 1998 as a hotel offering the highest standard of modern day amenities without sacrificing its intrinsic old world appeal. On the ground floor is a pretty restaurant called the Schneider Stube, which serves excellent food. It is quite a romantic place to dine in with handsome paneled walls, a combination of coved ceiling and beamed ceiling, wrought-iron light fixtures, and antiques. Another place to eat or enjoy a glass of beer, is the courtyard in the center of the hotel. The guestrooms are attractively decorated and have excellent reading lights, good mattresses, and top-notch bathrooms. The hotel also has a wellness center with sauna and fitness room. *Directions:* From the A13 take exit 94 into Görlitz. Follow signs to the hotel (watch for the twin spires of Peterskirche—the hotel is half a block away).

ROMANTIK HOTEL TUCHMACHER   ***New***
Manager: Martin Vits
Peterstrasse 8, Görlitz, Germany
Tel: (03581) 47310, Fax: (03581) 473179
48 Rooms, Double: €120–€164
Closed: Christmas & New Year's Eve
Credit cards: all major
Region: Sachsen, Michelin Map: 544
www.karenbrown.com/tuchmacher.html

Halberstadt was almost flattened by Allied bombers in January 1945 but the medieval area around the elegant cathedral of St. Stephanus, built from the 13th to the 15th centuries, has been carefully restored. Sadly, the ambiance of this area does not extend to the rest of the city, which contains many ugly apartment buildings. The Parkhotel Unter Den Linden, a totally modern hotel set behind a restored exterior, stands out as a rose amongst thorns. We were shown to the fireplace room for pre-dinner drinks and while we admired the richness of the dark paneled walls inlaid with interesting landscape paintings of the once historic Halberstadt, we felt ill at ease as we balanced in our uncomfortable red chairs placed regimentally every meter round the edge of the sculptured carpet. Things improved greatly in the much more comfortable restaurant, which overlooks an attractive grassy courtyard at the center of the hotel. Many of the bedrooms enjoy this same delightful garden vista. Bedrooms in the main building are spacious, decorated in a modern vein with art-deco-style headboards and furniture, each accompanied by a red-and-white-tile shower room. More glamorous gray-marble shower rooms are found in the modern extension where the bedrooms are smaller and uniform in size. *Directions:* Take the A2 85 km east from Hannover. Take exit 63 east of Helmstedt and travel south 45 km on the N245 to Halberstadt. The hotel is well signposted.

PARKHOTEL UNTER DEN LINDEN
Manager: Frank Butzke
Klamrothstrasse 2
38820 Halberstadt, Germany
Tel: (03941) 62540, Fax: (03941) 6254444
45 Rooms, Double: €105–€120
Open: all year, Credit cards: all major
Region: Sachsen-Anhalt, Michelin Map: 541
www.karenbrown.com/linden.html

The Hotel Abtei is one of the finest small city hotels in Germany. Situated on a quiet, tree-lined street north of the center of Hamburg, the hotel seems far removed from the confusion of the city, yet is quickly accessible either by car, subway, or boat. Every detail of the Abtei, originally a gracious private home, is of the highest quality and taste: gorgeous fabrics, exquisite antiques, fine linens, comfortable mattresses (replaced every two years), fresh-flower arrangements throughout, and exceptional service. Herr Lay's goal is to provide the old-fashioned quality of excellence rarely found today—his aim is to have the "smallest GRAND hotel" in Europe. The Abtei is not inexpensive, yet when compared with all the other hotels in the costly city of Hamburg, it offers real value for the price. It has been voted the best hotel with under 50 rooms in Germany—and was among the top 25 of all German hotels. The guestrooms are beautifully decorated suites with well-equipped, attractive en suite bathrooms. Guests may enjoy breakfast in their room, in one of the guest dining rooms, or, if the weather is warm, in the pretty garden behind the hotel. Homemade baked goods are offered in silver breadbaskets, and delicious coffee or tea is served in antique pots. In the evening, dinner is served in the intimate dining room. If you like refinement and exceptional service, you will love this tiny hotel. *Directions:* Ask the hotel for directions.

HOTEL ABTEI
Owners: Fritz & Petra Lay
Abteistrasse 14, 20149 Hamburg, Germany
Tel: (040) 442905, Fax: (040) 449820
11 Rooms, Double: €180–€260
Restaurant closed Sun & Mon
Open: all year, Credit cards: all major
Relais & Chateaux
Region: Stadtstaat Hamburg, Michelin Map: 541
www.karenbrown.com/hotelabtei.html

Hamburg is the hub of northern Germany. Far more than an important seaport and business center, it is a city of great beauty offering a rich and varied social and cultural menu. Just north of the city center you find Alster Lake: with this expanse of water at its front and a tranquil garden at its rear, the Hotel Prem occupies a handsome downtown Hamburg location. What were originally two large townhouses were converted into a small hotel by Herr and Frau Prem more than 75 years ago. The downstairs is small: a lounge area leads to a bar and, beyond, an airy restaurant overlooks the garden. The restaurant, decorated in shades of beige and white with arrangements of fresh flowers, brightens even the gloomiest Hamburg day. In summer the pretty garden is set with tables and chairs for outside dining. Accented with fine antiques, the bedrooms retain their high ceilings, which give a spacious feeling—a few lovely rooms even have their original ornate plasterwork ceilings. The staff speak excellent English and really care that you enjoy your holiday. You can easily walk to the heart of Hamburg, and for those who like to travel by boat, the ferry stop is very close by. Also, only steps from your front door are the walking paths that encircle the lake. The hotel provides discounted rates for guests staying on weekends. *Directions:* Located north of the city, on the southeastern shore of Alster Lake. Request directions from the hotel.

HOTEL PREM
Manager: Ulrich Voit
An der Alster 9, 20099 Hamburg, Germany
Tel: (040) 24834040, Fax: (040) 2803851
54 Rooms, Double: €115–€300*
*Breakfast not included: €15
Open: all year, Credit cards: all major
Region: Stadtstaat Hamburg, Michelin Map: 541
www.karenbrown.com/hotelprem.html

The Romantik Hotel Jagdhaus Waldidyll is so superb that if you are anywhere in the area, make a special effort to spend at least a few nights here. This small hotel, nestled in a fairy-tale-like forest, is most appealing with its steeply pitched roof, whimsical gables, stone-and-dark-wood façade, and cheery bright-red shutters. A tiny pond, manicured lawn, and colorful flowers complete the idyllic scene. From the moment you enter, the ambiance is of a cozy, elegant hunting lodge with beamed ceiling, wood paneling, and antlers on the walls. Carved double doors open from the reception area to two romantic paneled dining rooms, where local specialties are always available. The food is delicious and splendidly presented. The bedrooms are beautiful and of excellent quality in every detail, all lovingly decorated with gorgeous fabrics and fine furnishings. I fell in love with 102, which has three large windows and a balcony overlooking the forest. The marble bathrooms are very pretty with hand-painted washbasins and matching tile trim from Portugal. This is a family operation, which makes it very special, and all guests are greeted warmly as friends. Your charming hostess, Andrea Kahl (who worked at an inn in Vermont) oversees the operation of the hotel, assisted by her mother, Hertha Sellmair. *Directions:* Located 100 km southwest of Dresden. Take the Hartenstein exit from A72. The hotel is 1 km south of town.

ROMANTIK HOTEL JAGDHAUS WALDIDYLL
Owners: Hertha Sellmair & Andrea Kahl
Talstrasse 1, 08118 Hartenstein, Germany
Tel: (037605) 840, Fax: (037605) 84444
28 Rooms, Double: €119–€129
Open: all year, Credit cards: all major
Region: Sachsen, Michelin Map: 544
www.karenbrown.com/jagdhauswaldidyll.html

The Kronen Schlösschen offers deluxe accomodations. Completely redecorated in 2004, this attractive mansion, painted white with brown trim, is set in gardens across the highway from the Rhine. The Kronen Schlösschen has a whimsical look, with jaunty towers topped by peaked onion domes and a stepped roofline. From the courtyard, you enter into a pretty foyer with ornate stucco design and marble floors. A staircase leads up to the guestrooms, each one absolutely stunning in decor. Your choice of rooms depends upon what style appeals to you—some are smartly tailored in dark colors, others are spring-like with a pastel color scheme, some are modern, some antique. One of my favorites, mini-suite 29, has pale-yellow wallpaper, rich, natural-silk lemon-toned draperies, soft-green carpet, and comfortable, off-white matching sofas. No matter what room you choose, you will find glamorous marble bathrooms, truly fit for a king. The Kronen Schlösschen has two excellent restaurants: one an elegant gourmet dining room, the other, The Bistro, a less formal, pub-like room enclosed on two sides with windows. It is less than an hour from the Frankfurt airport, a convenient distance after a tiring transatlantic flight. *Directions:* Hattenheim is on the Rhine west of Eltville, 39 km west of Frankfurt airport. From Frankfurt take the A66 (changes to B42) towards Rüdesheim to Hattenheim.

KRONEN SCHLÖSSCHEN
Manager: H.B. Ullrich
Rheinallee, Eltville
65347 Hattenheim, Germany
Tel: (06723) 640, Fax: (06723) 7663
18 Rooms, Double: €140–€390*
*Breakfast not included: €14
Open: all year, Credit cards: all major
Region: Hessen, Michelin Map: 543
www.karenbrown.com/kronenschlosschen.html

The Weinhaus Zum Krug is located in Hattenheim, a tiny wine town along the Rhine. The village has many very old buildings with character, but only a few have been restored to reflect their historic past. Happily, the Weinhaus Zum Krug, dating back to 1720, is one of them. The first floor is painted white and has dark-green shutters framing leaded windows. The timbered second floor has a fairy-tale quality: it is painted dark green, merrily set off by an intricate design of gold grapevines. To add the finishing touch to this quaint house, bright-red geraniums overflow from green boxes below each of the windows. There is no doubt about what awaits the guest within—suspended over the entrance is a jug of wine, enclosed in a wreath of grapes (the restaurant has its own winery). Inside, the decor is appropriately rustic with a beamed ceiling, small tables with wooden chairs, Oriental throw rugs, and a dark-green tiled stove along the wall. Upstairs there are guestrooms which, although simple, all have their own private bathrooms. Reasonably priced, the Zum Krug offers great value, and the Laufer family extend a warm welcome and make this a very special place to stay. It is less than an hour's drive from the Frankfurt airport, a convenient distance after a tiring transatlantic flight. *Directions:* Hattenheim is on the Rhine west of Eltville, 39 km west of Frankfurt airport. From Frankfurt take the A66 (changes to B42) towards Rüdesheim to Hattenheim.

WEINHAUS ZUM KRUG
Owner: Josef Laufer
Hauptstrasse 34, Eltville
65347 Hattenheim, Germany
Tel: (06723) 99680, Fax: (06723) 996825
10 Rooms, Double: €120
Restaurant closed Mon
Open: all year, Credit cards: all major
Region: Hessen, Michelin Map: 543
www.karenbrown.com/weinhauszumkrug.html

In the first edition of this guide we recommended the Hotel Garni am Kornmarkt, but over the years maintenance became non-existent and we had to drop it. However, on our last research trip to Heidelberg we happened to walk by this hotel and could not believe our eyes—it was so fresh and pretty. We went inside and found the transformation total. Under new ownership and new management, the hotel has been totally rejuvenated and once again is an excellent choice for accommodation, largely thanks to the excellent, experienced manager, Markus Etzel. The hotel faces onto the Kornmarkt Platz, without a doubt one of the prettiest squares in Heidelberg, highlighted by lacy trees and a delightful fountain. The hotel is painted a dark, rust red and is very attractive with white shutters, small balconies, and steep roof with perky gables. There is no restaurant, but this is no problem in Heidelberg. Instead, on the ground floor with windows overlooking the fountain in the plaza, there is an intimate breakfast room with classic prints on the wall, antique mirrors, and pretty blue-and-yellow porcelain. The bedrooms have also been totally refurbished. If you want to splurge, the most expensive room with a balcony is exceptionally nice. Most of the guestrooms now have en suite bathrooms, but if you are really on a tight budget, ask for one of the rooms that share a bathroom down the hall. *Directions:* In the pedestrian section near parking lot 12.

HOTEL GARNI AM KORNMARKT
Manager: Markus Etzel
Kornmarkt 7, 69117 Heidelberg, Germany
Tel: (06221) 905830, Fax: (06221) 28218
20 Rooms, Double: €75–€125
Closed: first two weeks in Jan, Credit cards: MC, VS
Region: Baden-Württemberg, Michelin Map: 543
www.karenbrown.com/garni.html

The 300-year-old Gasthaus Backmulde enjoys a quiet location just off the main pedestrian street of Heidelberg's picturesque old town. This lovely small and atmospheric establishment offers an intimate restaurant and 16 bedrooms, a few of which were beautifully renovated in recent years. From the street, guests pass under the old stone-arched doorway to enter the softly lit restaurant filled with fresh flowers, antique pieces, old mirrors, photos, and paintings from Heidelberg. The restaurant, decorated in tones of red and green, offers excellent food in a cozy atmosphere. The hotel section faces its own quiet, enclosed courtyard. A staircase, whose pleasing soft-yellow walls are brightened by an overhead skylight, leads up one floor to the reception area and the breakfast room. A blue color scheme prevails throughout, including a patterned carpet of excellent quality. Each of the bedrooms is attractively decorated in pretty, blue floral draperies (with white sheer curtains beneath) and color-coordinated fabrics on the bedcovers (rooms 23 and 24 are special favorites). The bathrooms are not large, but each is new and spotlessly clean. The Gasthaus Backmulde is our favorite small hotel in Heidelberg. *Directions:* At the heart of the Altstadt, the Backmulde is located just a block off the river.

GASTHAUS BACKMULDE
Owners: Bernhard Zepf & Alex Schneider
Schiffgasse 11, 69117 Heidelberg, Germany
Tel: (06221) 53660, Fax: (06221) 536660
16 Rooms, Double: €99–€110
Restaurant closed Sun
Open: all year, Credit cards: all major
Region: Baden-Württemberg, Michelin Map: 543
www.karenbrown.com/gasthausbackmulde.html

Heidelberg is so popular, particularly in the high season, that it is often very difficult to find accommodation, so we were excited to find the KulturBrauerei Hotel on our last visit to Heidelberg. As you might guess from the name, the hotel is closely involved with a brewery. The property is actually a complex made up of a brewery, a beer hall, a beer garden, and the hotel. The white building on the left with rust-red shutters houses the very modern, sleek reception area for the hotel. The nostalgic, bright-yellow building, on the right, with red trim, is a cozy, typical German beer hall. Between the two buildings a pathway leads to a charming, enclosed beer garden where guests dine informally (accompanied by huge mugs of cold beer) on wooden tables shaded by a wonderful old tree. In the KulturBrauerei you can look out through large plate-glass windows to the machinery that produces the excellent beer for which the hotel was named. A staircase leads to the bedrooms, which are located above the brewery. The bedrooms all have a light and airy ambiance and a modern, sophisticated, uncluttered look with hardwood floors, built-in headboards, and lots of light. Everything is fresh and new and attractive. Some of the bedrooms on the top floor have enormous windows that make them especially appealing. *Directions:* Located just outside the pedestrian section, one block up from the river, near parking areas 12 and 13.

KULTURBRAUEREI HOTEL
Owner: Jurgen Merz Family
Leyergasse 6, 69117 Heidelberg, Germany
Tel: (06221) 502980, Fax: (06221) 5029879
34 Rooms, Double: €116–€135
Open: all year, Credit cards: MC, VS
Region: Baden-Württemberg, Michelin Map: 543
www.karenbrown.com/kulturbrauerei.html

Heidelberg is a romantic, beguiling old university town with a pedestrian street, the Hauptstrasse, the dynamic heart of the action. It is here that you will find the Romantik Hotel Zum Ritter St. Georg occupying one of the best positions in town. In fact, the Zum Ritter's convenient location is its greatest enticement. The hotel's stately façade dates from 1592, when the master builder, Carolus Belier, imprinted the gold sign still hanging above the door. Official records show the building served as a fabric trade house for a decade before it became the Hotel Zum Ritter. Because of its impressive façade and central location, the lovely paneled dining room is popular with the throngs of tourists that flock to Heidelberg—this gives the hotel a very bustling atmosphere in the evenings. The hotel has been extended to the rear and in the newer wing you find seven spacious, modern bedrooms with fitted furniture and floor-to-ceiling draperies. The remainder of the rooms vary from little single rooms to large bedrooms overlooking the busy main street, with a decor that is both modern than old-world. The majority of the rooms have recently been renovated. *Directions:* If driving, follow signs to parking area 12. From there it is only a few blocks to the hotel.

ROMANTIK HOTEL ZUM RITTER ST. GEORG
Owner: Nicolaas Bootsma
Hauptstrasse 178, 69117 Heidelberg, Germany
Tel: (06221) 1350, Fax: (06221) 135230
39 Rooms, Double: €161–€241*
*Breakfast not included: €10
Open: all year, Credit cards: all major
Region: Baden-Württemberg, Michelin Map: 543
www.karenbrown.com/zumrittersaintgeorg.html

Staying in a castle almost always guarantees an adventure, but not always a comfortable night's accommodation. All too often the knights in armor are ever-present, but not the firm mattress and the welcome hot and cold running water. Near the River Neckar there are numerous castle hotels. One of these, Schloss Heinsheim (in the von Racknitz family for hundreds of years), is especially appealing because of its excellent accommodations and outstanding cuisine. The hotel is surrounded by a forest and has all the ambiance of a large country estate. Horses frequently frolic in the fields visible from your bedroom window, enhancing the country mood. There is a small, circular pool that is favored by children and a lovely terraced area set with tables for enjoying meals outside in warm weather. There are two attractive restaurants: one has a rustic decor and the other is a bit more modern. The bedrooms are beautifully furnished with fine fabrics and many antiques—one of my favorites, room 15, is especially pleasing. There is a small, baroque chapel on the grounds, and on weekends, you might well witness a wedding celebration. *Directions:* Located 55 km east of Heidelberg, the town of Heinsheim is quite small and not on many maps. From Bad Rappenau (which you can find on most maps), go east for 5 km to Heinsheim (signposted for Gundelsheim, a town beyond Heinsheim).

SCHLOSS HEINSHEIM
Owner: Yvonne von Racknitz
Gundelsheimer Strasse 36, Bad Rappenau
74906 Heinsheim, Germany
Tel: (07264) 95030, Fax: (07264) 4208
41 Rooms, Double: €85–€150
Restaurant closed Mon & Tues
Closed: Jan, Credit cards: all major
Region: Baden-Württemberg, Michelin Map: 543
www.karenbrown.com/schlossheinsheim.html

Overlooking the village green in the center of Hinterzarten, two traditional chalet homes form the core of the luxurious Hotel Reppert. This small resort, run by dedicated brothers Thomas and Volker Reppert, typifies the very best of small luxury German hotels. Volker ensures that guests are well taken care of while Thomas is in charge of the kitchen, making sure that guests are well fed. Plan your day's activities in the luxurious lobby lounge, where elegant chairs are arranged into small groups facing the room-wide view of a little lake and pastoral countryside. Bedrooms are traditionally furnished and a spacious bathroom accompanies each. The most impressive feature of the hotel is its luxurious award-winning health club. Beyond the saunas, Jacuzzis, and small swimming pool lies the elegant salt-water swimming pool and there is a third pool in the garden area. After aquatic disport, soak up the soothing warmth of the surrounding heated tile benches or relax in an aromatherapy room. I suggest you choose your room by temperature rather than scent—the 60°C lemon room was too hot for me while the cooler herb room was just perfect. Most European guests come for a week—after a day you will wish you had. Volker offers escorted tours of the Black Forest byways in his eight-seater minibus—ideal if you want to take a break from driving or have traveled here by train. *Directions:* Hinterzarten is located 30 km west of Donaueschingen on the B31.

HOTEL REPPERT
Owners: Thomas & Volker Reppert
Am Adlerweg 21–23
79856 Hinterzarten, Germany
Tel: (07652) 12080, Fax: (07652) 120811
43 Rooms, Double: €166–€270
Closed: Nov 10 to Dec 6, Credit cards: all major
Region: Baden-Württemberg, Michelin Map: 545
www.karenbrown.com/hotelreppert.html

Hinterzarten is a small Black Forest resort famous for its healthy air where people come for family holidays with long country walks or cross-country skiing. Set beside the village green you find the Sassenhof. If your arrival is in the early afternoon, you will most likely find the Lück family supervising the presentation of each of the guestrooms, striving to achieve the atmosphere of a private home with very personalized service. Richly polished woods and antiques adorn the public rooms and artistic flower arrangements prepared by Frau Lück add splashes of color. Everything is spic-and-span and well cared for. From the attractive dining room, where breakfast and supper are served, you can see the mountains of Hinterzarten. You can help yourself to drinks in the kitchen bar (which is always open) and enjoy the nostalgic tea hour each day. Each room is thoughtfully provided with dishes and freshly pressed linen napkins. The halls that lead to the bedrooms are warmed by soft lighting, handsome prints, red carpet covered in Oriental throw rugs, and heavy wooden doors and doorways. Each room is individual in its decor but all are tastefully decorated. For relaxation, there is an indoor swimming pool, sauna, and solarium. *Directions:* From Freiburg via B31 in the direction of Donaueschingen, exit at Hinterzarten. The hotel is beside the village green.

HOTEL SASSENHOF
Owner: Lück Family
Alderweg 17, 79856 Hinterzarten, Germany
Tel: (07652) 918190, Fax: (07652) 9181999
22 Rooms, Double: €98–€120
Open: all year, Credit cards: MC, VS
Region: Baden-Württemberg, Michelin Map: 545
www.karenbrown.com/sassenhof.html

Visitors flock to Hohenschwangau to visit the fanciful Schloss Neuschwanstein, the astonishing fantasy castle that Bavarian King Ludwig II built as a retreat from the world. Sitting directly between the castle and Schloss Hohenschwangau, the delightful village of Hohenschwangau throngs with day visitors. Consider staying for a night or two because after the day-trippers leave, the castles are yours to admire, particularly Neuschwanstein hovering high above the valley on its hilltop perch. Bedrooms 25 and 45, as well as suites 24 and 30, offer you Neuschwanstein views from your bed but many afford a glimpse from your balcony. I was also captivated by rooms looking up to Hohenschwangau Castle: room 55, a great value as a standard room with a spectacular view and room 16, a superior room with its own terrace. Whichever room you stay in, you will enjoy your sojourn at this delightful hotel built in 1910 and extended with a wing of traditional rooms in the 1980s. Bedrooms in the old house have high ceilings and a tailored look, while those in the new have a traditional Bavarian decor. Horse-drawn carriage rides to Neuschwanstein leave from doorstep. A perfect base from which to explore Bavaria, the Hotel Müller also affords accommodation with memorable views and a staff that ensures a warm welcome and comfortable stay. *Directions:* From Füssen take the Munich road, turn right to Hohenschwangau, and the Müller is on the right.

🍺 ⚞ 💳 ☎ 🐕 ♿ P 🍴 🚭 🖼 ♿ 🎿

HOTEL MÜLLER
Owner: Müller Family
Alpseestrasse 16
87645 Hohenschwangau, Germany
Tel: (08362) 81990, Fax: (08362) 819913
42 Rooms, Double: €140–€180
Open: Mar 15 to Jan, Credit cards: all major
Region: Bayern, Michelin Map: 546
www.karenbrown.com/hotelmueller.html

The Schlosshotel Lisl and the Jaegerhaus are conveniently located at the base of the road that climbs to Neuschwanstein in the shadow of Hohenschwangau. Many of the rooms give you unobstructed views up to one or both of the castles and it is especially nice when you can open your windows to see them dramatically lit against a night sky long after the crowds of day visitors have departed. The three-star Schlosshotel Lisl dates back over one hundred years to when it was a guesthouse for the castle workers. Guestrooms here are functional in their decor and enjoy modern bathrooms. Be sure to ask for room 10 or 20, larger corner rooms (not priced at a premium) with windows boasting incredible views of both castles. The breakfast room, an à-la-carte restaurant, cozy stube, and terrace bar are all located in the Schlosshotel Lisl. The four-star Jaegerhaus just across the street offers twelve luxurious rooms and junior suites with modern, spacious bathrooms. The large corner rooms 42, 52, and 62 are exceptional in terms of space and castle views and again, are not priced at a premium. Third-floor rooms are tucked under the eaves. The buildings are elegant but do show a bit of wear, having accommodated large numbers of guests. *Directions:* From Füssen take the Munich road for 2 km, turn right, and drive 2 km to Hohenschwangau. The Schlosshotel Lisl and Jaegerhaus are at the end of town just as the road climbs to Neuschwanstein.

SCHLOSSHOTEL LISL & JAEGERHAUS
Manager: Guenter Meyer
Neuschwansteinstrasse 1–3
Hohenschwangau, Germany
Tel: (08362) 8870, Fax: (08362) 81107
47 Rooms, Double: €110–€200*
*Breakfast not included: €12
Closed: Christmas, Credit cards: all major
Region: Bayern, Michelin Map: 546
www.karenbrown.com/lisl.html

Located just off the A4 and nestled in a wooded park, the Hotel Hohenhaus is a convenient base for exploring the many sights in Eisenach, Weimar, and Erfurt. However, many guests come to just relax, take strolls in the surrounding forest, enjoy the gourmet meals, and swim in the large, indoor pool that overlooks the gardens. The hotel sits at the edge of the tiny pretty village of Holzhausen, 5 kilometers from Herleshausen. As you drive up, your first glimpse of the tan stone manor is seen through intricate, wrought-iron gates flanked by stone pillars. Six of guestrooms are in this manor, but they have not yet been renovated so they are only rented when the hotel is full. The majority of the guestrooms are in the newer left wing, contemporary in architecture yet with a traditional, understated elegance. The ground floor is devoted to the reception area, a cute sitting nook in front of a handsome fireplace, a sunroom, and the dining rooms. The front of the building has large windows overlooking the lawn. The dining rooms and conference rooms have the better view of the beautiful forest that wraps around the hotel. Taking advantage of this lovely setting, dining tables and chairs are set on a lower cobblestone terrace where rolling hills stretch to the edge of the forest. *Directions:* From the A4, take the Herleshausen exit 37. Turn toward Sontra. Follow signs toward Nesselroden, then Holszhausen. The hotel is located just a few minutes north of the A4.

RELAIS CHATEAU HOTEL HOHENHAUS   *New*
Manager: Hannes Horsch
Holzhausen 37293 (near Herleshausen) Germany
Tel: (05654) 9870, Fax: (05654) 1303
26 Rooms, Double: €170–€240*
*Breakfast not included: €18
Restaurant closed Sun eve, Mon & Tues
Closed: Jan 3 to 30, Credit cards: all major
Relais & Chateaux
Region: Hessen, Michelin Map: 546
www.karenbrown.com/hotelhohenhaus.html

High above the beautiful Mosel Valley is one of those rare, perfect hideaways—the Historische Schlossmühle, once an old mill. This lovely cream stone building with its handsome teal trim enjoys a peaceful riverside setting. Bedrooms in the old mill (named after country animals) are stocked with thoughtful little extras like sewing kits and hair spray. The four new rooms in the granary are equally as lovely. It is just a short stroll along the river to the recently renovated farmhouse and eight more attractive rooms. Rüdiger and Anne Liller are your charming hosts—Anne is responsible for the creative decor and Rüdiger oversees the cuisine. The restaurant is wonderful and understandably quite popular with locals. Enjoy an aperitif at tables set in the shade in the garden and then dine at tables on different terraced levels of the dining room. A little sitting room honors Napoleon who, so the story goes, sold the mill in 1804 to raise money. The enterprising new owner realized that once Napoleon had left, the original owner would reclaim his property, so to prevent this, he had the mill taken apart and erected 25 kilometers away in this quiet green valley outside Horbruch. *Directions:* 20 km east of Bernkastel-Kues. A detailed map will help you to find the Rhaunen turnoff from road 327 that runs to the south of the Mosel. The Historische Schlossmühle is a short drive from the junction, roughly a kilometer beyond Horbruch.

HOTEL HISTORISCHE SCHLOSSMÜHLE
Owners: Anne & Rüdiger Liller
55483 Horbruch, Germany
Tel: (06543) 4041, Fax: (06543) 3178
18 Rooms, Double: €120–€180
Restaurant closed Mon
Closed: Jan 2 to Jan 15, Credit cards: MC, VS
Region: Rheinland-Pfalz, Michelin Map: 543
www.karenbrown.com/schlossmuehle.html

Just 30 kilometers from the fascinating city of Würzburg, the Zehntkeller, Romantik Hotel and wine house, is also convenient to the wine region at the foot of the Schwan Mountain. Once a tax-collection point for the church, and hence a most unpopular building, the Zehntkeller (made into a hotel in 1910) is now the chosen destination of many. Iphofen is a small, quiet village, and it is amazing to find the traffic coming and going from the inn: the specialties of the menu attract diners from outlying regions. The restaurant is actually a number of rooms on the first floor, serviced by gracious girls dressed in attractive dirndls. The 5 single and 11 double rooms housed in the main building above the restaurant, are all lovely and well-appointed with modern bathrooms. The Kelterhaus, Gartenhaus, and Hofhaus are all newly constructed buildings that are accessed off the courtyard and back onto a walled garden. Guestrooms in the newer buildings are spacious and charming—perfect for guests who want to linger for a stay of more than a few days. The four suites in the Kelterhaus are luxurious, and each has its own special luxury such as garden terrace or separate salon. The Wedding Suite is housed in a separate cottage with its own entrance. *Directions:* Iphofen is located just to the north of the N8, 30 km southeast of Würzburg.

ROMANTIK HOTEL ZEHNTKELLER
Owner: Heinrich Seufert
Bahnhofstrasse 12, 97346 Iphofen, Germany
Tel: (09323) 8440, Fax: (09323) 844123
58 Rooms, Double: €105–€200
Open: all year, Credit cards: all major
Region: Bayern, Michelin Map: 546
www.karenbrown.com/zehntkeller.html

Ambling from village to village on Die Deutsche Weinstrasse (The German Wine Road), with stops for winetasting at taverns and vineyards, is great fun. A most appropriate place for such pursuits is the Weinkastell "Zum Weissen Ross" which dates back to 1553, though most of what you see today as a lovely traditional building dates only from 1958. I particularly admired the timbered exterior where each vertical timber is supported by a colorfully painted carved figure and the beams are carved and painted with flowers. The same traditional craftsmanship continues in the interior where the dining room has a fan-vaulted ceiling set above a traditional tiled stove. The hunters' corner with its almost circular seating beneath an intricate wood ceiling is a snug place to dine. Jutta has added her own touches—over 1300 ducks of all shapes and sizes. The bedrooms all have oak furniture in either a rustic modern or a traditional style—several have four-poster beds and one has two single alcove beds. All have modern white-tile bathrooms or shower rooms. Brother Philippi carries on the family tradition of winemaking across the courtyard. Popular activities in the area include bike riding on paved paths through the vineyards and walking on many kilometers of well-marked footpaths in the Pfälzer Wald (forest). *Directions:* 26 km west of Mannheim, 37 km east of Kaiserslautern. From the A6 exit at Grünstadt follow signs to Bad Dürkheim.

WEINKASTELL "ZUM WEISSEN ROSS"
Owners: Jutta & Norbert Kohnke
Weinstrasse 80/82, 67169 Kallstadt, Germany
Tel: (06322) 5033, Fax: (06322) 66091
14 Rooms, Double: €80–€105
Restaurant closed Mon & Tues
Open: mid-Feb to Dec, Credit cards: all major
Region: Rheinland-Pfalz, Michelin Map: 545
www.karenbrown.com/weissen.html

Sylt, a sand-dune island located in the northernmost tip of Germany, is reached by taking the car-train across the narrow causeway linking the island to the mainland—a 45-minute ride. The Benen Diken Hof is comprised of several squat, Friesian farmhouses joined into a complex by means of glass corridors that appear to bring the outdoors indoors. Decorated throughout in white and cream with accents of pale pink and blue, the hotel is light and welcoming. A playground at the front of the inn is evidence of the welcome the hotel extends to families. After a walk along the sand dunes in the bracing sea air, you return to the hotel to pamper yourself with a sauna and a massage or a relaxing swim. The hotel's greatest assets are its gracious young owners Claas-Erik and Anja Johannsen who continue to offer the same friendly hospitality that Claas-Erik's parents did. In the evening Claas-Erik can often be found hosting the hotel's cozy bar. His warmth and graciousness transcend the language barrier and make you feel at home. The restaurant serves breakfast without a time limit so that guests can enjoy sleeping late. In the evenings a creative menu is offered in the restaurant. *Directions:* Take the train from the mainland to the Island of Sylt, 160 km northwest of Hamburg. If traveling by car, drive onto the train and stay in your car for the duration of the trip. To reach Keitum travel the one road east for 4.5 km to the hotel.

HOTEL BENEN DIKEN HOF
Owners: Anja & Claas-Erik Johannsen
Süderstrasse 3, Sylt, 25980 Keitum, Germany
Tel: (04651) 93830, Fax: (04651) 9383183
40 Rooms, Double: €162–€386
Restaurant closed Tues
Open: all year, Credit cards: all major
Region: Schleswig-Holstein, Michelin Map: 541
www.karenbrown.com/benendiken.html

The lush Ruhr region is beautiful. Especially appealing is the landscape around Kettwig. Here, far from the smokestacks of the industrial area, you find the Schloss Hugenpoet, an imposing fortress surrounded by a water-filled moat where large carp swim lazily. There has been a fortification on this site for over one thousand years, and during violent periods of history several castles on the site were destroyed. The present structure has existed since 1650. The interior, rich in tradition, presents a castle in tiptop condition. An impressive black-marble staircase dominates the lobby; a grouping of fine furniture stands in front of the huge carved fireplace, while the surrounding walls host a picture gallery of fine oil paintings. This is a grand castle where the bedchambers were given spacious proportions. Many are furnished with authentic 17th-century furniture. Downstairs, the dining rooms, baronial in size, are each dominated by a grand carved fireplace. Boasting famous chefs and an incredible wine list, the hotel offers two restaurants, the French inspired "Nesselrode" and the "Hugenpottchen" which serves local cuisine. *Directions:* Take the A52 from Düsseldorf to Kreuz Breitscheid, exit at Ratingen-Breitscheid. At the first traffic light turn right towards Velbert on the B227. Go 1.8 km to the roundabout, turn left after 1.3 km and drive 3.3 km to the schloss entrance.

SCHLOSS HUGENPOET
Owner: Michael Lübbert
August-Thyssen Strasse 51, Essen
45219 Kettwig, Germany
Tel: (02054) 12040, Fax: (02054) 120450
25 Rooms, Double: €235–€550
Open: all year, Credit cards: all major
Relais & Chateaux
Region: Nordrhein-Westfalen, Michelin Map: 543
www.karenbrown.com/schlosshugenpoet.html

The Alte Försterei has been giving shelter to many illustrious guests during its 200-year history—Frederick the Great, for example. Today you can lodge in one of the 20 wonderful guestrooms of this renovated farm complex, each tastefully decorated with country furniture and antiques. Each bedroom has its own particular charm with majestic oak timber roofs, knotty-pine floors, wrought-iron beds, and lovely antiques. The most exquisite room is the Wedding Suite (room 15), with a sunken four-poster bed and headboard of myrtle leaves. The hotel is built around a large courtyard where tables are set in summer for lunch and dinner. You also can dine in either the Friedrichs Stuben, serving a variety of imaginative meat, fish, and vegetarian dishes, or in the more informal 12 Monche—a former stable where you can sample beer on draft or a fresh glass of wine. A bountiful buffet breakfast is served in the kitchen on a tiled stove from the last century. Your genial host, Roland Frankfurth, will probably be there to greet you. His warm welcome, excellent English, and concern for his guests' comfort add to an enjoyable stay. Don't let the nondescript exterior of the hotel discourage you—it does not hint at the inn's engaging interior, which is further brightened by baskets of dried and fresh flowers. Try to hear a concert at the old monastery. *Directions:* The hotel is a 50-minute drive south of Berlin on B101 between Luckenwalde and Jüterbog.

HOTEL ALTE FÖRSTEREI
Owner: Roland Frankfurth
Markt 7, 14913 Kloster Zinna, Germany
Tel: (03372) 4650, Fax: (03372) 406577
20 Rooms, Double: €95–€105
Open: all year, Credit cards: all major
Region: Brandenburg, Michelin Map: 544
www.karenbrown.com/forsterei.html

The enchanting, cozy Romantik Hotel Zur Krone is owned by the Breitenbach family, whose genuine warmth of welcome and passion for perfection guarantee a wonderful stay. Laudenbach is a small town on the River Main with just a cluster of houses, several of which are nicely restored historic buildings—of these the Zur Krone is one of the finest. The 300-year-old inn is as pretty as a picture—a two-story, creamy-yellow building with a steeply pitched, mansard-style roof, and leaded windows enhanced by windowboxes full of red geraniums. As you enter, notice the intricately carved front door—this masterpiece was created by Karl Breitenbach's father, whose carvings and woodwork are seen throughout the house. Inside, a cozy ambiance prevails. The dining room is especially romantic, with a low, beamed ceiling, white walls, fresh flowers on the tables, and a stunning antique ceramic stove. Herr Breitenbach is a talented chef who produces the most delicious food. In mild weather, meals are also served outside on the terrace surrounded by a meticulously tended garden. The bedrooms are all attractively furnished. If you want to splurge, room 16 is especially delightful: it has a spacious living room with floor-to-ceiling windows overlooking the charming garden. *Directions:* Forty minutes from Frankfurt. Take the A3 towards Würzburg, exit at Stockstadt onto the B469, travel south to Miltenberg, then west on B47 to Laudenbach.

ROMANTIK HOTEL ZUR KRONE
Owners: Gabriele & Karl Breitenbach
Obernburger Strasse 4
63925 Laudenbach, Germany
Tel: (09372) 10882, Fax: (09372) 10112
16 Rooms, Double: €105–€175
Open: all year, Credit cards: all major
Region: Bayern, Michelin Map: 543
www.karenbrown.com/krone.html

If you are a castle connoisseur, the Schlosshotel Lembeck is worth a detour—it is a real winner. This 12th-century moated castle is awesome in size yet not in the least foreboding as some German castles tend to be. Somehow, as you approach over the moat and through the gate, this massive building of mellow, cut stone and dark-gray slate roof with perky, pointed, cap-like domed towers is irresistible. The castle is also a sightseeing attraction—the museum and grounds are open to the public—but at the gate just say you are a guest of the hotel and there is no charge to enter. A door in the gate leads down to the small restaurant, which is also where you register. The restaurant is informal and very inviting with a vaulted brick ceiling, wooden chairs and tables, soft lighting from rustic chandeliers, and a cozy fireplace. In the summertime, snacks are also served outside on the lawn overlooking the moat. The guestrooms are located in the rear wing of the castle. Splurge on one of the best rooms and you will be treated to antique furniture and an ambiance of days gone by. The Bridal Suite (Hochzeitszimmer mit Himmelbett) has a large canopied bed, tapestry chairs, and windows looking out over the countryside. The Schlosshotel Lembeck is surrounded by lovely grounds and woods where many kilometers of footpaths meander beneath the trees. *Directions:* Located 10 km north of Dorsten, 29 km north of Essen.

SCHLOSSHOTEL LEMBECK
Owner: Josef Selting
Dorsten, 46286 Lembeck, Germany
Tel: (02369) 7213, Fax: (02369) 77370
17 Rooms, Double: €89–€120
Open: all year, Credit cards: MC, VS
Region: Nordrhein-Westfalen, Michelin Map: 543
www.karenbrown.com/lembeck.html

Just inside Bavaria, this delightful island is the Bodensee's (Lake Constance) most scenic resort, joined to the mainland by railway and road. The Hotel Lindauer Hof, sitting right on the harbor—a perfect location—began life in the 1600s as two granaries for storing oats awaiting transportation across the Bodensee. It is owned by the energetic Wimpissinger family and Claudia is responsible for the smart, modern decor, which gives a welcoming feeling to the public rooms and a restful one to the bedrooms. Pale-lemon walls contrast with cool-gray terrazzo floors in the appealing ground-floor lounge and bar where little tables and chairs spill out onto the quayside. Up the broad staircase you come to the restaurant, which specializes in locally caught fish. If it's a warm evening, dine on the terrace overlooking the harbor and distant shore. While all the bedrooms are most attractive, five special rooms command the highest tariff. Santis (room 207), decorated in jade green, has a lovely paneled pine ceiling with a large crest in the center and a separate sitting room with views to the lake. Rooms 401 to 404 have been added under the eaves, each with its own large terrace—perfect for sitting and watching the activity of the harbor below. *Directions:* Located on an island on the north shore of the Bodensee. The hotel's brochure has a map that directs you to the hotel's back entrance.

HOTEL LINDAUER HOF
Owners: Gert, Karin & Claudia Wimpissinger
Seepromenade, 88131 Lindau, Germany
Tel: (08382) 4064, Fax: (08382) 24203
30 Rooms, Double: €115–€215
Open: all year, Credit cards: all major
Region: Bayern, Michelin Map: 545
www.karenbrown.com/lindauerhof.html

An absolutely fascinating niche in Germany is the Spreewald, an area midway between Dresden and Berlin where the River Spree fans out into a spider web of waterways bordered by quaint houses, many accessible only by boat. If you plan to overnight in the area, we heartily recommend a large private estate, the Schloss Lübbenau, within walking distance of the boat dock. The Schloss has been owned by the Lynar family since 1621. During the days of the wall, the castle became a school and later a hotel. After the reunification, the Lynar family reclaimed their property and restored everything to its former glory. Guestrooms are bright and cheerful. Italian, antique-style furniture gives a pleasing traditional look, enhanced by fine-quality carpets and drapes in restful tones of green. The most expensive bedrooms are very spacious (request one like room 214), while the least expensive rooms appear small and boxy by comparison. The Countess of Lynar's hobby is dried-flower arranging, and she is personally responsible for the pretty floral displays in the hotel. *Directions:* Take the A13 Berlin to Dresden autobahn. Exit at Lübbenau, turn left to the old town, and follow signs to the schloss.

SCHLOSS LÜBBENAU
Owner: Count of Lynar
Schlossbezirk 6, 03222 Lübbenau, Germany
Tel: (03542) 8730, Fax: (03542) 873666
46 Rooms, Double: €88–€200
Open: all year, Credit cards: all major
Region: Brandenburg, Michelin Map: 542
www.karenbrown.com/lubbenau.html

The Hotel Jensen enjoys a choice location just across the river from the dramatic walled entrance to the town of Lübeck. The hotel is one of many tall, narrow buildings lining the canal and, like its neighbors, this slim and appealing structure has the characteristic steep roof that forms a "stair step" gabled effect in the front. The main thrust of the Jensen seems to be the dining rooms—The Cabin, the Yacht Room, the Fireside Room, and the Patrician's Room—each with its own personality. The bedrooms are located up a stairway leading from the reception area (there's also an elevator). We found them to be small and characterless but we understand that they have been totally renovated. The rooms in the front of the building overlook the canal, and the twin-towered Holstentor (Holsten Gate), affords good views of the boats and quayside activity. Although these front rooms face the busy street, they are very quiet due to well-insulated windows. Handily, the pier for the ferry excursion boats (a must for enjoying the colorful town of Lübeck) is located just across the street from the hotel. Recommended mainly for travelers seeking a convenient location for enjoying Lübeck, the Jensen is a very modest hotel offering friendly management and a fun place to stay. *Directions:* Located 66 km northeast of Hamburg, 92 km southeast of Kiel.

HOTEL JENSEN
Innkeepers: Marnie & Markus Stillert
An der Obertrave 4-5, 23552 Lübeck, Germany
Tel: (0451) 702490, Fax: (0451) 73386
42 Rooms, Double: €85–€164
Open: all year, Credit cards: all major
Region: Schleswig-Holstein, Michelin Map: 541
www.karenbrown.com/hoteljensen.html

The Hotel Kaiserhof is just across the canal and a short walk from the historic old city of Lübeck. The hotel is a clever combination of two stately 19th-century homes joined with a central core serving as lobby and reception area. The hotel has grown over the years yet still retains the homespun ambiance and warmth of a small hotel. The staff is carefully chosen and taught to give "service with heart", thus making this a hotel with a special level of service. The reception area is light and airy with Oriental carpets setting off the polished marble floor. The intimate lounge has a magnificent sculpted ceiling, fully restored including the 24-carat gilt paint, but this room's pièce de résistance is a superb, intricately formed Meissen porcelain fireplace. Each of the bedrooms is individually decorated and the ones I saw were spacious and filled with light from large windows. The Hotel Kaiserhof is not a showplace of antique furniture or a decorator's dream, yet these two lovely old buildings are beautiful and have been restored to their original elegance. *Directions:* Leave the A1 at Lübeck Zentrum. At the Lindenplatz take the third right off the circle, then cross over Puppenbridge towards the Holstentor. At the first light, turn right on Posselhlstrasse, at the second light turn left onto Wallstrasse to its end. Turn right, cross the bridge, take the first right off the traffic circle and the hotel is 200 meters down on the left.

HOTEL KAISERHOF
Owner: Michael V. Iwanschitz
Kronsforder Allee 11-13
23560 Lübeck, Germany
Tel: (0451) 703301, Fax: (0451) 795083
60 Rooms, Double: €100–€215
Open: all year, Credit cards: all major
Region: Schleswig-Holstein, Michelin Map: 541
www.karenbrown.com/kaiserhof.html

One often hears about the town of Iphofen just a few kilometers away, but the walled town of Mainbernheim with its gateway turrets and authentic simplicity is also a pleaser. You won't find the horse-drawn carriages or many gift shops, but you can walk the cobbled streets and explore the ramparts. Another asset of the town is its charming Gasthof Zum Falken, lovingly managed by mother and daughter, Greta and Christine Jaeger, whose family has owned it for over 120 years. The wide front hallway hung with handsome old farming implements serves as the casual reception area. Each of the restaurant's dining rooms is cozy with wood paneling, heavy old beams, and country tablecloths. The menu features regional and seasonal specialties. Guestrooms are found up the staircase that winds from the entry. The rooms fresh and comfortable with good mattresses, large pillows, down comforters, television, telephone, and modern bathrooms. Rooms are simple but pretty with well-chosen fabrics for the curtains, and the housekeeping is impeccable. Greta is most welcoming and daughter Christine, who has a sincere warmth in her smile, loves to practice her English. You are assured of a quiet night's sleep here for a very reasonable price that includes a full breakfast buffet. *Directions:* 26 km southeast of Würzburg on the Frankische Weinstrasse. Take the B8 into the village and the hotel is at its heart next to the fountain.

GASTHOF ZUM FALKEN
Owners: Greta & Christine Jaeger
Herrnstrasse 27
97350 Mainbernheim, Germany
Tel: (09323) 87280, Fax: (09323) 872828
15 Rooms, Double: €65–€70
Restaurant closed Tue
Open: Mar 20 to Aug 26 & Sep 12 to Feb 20
Credit cards: none
Region: Bayern, Michelin Map: 546
www.karenbrown.com/zumfalken.html

Marienthal, at the heart of the Lower Rhine parkland region, offers the ultimate idyllic setting, with delightful trails and well-signposted bicycle routes. The Romantik Hotel Haus Elmer, a lovingly developed ancient cloister garth, is an oasis of peace and quiet in a historic region offering a wealth of contrasts. The hotel is a clever blend of an old and a new building and each of the individually appointed rooms contributes its own distinct character to the hotel's unique atmosphere. Bedrooms in the old house are smaller and exude country charm, while those in the new section are larger and decorated with new, country-style furniture. Each room is unique and often the decor cleverly incorporates the work of a particular artist. There are several dining rooms: one is on the upper story of the new wing and has delightful views of the surrounding countryside through its large picture windows, while another is paneled and cozy. The select cuisine and the well-stocked wine cellar will delight every gourmet. The outstanding cabaret performances that are presented in front of the cloister church in the summer have attained cult status. Beside the old oak trees trail you'll find love poems; another trail shows you wonderful sculptures. *Directions:* From the A3 exit at Wesel/Schermbeck. Travel 2 km towards Schermbeck, turn left at the light, drive 500 meters, then turn right towards Marienthal. The hotel is 7 km farther beside the church.

ROMANTIK HOTEL HAUS ELMER
Owner: René Nicke
An der Klosterkirche 12
46499 Marienthal, Germany
Tel: (02856) 9110, Fax: (02856) 91170
30 Rooms, Double: €102–€168
Open: all year, Credit cards: MC, VS
Region: Nordrhein-Westfalen, Michelin Map: 543
www.karenbrown.com/hauselmer.html

To the north of Berchtesgaden, halfway to Salzburg, is a dear, family-run inn that affords a quiet respite from the crowds of Berchtesgaden and the Königssee. The inn sits across from the oldest existing marble mill in Germany (constructed in 1683) on the banks of the rushing River Almbach. While many people come during the day to enjoy the serenity of the setting and the wonderful lunches and afternoon cakes; in the evenings, the population shrinks to just the guests staying in the seven bedrooms and the attentive staff and family. Day guests enjoy a lovely, large dining room, while an intimate, four-table stube is reserved for residents. All the guestrooms overlook the front terrace and river and five have either a balcony or shared terrace. I especially liked number 24 with its own balcony. Rooms are simple and clean, with white duvets decking pine beds. Bathrooms are functional and small, but again spotlessly clean. After breakfast in the charming dining room or on the riverfront terrace you can cross the little pedestrian bridge to see the workings of the old mill, still churning away just up from the garden terrace, or take a walk on the hiking trails that beckon you into the woods. This was a reader recommendation, for which we are most grateful! *Directions:* From Berchtesgaden, drive towards Salzburg and just before Marktschellenberg watch for a sign pointing left to the Gasthof Zur Kugelmühle. The road ends at the mill.

GASTHOF ZUR KUGELMÜHLE
Owner: Pfnür-Anfang Family
Berchtesgaden
83487 Marktschellenberg, Germany
Tel: (08650) 461, Fax: (08650) 416
7 Rooms, Double: €60–€80
Open: Mar to Oct, Credit cards: none
Region: Bayern, Michelin Map: 546
www.karenbrown.com/kugelmuehle.html

Michael Gilowsky is especially proud that the Gasthof Zum Bären, a picture-perfect 15th-century inn has been in his family for five generations. The hotel is in the heart of Meersburg, an absolutely stunning little medieval town hugging the shore of Lake Constance. Upstairs, a treasure chest of bedrooms awaits: our room had a beautifully carved wooden ceiling, country-pine furniture, dainty print wallpaper, and lace curtains. Some rooms have old painted furniture and all have antique touches and pretty wallpapers. Every bedroom is equipped with telephone and color television as well as a snug shower or bathroom. Downstairs, the two cozy dining rooms are decorated with pewter plates and typical blue stoneware filling shelves above carved wooden furniture, fresh flowers, and comfy window benches with pretty print pillows. A wood parquet floor, low, beamed ceiling, and white tiled stove add to the pervading feeling of gemütlichkeit. Both dining rooms contain only large tables for six to eight persons, which encourages guests to share a table and good conversation. The gasthof has its own parking garage nearby. *Directions:* Located 170 km southeast of Stuttgart, 31 km southwest of Ravensburg. Follow the main street, the B33, through Meersburg. At the traffic light by the church, turn right when coming from the ferry or left from all other directions.

GASTHOF ZUM BÄREN
Owner: Michael Gilowsky
Marktplatz 11, 88709 Meersburg, Germany
Tel: (07532) 43220, Fax: (07532) 432244
17 Rooms, Double: €78–€104
3 single rooms: €46
Restaurant closed Mon
Open: Mar 1 to Nov 20, Credit cards: none
Region: Baden-Württemberg, Michelin Maps: 545, 546
www.karenbrown.com/gasthofzumbaren.html

The Hotel Weinstube Löwen, located in the heart of the pedestrian section of the fairy-tale-like walled town of Meersburg, sits just across the street from another of our favorite small inns, the Gasthof Zum Bären. Both adorable hotels are similar in ambiance, with dining rooms filled with charm and guestrooms that are simple, but very comfortable. The Hotel Löwen's appeal is immediate: you can't help being captivated by the wisteria-laden, deep-salmon-colored façade, green shutters, and steep gabled roof. You step inside to an attractive foyer where the gracious receptionist will probably be at the desk to greet you. The Hotelier, Sigfrid Fischer, is also exceptionally friendly, and although he speaks little English, his warmth of welcome crosses all language barriers. The romantic dining room with its low, beamed ceiling and cozy tables set with fresh flowers serves marvelous food, including many fresh fish specialties from adjacent Lake Constance. The modern guestrooms are simple, but very nice. Ask for one of the recently renovated bedrooms—these are especially attractive. The hotel also has apartments available off-site. Although in the pedestrian area, the hotel will give you an entry permit for the nearby public parking garage. *Directions:* Located 191 km southeast of Stuttgart, on Lake Constance. From the B31 turn off to the center of town. Past the Obertor, at the traffic light opposite the church, turn left to the hotel.

HOTEL WEINSTUBE LÖWEN
Manager: Sigfrid Fischer
Marktplatz 2, 88709 Meersburg, Germany
Tel: (07532) 43040, Fax: (07532) 430410
21 Rooms, Double: €80–€118
Restaurant closed Wed Nov to Apr
Open: all year, Credit cards: all major
Region: Baden-Württemberg, Michelin Maps: 545, 546
www.karenbrown.com/hotelweinstubelowen.html

If you are at all interested in porcelain, be sure to visit Meissen to see its fascinating porcelain museum. You can easily visit Meissen as a side trip from Dresden, but if you want to spend the night, the best choice is the Mercure Parkhotel Meissen. When you first see the hotel, you can't help smiling at its whimsical design. The two-story villa is a fantasy of fairy-tale turrets, fancy chimneys, and a steep roof punctuated by perky little gables. However, what makes this building so incredibly different is that the façade is totally covered with tiny, shiny tiles, many of them in intricate, brightly colored designs. Questioning what inspired this most unusual-looking 18th-century villa, I found the answer to be quite logical—the owner's son-in-law had a tile factory. The villa forms the heart of the hotel, housing the restaurant and a few of the bedrooms. Most of the guestrooms are in a newly built annex. These are all similar in decor, nicely furnished with a typical hotel look, and have large modern bathrooms. Request one of the rooms (such as 15) overlooking the river, which capture a romantic view of the castle and the cathedral spires. One of the nicest features of the hotel is that the villa sits directly on the Elbe. Behind the hotel there is a garden with a lawn that stretches down to the banks of the river. *Directions:* 18 km northwest of Dresden traveling the N6. The hotel is across the river from the castle.

MERCURE PARKHOTEL MEISSEN
Director: Peter Payr
Hafenstrasse 27-31, 01662 Meissen, Germany
Tel: (03521) 72250, Fax: (03521) 722904
97 Rooms, Double: €67–€97*
*Breakfast not included: €14
Open: all year, Credit cards: all major
Region: Sachsen, Michelin Map: 544
www.karenbrown.com/meissen.html

Set on Schützenstrasse, a pedestrian street that runs between Munich's main train station and Karlsplatz, the Hotel Excelsior occupies an enviable downtown location. Step into the hotel and leave the bustle of Munich behind you as you enter regional Bavaria with ornate ironwork, pastel friezes, and classic Bavarian decor, a style continued into the absolutely delightful breakfast room with its Alpine-hunting-lodge motif. The muted colors of the lobby are echoed in the bedrooms, which are all individually decorated in soft pastels and accompanied by top-of-the-line bathrooms. The bedrooms are soundproofed and include all the amenities of a mini-bar, hairdryer, phone, and cable TV. To ensure a quiet night's sleep on a summer evening, request an inside room that overlooks the central courtyard, or preferably a front room, where you can enjoy people watching on the pedestrian Schützenstrasse. The front rooms are quieter than those at the back for the back of the hotel overlooks the bustling Bayerstrasse with its traffic and streetcars. *Directions:* Schützenstrasse is located opposite the main entrance to the train station. If arriving by car, drive into the pedestrian-only zone and park outside the hotel (on your right) where the porter will assist you with your luggage. Your car will then be taken to the hotel's private garage just down the street.

HOTEL EXCELSIOR
Owner: Geisel Family
Schützenstrasse 11, 80335 Munich, Germany
Tel: (089) 551370, Fax: (089) 55137192
113 Rooms, Double: €150–€310*
*Breakfast not included: €16
Open: all year, Credit cards: all major
Region: Bayern, Michelin Map: 546
www.karenbrown.com/excelsior.html

The Hotel Königshof sits at the heart of Munich on the bustling Karlsplatz with its dancing fountains. This is only the square's official name—the locals always refer to it as the Stachus in honor of Foderl Stachus, who was held in such high regard that they named the square after him in 1730. The Königshof's unique location enables its guests to enjoy the history, entertainment, and business life of this lovely city, with the greatest convenience. It's one of those classic "Grand hotels" where everyone from the doorman to the maid who turns down your bed at night seems to take personal pride in making you feel welcome. The Königshof Restaurant is one of Munich's premier dining spots, not only for its simply wonderful view of the Stachus, but also for its classic French with, of course, a touch of German cuisine. The restaurant has been awarded a coveted Michelin star. The same magnificent view of the Stachus is offered from several of the top-of-the-line bedrooms and suites. The city noise is kept at bay with soundproofing and all of the rooms are air-conditioned. *Directions:* Karlsplatz is well-signposted on Munich's inner ring road. The hotel has an adjacent underground parking garage.

HOTEL KÖNIGSHOF
Owner: Geisel Family
Karlsplatz 25, 80335 Munich, Germany
Tel: (089) 551360, Fax: (089) 55136192
87 Rooms, Double: €270–€765*
*Breakfast not included: €19.50
Open: all year, Credit cards: all major
Region: Bayern, Michelin Map: 546
www.karenbrown.com/konigshof.html

The Torbräu, Munich's oldest hostelry, has been offering a warm welcome to guests since 1490. Its location is excellent: a short walk down the Tal from Marienplatz, in the heart of Munich at the historic Isartor (one of Munich's original main tower gates). The Kirchlechner family, owners for over one hundred years, are dedicated to ongoing improvements. Rooms range in size from snug singles, through spacious doubles, to two-room suites. I was charmed by room 501, a lovely corner room with a cozy sitting area that enjoys the morning sun. A new wing of rooms, located in what was once the servants' quarters, is banded by quiet side streets. The most expensive double rooms and suites have complimentary drinks and tea- and coffee-making facilities. All the rooms have modern bathrooms and air conditioning. Breakfast is served each morning in an especially attractive dining room with a balcony overlooking the street. At 11 am this room converts to a tea room, where a stunning selection of scrumptious pastries, fresh from the hotel's own bakery, is served. In summer the hotel's Italian restaurant, La Familia, overflows to outside seating. The cellar bar, La Cantinetta, is cozy and offers late-night snacks for those not yet on Germany time. *Directions:* Follow signs to "Zentrum" and then "Altstadtring." Look for the Isartor and the Torbräu is on the corner. From the airport take the S-Bahn No. S 8.

HOTEL TORBRÄU
Owners: Werner & Walter Kirchlechner
Director: Manfred Fritsch
Tal 41, 80331 Munich, Germany
Tel: (089) 242340, Fax: (089) 24234235
92 Rooms, Double: €175–€320
Open: all year, Credit cards: all major
Region: Bayern, Michelin Map: 546
www.karenbrown.com/hoteltorbrau.html

Situated in the little village of Handorf just outside the town of Münster, the Hof Zur Linde is as lovely inside and out as the brochure depicts. It is a complex of old farm buildings connected by courtyards and surrounded by grassy lawns and woodlands leading down to a river. At dinnertime you can choose from a selection of dining rooms. These are all actually adjoining, but each has been done in a totally different style so that you move from a light-pine-paneled room with gay red-gingham curtains where you dine in cozy booths to one with stucco walls and beams, a huge walk-in fireplace, flagstone floors, and hams hung from the ceiling. The main dining room is more formal with its tapestry-covered chairs and starched white linens. The menu is extensive, the food delicious, and the service friendly and efficient. Bedrooms are upstairs in the main building, in a lovely old farmhouse just a few steps away, or in one of the charming cottages located on the river's edge. You may find yourself sleeping in a bed that was made for British royalty or in a rustic pine bed beneath a curtained canopy. Summer mornings find Herr Löfken, the hotel owner, busy adjusting bicycles and providing maps for guests setting off to explore the area. *Directions:* Exit the A1 at Münster-Ost/Greven, and travel south towards Münster. After 15 km, at the first set of traffic lights, turn left to Handorf. The hotel is opposite the Shell station on the left.

ROMANTIK HOTEL HOF ZUR LINDE
Owner: Otto Löfken
Handorf, 48157 Münster, Germany
Tel: (0251) 32750, Fax: (0251) 328209
49 Rooms, Double: €127–€220
Open: all year, Credit cards: all major
Region: Nordrhein-Westfalen, Michelin Map: 543
www.karenbrown.com/romantikhotelhofzurlinde.html

The Hotel Schloss Wilkinghege is located just 6 kilometers from Münster (with regular bus service available to the city). Although considered a castle, the handsome red-brick building with red-tiled roof is really more reminiscent of a country estate. A pretty moat and lots of trees and gardens surround the castle, and it has an 18-hole golf course in the rear. The castle has changed hands many times and undergone several architectural alterations in the years since being built in 1719. Lubert Winnecken turned the property into a hotel and restaurant in 1955, meticulously preserving the style and feeling of this romantic home's former grandeur. The restaurant at Schloss Wilkinghege is renowned for the quality of it cuisine. Reservations are needed to dine in this atmospheric restaurant, which has been completely renovated, reflecting the authentic mood of the late Renaissance period. There are some guestrooms in the main house with lofty ceilings and fancy decor. Especially dramatic is one suite that resembles the style of 1759 with original furniture of the epoch that belonged to the commander General d'Armentier. There are also some apartments furnished in modern style in the annex. *Directions:* The Hotel Schloss Wilkinghege is not located in the heart of town, but just on the outskirts, signposted off road 54.

HOTEL SCHLOSS WILKINGHEGE
Owners: Lubert & Rembert Winnecken
Steinfurter Strasse 374
48159 Münster, Germany
Tel: (0251) 166270, Fax: (0251) 212898
35 Rooms, Double: €145–€305
Open: all year, Credit cards: all major
Relais & Chateaux
Region: Nordrhein-Westfalen, Michelin Map: 543
www.karenbrown.com/wilkinghege.html

From the moment you step through the front door of the Spielweg Romantik Hotel, you are surrounded by the warmth of a wonderful old farmhouse, lovingly converted into a small luxury hotel. To the left of the reception is a comfortable sitting area with chairs set around small tables for afternoon tea. To the right of the lobby is a series of dining rooms, each a masterpiece of country-cozy with antique paneling covering the walls and low ceilings, ceramic plates and pictures, hunting trophies, tiled stove, and pretty hanging lamps. All the dining rooms look like settings for Gourmet magazine. As the hotel has grown, the bedrooms have expanded from the original home to two additional wings. The rooms in the older part are smaller and more old-fashioned in decor, but very good value for the money. The rooms in the newer wings are larger, have more modern furnishings, and are more costly. For those traveling with children, there is an enormous playroom for your little ones with all kinds of toys to keep them happy on a rainy day. Connected to the hotel by an underground passage is an indoor swimming pool and just beyond, in the garden, you'll find an outdoor pool. At the end of the valley, with a backdrop of the lush Black Forest, the Spielweg is a wonderful base from which to hike and explore the region. *Directions:* 27 km south of Freiburg. Drive south on N3 and turn east at Bad Krozingen, traveling to Staufen and on to Münstertal.

SPIELWEG ROMANTIK HOTEL
Owner: Karl Josef Fuchs
Spielweg 61, 79244 Münstertal, Germany
Tel: (07636) 7090, Fax: (07636) 70966
42 Rooms, Double: €110–€269
Open: all year, Credit cards: all major
Region: Baden-Württemberg, Michelin Map: 545
www.karenbrown.com/spielwegromantikhotel.html

The Romantik Hotel am Josephsplatz has a prime location facing onto a small plaza (Josephsplatz) in the historic heart of Nürnberg, within easy walking distance of the many gorgeous churches and interesting sights of this colorful city. The hotel is made up of three quaint, 17th-century, narrow, five-story patrician houses that have been joined together to form the hotel. There is an old-fashioned, faded glamour to this family-owned and-managed hotel, where many antique knickknacks, old chests, spinning wheels, clocks, Oriental carpets, silk flowers, and fine oil paintings decorate the narrow hallways and public rooms. A bountiful buffet breakfast is served in a pretty dining room where the high ceiling, light blue/gray paneled walls, and large windows create a most inviting ambiance. An elevator leads up to the bedrooms, which are individual in size and decor, each having its own personality. Some have light-pine, modern furnishings, while others reflect a more traditional style. Arrangements of silk flowers and ribbons adorn many of the walls. The hotel has a rooftop sun terrace as well as a sauna, solarium, fitness room, and winter garden. *Directions:* Follow signs through the city walls to the historic center and then follow signs to the hotel.

ROMANTIK HOTEL AM JOSEPHSPLATZ
Owner: Reuter Family
Josephsplatz 30-32, 90403 Nürnberg, Germany
Tel: (0911) 214470, Fax: (0911) 21447200
36 rooms, Double: €106–€146
Open: all year, Credit cards: all major
Region: Bayern, Michelin Map: 546
www.karenbrown.com/josephsplatz.html

The Romantik Hotel Gasthaus Rottner is located on the outskirts of Nürnberg, about a 20-minute drive to its historic center. The hotel is divided among three buildings: one houses the reception and breakfast room, one the guestrooms, and one the restaurant. The reception and guestrooms are in contemporary, rust-colored stucco buildings with ultra-modern interiors. The compact bedrooms have a gray and white decor and modern built-in furnishings that create good use of the space. However, what makes the Romantik Hotel Gasthaus Rottner so special is its restaurant, which oozes charm. It is snuggled into a darling, very old timbered house with dormer windows peeking out of a steep tiled roof and windowboxes cascading bright-red geraniums. Inside you find a series of intimate dining rooms, each with antique decor, low-beamed ceilings, soft lighting, and fresh flowers. The food is excellent, featuring fine regional cuisine. On warm evenings guests frequently opt to eat in the delightful garden behind the hotel. For less formal dining, there is a sweet, traditional beer garden just across from the restaurant serving wonderful simple Franconian-style light meals. *Directions:* Located in the southwest part of Nürnberg. From A73, take the Gebersdorf/Grossreuth exit toward Grossreuth. At the second traffic light turn left into Alte Wallensteinstrasse and then immediately right onto Winterstrasse.

ROMANTIK HOTEL GASTHAUS ROTTNER
Owner: Rottner Family
Manager: Jürgen Baumgratz
Winterstrasse 15, 90431 Nürnberg, Germany
Tel: (911) 658480, Fax: (911) 65848203
37 rooms, Double: €140–€170
Closed: Dec 24 to Jan 6, Credit cards: all major
Region: Bayern, Michelin Map: 546
www.karenbrown.com/gasthausrottner.html

The Hotel Alte Post, which dates back to 1612, holds a prime position on the main square of Oberammergau, just up from the Heimat Museum. It is a charming three-story white-stucco building with a colorful painted façade and paned windows framed by green shutters. Just outside its entry gingham cloths deck tables set under pale-blue umbrellas. We visited on a gorgeous summer afternoon when all the outside tables were full but it wouldn't take much of a drop in temperature to tempt one inside into one of the many cozy restaurants and dining nooks where beautiful pewter accents are set against the backdrop of old paneled walls under heavy beamed ceilings—all with that wonderful patina of age. Incredibly, the inn is managed by the fifth generation of the Preisinger family, who extend a warm welcome and set a wonderful example to their gracious, helpful employees. The inn has 32 guestrooms, most of which are found in the original hotel. I especially liked number 44, a very pretty room overlooking the square with a sitting area whose sofa could convert to a third bed. There are six rooms located in a back annex off the hotel parking area that are termed family rooms (a few with kitchenettes) but, aside from the comfort of space, I found these not as charming as the reasonably priced standard rooms in the original house (Hauptgebaude). *Directions:* Located 19 km north of Garmisch. In Oberammergau, follow signs to the town center.

HOTEL ALTE POST
Innkeepers: Anton Preisinger Family
Dorfstrasse 19, 82487 Oberammergau, Germany
Tel: (08822) 9100, Fax: (08822) 910100
32 Rooms, Double: €60–€90
Open: mid-Dec to Nov, Credit cards: all major
Region: Bayern, Michelin Map: 546
www.karenbrown.com/altepostoberammergau.html

A hallway full of family antiques leads to a reception desk brightened by a bouquet of fresh flowers at the charming Gasthof Zur Rose, well located on a quiet street one block from the central square. Formerly a farmer's stable, the gasthof is almost 200 years old and has been in the Stückl family for many years—Renata is the third generation of her family to welcome guests here and is assisted by her husband, Ludwig, and her parents, Roswitha and Peter. All the family members are experts on local sights and history. Artistic touches are found throughout the Zur Rose, from colorful dried-flower arrangements and strategically placed paintings to pleasing combinations of fabrics. The two dining rooms are bright and cheerful, filled with pretty fabrics, rustic furniture, and green plants, and offer many Bavarian specialties. Some of the simple guestrooms have antique accent pieces. All the bedrooms have small shower cabinets. For longer rentals, the Stückl family offers three Bavarian houses with apartments for up to six persons. For warmth of welcome and super-caring hosts, the Gasthof Zur Rose is a real winner. *Directions:* 92 km southwest of Munich, 19 km north of Garmisch. In Oberammergau, follow signs to the Oberammergau House Tourist Office, which shows the exact location of Gasthof Zur Rose several streets away.

GASTHOF ZUR ROSE
Owners: Renata Stückl & Ludwig Frank
Dedlerstrasse 9
82487 Oberammergau, Germany
Tel: (08822) 4706, Fax: (08822) 6753
20 Rooms, Double: €58–€62
Restaurant closed Mon
Closed: end-Oct to mid-Dec, Credit cards: all major
Region: Bayern, Michelin Map: 546
www.karenbrown.com/gasthofzurrose.html

Most of the hotels in Oberammergau are irresistible outside, with intricately painted façades and windowboxes overflowing with brightly colored geraniums; but unfortunately, inside most of the cozy ambiance usually evaporates. An exception is the Hotel Turmwirt, where from the moment you enter, a rustic mood is established by the use of pine paneling, antique trunks, Oriental carpets, colorful draperies, and carefully selected fabrics on comfortable chairs. There are two dining rooms, both very attractive. Especially cozy is one with 200-year-old paneled ceiling and walls. In 1998 the restaurant was voted one of the 20 restaurants offering best value for money in Germany. The Glas family has owned and operated the Hotel Turmwirt for over 60 years. Georg Glas now manages the hotel, and the mouth-watering display of cakes and marvelous pastries are baked following his mother's traditional recipes. Some of the guestrooms are located in the original house, others in a newer wing, and all have been newly renovated. Bedrooms have built-in beds and modern, Danish-style chairs. The rooms with the best views are those in the new wing, with balconies looking out to the mountains, but I think that my favorite is number 11, a front-facing room, which has lovely, hand-painted, Bavarian-style furniture dating back to the turn of the last century. *Directions:* 92 km southwest of Munich, 19 km north of Garmisch. The hotel is in the center of town.

HOTEL TURMWIRT
Owner: Georg Glas
Ettaler Strasse 2
82483 Oberammergau, Germany
Tel: (08822) 92600, Fax: (08822) 1437
22 Rooms, Double: €88–€103
Closed: Mar, Credit cards: all major
Region: Bayern, Michelin Map: 546
www.karenbrown.com/hotelturmwirt.html

The Auf Schönburg is the perfect castle hotel. High atop a rocky bluff, the façade is a fairy-tale picture of towers and battlements reached by crossing a narrow, wooden bridge. Cobbles worn smooth by feet through the ages wind through the castle to the summit. The terrace view is superb, dropping steeply to the Rhine below. The bedrooms are shaped by the unusual castle buildings—tower rooms sit atop steep winding staircases and several rooms have balconies (one leads to a long drop). Through tiny lead-paned windows you catch glimpses of the Rhine or vineyards far below. While several rooms have views to the Rhine, you are assured a quieter night's sleep if you have a vineyard view. Be aware that, whichever room you select, you will hear the trains rushing along beside the river. Guestrooms do vary in size and are located down a maze of corridors and up and down winding turret squares. The most spectacular rooms are the beautiful, spacious rooms enjoying window seats, balconies, and river views; but even those more intimate in size have their own special appeal and some even have hidden rooms. The romance extends to the lovely dining rooms where you dine by candlelight. The Ritterstube restaurant has lovely views to the vineyards while the newly renovated dining room has medieval charm. *Directions:* Oberwesel is on the B9, 18 km northwest of Bingen. At the church turn up the hill to the castle.

AUF SCHÖNBURG
Owners: Barbara & Wolfgang Hüttl
55430 Oberwesel, Germany
Tel: (06744) 93930, Fax: (06744) 1613
22 Rooms, Double: €150–€210
Restaurant closed Mon
Closed: Jan and Feb, Credit cards: MC, VS
Region: Rheinland-Pfalz, Michelin Map: 543
www.karenbrown.com/aufschonburg.html

A picturesque drive past green meadows and flower-bedecked chalets leads to the Gasthof Hirschen, located about 6 kilometers beyond Wolfach in the tiny hamlet of Oberwolfach-Walke. Colorful geraniums adorn the Hirschen's many windowboxes and a small stream flows by across the street. This inn is one of the oldest in the Black Forest, dating from 1609. Its attractive restaurant encompasses a series of cozy rooms, each decked out in an inviting, old-fashioned style. The menu is enticing, offering a delicious variety of local dishes. Follow the Oriental rug runners up the old staircase to a small lobby area, which displays an antique clock and a cabinet filled with antique dolls. There are 17 guestrooms in the main building, all with private baths. These bedrooms are not overly large, but are pleasantly furnished. My favorite rooms are found in the lovely new wing of more modern rooms, many of which have balconies overlooking the garden. You can enjoy sunny days on the flower-filled terrace or in the tranquil garden, the only sounds the birds in surrounding trees. In winter cross-country skiing is a popular sport in this region of forests and rolling hills. The quiet rural location and warm welcome of the Junghanns family make it easy to see why the Gasthof Hirschen is a popular country inn for travelers "in the know." *Directions:* The town is located 6 km north of Wolfach, 40 km northeast of Freiburg.

GASTHOF HIRSCHEN
Owner: Junghanns Family
Schwarzwaldstrasse 2
77709 Oberwolfach-Walke, Germany
Tel: (07834) 8370, Fax: (07834) 6775
38 Rooms, Double: €68–€94
Closed: Jan 6 to 31, Credit cards: all major
Region: Baden-Württemberg, Michelin Map: 545
www.karenbrown.com/gasthofhirschen.html

The Hotel Schwan, with its gray-tile roof and timbered façade, has been around since 1628 when it was a travelers' inn along the River Rhine. Today both the road and the river in front of the hotel are a lot busier than in the days of carriages and river barges. Fortunately, the hotel is saved from being overwhelmed by the busy Rhineside road by a broad band of garden that separates it from the highway. The Wenckstern family has owned and managed the inn for many generations. They produce their own wine, which you can sample with dinner in the dignified dining room or sip on the outdoor terrace while watching the river. The Schwan has grown to a substantial hotel, and the joy of staying here is that you can obtain a Rhine-facing room. All the bedrooms are decorated in a rather unmemorable pastel-modern decor. Quite the nicest room is the tower room whose seven little windows command lovely river views. A major renovation project was underway when we last visited and we will be eager to share the improvements with you. The Hotel Schwan is only about an hour's drive from the Frankfurt airport, a convenient distance after a tiring transatlantic flight. Its location on the Rheingau Riesling Road makes it an ideal base for touring the region. *Directions:* 55 km west of Frankfurt, 21 km west of Wiesbaden. Take the A66 from Wiesbaden towards Rüdesheim, then the B42 towards Rüdesheim. Get off at the second exit marked Oestrich.

HOTEL SCHWAN
Owners: Wenckstern Family & Franz Winkel
Rheinallee 5-7
65375 Oestrich-Winkel, Germany
Tel: (06723) 8090, Fax: (06723) 7820
42 Rooms, Double: €115–€160
Open: all year, Credit cards: all major
Region: Hessen, Michelin Map: 543
www.karenbrown.com/schwan.html

As the name implies, this charming thatched roadside inn dating back to 1519 has witnessed a lot of history, but, remarkably, it is still in the hands of the same family. In a region that has fluctuated between German and Danish domination, the hotel combines both influences. Under a thick thatched roof, the main building of the Historicher Krug is especially lovely with its beamed walls, rich wainscoting, and handsome antiques. The Bauernstube restaurant is excellent and extremely intimate, and the more formal gourmet restaurant is quite elegant. In the mornings the breakfast room seems to be the gathering spot for all the locals as well as hotel guests—and it is no wonder, for breakfast is a real feast. Guestrooms are found in newly constructed stucco buildings removed from the street noise. I was able to see a "standard" room in the building closest to the creek, and it was charming, with down-decked beds overlooking the tranquil rushing water. In another building just up from the creek, guestrooms also open onto the back gardens and not the road. Tucked just below the road is a series of suites housed in a building that overlooks a lovely stretch of lawn. The rooms are buffered from the highway noise by double doors. Dinner is a gourmet treat. *Directions:* Take A7 north from Hamburg to Flensburg, exit at Tarp, go left towards Ostsee and Sörup. At the roundabout head for Flensburg for 4 km. The hotel is on the left.

ROMANTIK HOTEL HISTORISCHER KRUG
Owner: Lenka Hansen-Mörck
Am Graze Platz 1, 24988 Oeversee, Germany
Tel: (046) 309400, Fax: (046) 30780
40 Rooms, Double: €102–€168
Open: all year, Credit cards: all major
Region: Schleswig-Holstein, Michelin Map: 541
www.karenbrown.com/historischerkrug.html

At the base of Falkenstein Mountain, at the edge of a forest, the Berghotel Schlossanger Alp is nestled in a high Alpine meadow. Muck and Toni Schlachter (who have been offering a traditional Bavarian welcome for over 30 years) have been joined here by daughter, Barbara, and her husband, Bernhard Ebert. Together they made great improvements, adding 16 suites in addition to an incredible indoor fitness center complete with pool, saunas, and massage rooms. Guestrooms are as fresh and pretty as can be, with pine furniture, lovely fabrics that color-coordinate with wallpaper trim, and beautiful large bathrooms and kitchenettes. Every detail exudes quality. Rooms are individual in theme and I especially liked the Burgblick Suite, which enjoys wonderful views and a very cozy ambiance. The dining room and lounges display an old-fashioned, lived-in comfort. Barbara and Bernhard welcome families wholeheartedly and many of the suites have an extra bedroom for children. You will be captivated by the glorious setting at the edge of the pines overlooking the rolling green meadow and distant mountain peaks. The setting is superb, but it is the genuine warmth of hospitality that will win your heart. *Directions:* Turn for Pfronten from the Füssen/Kempten road and from the roundabout take the first left towards Falkensein/Schlossanger Alp. Do not go into Pfronten.

BERGHOTEL SCHLOSSANGER ALP
Owners: Barbara & Bernhard Ebert
Am Schlossanger 1, 87459 Pfronten, Germany
Tel: (08363) 914550, Fax: (08363) 91455555
30 Rooms, Double: €130–€220
Open: all year, Credit cards: all major
Region: Bayern, Michelin Maps: 545, 546
www.karenbrown.com/berghotelschlossangeralp.html

King Ludwig II looked out of his bedroom window at Neuschwanstein to the ruins of Falkenstein Castle, crowning a distant mountaintop. He was captivated by the romantic setting and decided he must build his fourth, and most fanciful, castle there. Plans were drawn up and workmen laid a narrow road with hairpin curves through the forest to the rocky precipice, but before construction could begin, Ludwig died. The Burghotel Falkenstein now occupies this stunning site. It was built by the Schlachter family for son Toni (a talented chef) and his family. The core of the Burghotel dates to 1896 and while the theme is decidedly old-world, the comfort and appointments reflect the new construction. I adored the lovely dining room and longed to dine on a warm summer evening on the narrow terrace which overhangs a sheer precipice dropping to the Austrian-German border post far below. Toni not only demonstrates a flair in the kitchen but also an artistry in the decor of the bedrooms. Like Ludwig, he is redecorating rooms, one by one, with quite fanciful themes. Guestrooms are dramatically individual so be sure to discuss the decor to determine the room of your preference. A small fitness room offers a sauna, solarium, and laundry room. *Directions:* Follow directions as given for sister hotel, the Berghotel Schlossanger Alp. A narrow, winding road on the last stretch delivers you to the top of the hill.

BURGHOTEL FALKENSTEIN
Owners: Hertha & Toni Schlachter
Falkenstein 1, Obermeilingen
87459 Pfronten, Germany
Tel: (08363) 914540, Fax: (08363) 9145444
10 Rooms, Double: €124–€180
Open: all year, Credit cards: all major
Region: Bayern, Michelin Maps: 545, 546
www.karenbrown.com/burghotelfalkenstein.html

The heart of Pirna (a pedestrian-only zone) is a charming medieval town with cobbled streets, colorful houses, and historic buildings—plus, a superb location. You can stay in Pirna and take the train into Dresden for a day of sightseeing or take a boat to explore one of our favorite areas in East Germany, the fascinating Swiss Saxony (Sächsische Schweiz). The Romantik Hotel Deutsches Haus, adjacent to the beautiful St. Marien church, occupies three Renaissance houses, one painted pink, another off-white, and the other yellow. Over the doorway is a crest of the famous stone mason, Wolf Blechschmidt, who lived in the house in the 16th century, and not only designed his own home, but was also responsible for the architectural design of the church across the street and many houses in town. Not a pretentious hotel, the Deutsches Haus is a homey place to stay with great hospitality, historic ambiance, wonderful restaurant, inviting garden courtyard, wellness center, and nice accommodations (some guestrooms are decorated with Biedermeier furnishings). The owner, Herr Riedel, (born here when his parents had a restaurant with a few rooms) took possession of the property which was derelict after the Russian occupation. With great devotion to its rich heritage, he lovingly transformed it into a first-class hotel. *Directions:* On the edge of the pedestrian-only zone, next to St. Marien church. Access is tricky, so ask for detailed instructions.

ROMANTIK HOTEL DEUTSCHES HAUS　　*New*
Owner: Herr Riedel
Niedere Burgstraße 1, 01796 Pirna, Germany
Tel: (03501) 46880, Fax: (03501) 468820
40 Rooms, Double: €92–€98
Open: all year, Credit cards: all major
Region: Sachsen, Michelin Map: 544
www.karenbrown.com/deutschhaus.html

No sightseeing excursion to the Berlin area would be complete without a visit to the nearby town of Potsdam to see the sensational palaces and gardens of Sanssouci and Schloss Cecilienhof. Most tourists linger along the paths of the Schloss Cecilienhof, never realizing that if they had planned ahead, they could have spent the night there. This historic manor house, the very place where Truman, Churchill, and Stalin signed the Potsdam Agreement in 1945, now takes overnight guests. The setting of this large timbered, English country house-style hotel is magnificent—not one, but two lakes are on the property plus beautiful forests laced with walking paths. Only a part of the castle is operated as a hotel—the remainder and the surrounding park are open to the public. The bedrooms have a very nice, traditional decor. Room 49 is an especially attractive larger room. There is also an old-fashioned bridal suite (room 33) with heavy wooden furniture and a canopied, king-size bed. The views to the park and gardens make all the bedrooms most appealing. The paneled dining room is very attractive, especially in the evening when the cozy room glows from the candles on each table. On warm days, lunch is served on a pretty garden terrace. This is a serene, pleasant hotel that offers a wonderful alternative to staying in nearby Berlin. *Directions:* 24 km southwest of Berlin. Follow signs for Potsdam Zentrum, then street signs to Cecilienhof.

SCHLOSSHOTEL CECILIENHOF
Manager: Christina Aue
Neuer Garten, 14469 Potsdam, Germany
Tel: (0331) 37050, Fax: (0331) 292498
41 Rooms, Double: €150–€610*
*Breakfast not included: €10, Service: 10%
Open: all year, Credit cards: all major
Region: Brandenburg, Michelin Map: 542
www.karenbrown.com/cecilienhof.html

Romantik Hotel Am Brühl is an exceptional inn located in one of Germany's picture-perfect, fairy-tale villages. The Russians confiscated the Schmidts' house after World War II; but after reunification, Reinhard Schmidt reclaimed the property. He and his talented wife, Ursula, converted the original 1920s stucco home into a delightful hotel, and the connecting warehouse into an outstanding restaurant that absolutely oozes cozy charm. When the adjacent 350-year-old timbered farmhouse became available, the Schmidts bought it and expanded their flourishing business. The original house, the warehouse, and the old farm enclose an enchanting courtyard where a timbered ivy-covered wall, colorful flower gardens, and a cobblestoned floor create a romantic ambiance. Inside you enter into a spacious, uncluttered room that exudes a mellow glow. Natural light streams through arched windows, gently highlighting walls of exposed honey-toned stone. Beautifully upholstered, light-wood furniture, soft lighting, a few antiques, and large bouquets of fresh flowers complete the picture of quiet luxury. This light, airy ambiance continues in the guestrooms, each having been lovingly decorated by Frau Schmidt. My favorite guestrooms are the non-smoking ones in the timbered farmhouse, which have more of an informal, country flair. *Directions:* 71 km southwest of Magdeburg. Take N81 southwest to Halberstadt and then the 79 to Quedlinburg.

ROMANTIK HOTEL AM BRÜHL
Owners: Ursula & Reinhard Schmidt
Billungstrasse 11
06484 Quedlinburg, Germany
Tel: (03946) 96180, Fax: (03946) 9618246
48 Rooms, Double: €100–€145
Open: all year, Credit cards: all major
Region: Sachsen-Anhalt, Michelin Map: 542
www.karenbrown.com/hotelambruehl.html

If you are using Hamburg airport and have a car, the Jagdhaus Waldfrieden is a splendid choice for your first or last night in Germany. Although the hotel is set peacefully in a lovely wooded park, the highway is conveniently close. During his career as the manager of large hotels, Siegmund Baierle formulated his plans for a small hotel with a first-rate restaurant—the result is the delightful Jagdhaus Waldfrieden. The latest renovation has added a glass-enclosed, greenhouse-style restaurant where you dine elegantly, yet feel as if you are in the garden. Just beyond the intimate bar there is a second high-ceilinged dining room with gleaming polished wood, Oriental carpets, and groupings of tables laid with crisp white linen before a roaring log fire. Dinner is an event where guests linger at their tables after a splendid meal before retiring for a contented night's sleep. A few bedrooms are found in the main building, with the remainder across the courtyard in what were once the stables. All the rooms have been lovingly decorated with a traditional look of comfortable sophistication achieved through the use of beautiful, color-coordinated fabrics and fine furniture. My favorite, room 45, is especially fantastic—a corner room on the ground floor of the stables with French doors leading out to the garden and, just beyond, to the forest. *Directions:* Located 23 km north of Hamburg traveling the N4.

ROMANTIK HOTEL JAGDHAUS WALDFRIEDEN
Owner: Siegmund Baierle
Kieler Strasse B4, 25451 Quickborn, Germany
Tel: (04106) 61020, Fax: (04106) 69196
25 Rooms, Double: €138–€155
Restaurant closed Mon lunch
Open: all year, Credit cards: all major
Region: Schleswig-Holstein, Michelin Map: 541
www.karenbrown.com/jagdhaus.html

Hotel der Seehof is the "sister" hotel of the Schlosshotel Rheinsberg, just a few steps up the street. Both are owned by Titus-Rex Gièse who opened them in 2003. If you prefer an elegant décor, the Schlosshotel would be the better choice. If a more rustic, casual flair appeals to you, the Hotel der Seehof is equally attractive in its own way. The location is excellent: half a block up from the wharf where the ferryboats ply the lake, very near to the charming village green, and close to the famous Rheinsberg—a dramatic castle that sits on the edge of the lake and is surrounded by a splendid park. The exterior of the Hotel der Seehof is exceptionally pretty—a two-story pastel blue house with casement windows trimmed in white, dark green shutters, gabled red-tile roof, and a lacy tree in front shading small tables and chairs. As you enter the hotel, there is a combination bar and restaurant to your left that has a smart, modern, uncluttered look with black chairs, light wood bar, and terracotta floor. The room wraps a corner and opens to a charming cobblestone courtyard where guests dine in a garden setting when the weather is warm. For private parties there is a romantic dining room set in the wine cellar. This is a small hotel with only twelve guestrooms, including one particularly nice suite that is definitely worth the extra cost—a sunny corner room decorated in cheerful blues and reds. *Directions:* In the center of Rheinsberg, a half block from the boat dock.

HOTEL DER SEEHOF   **New**
Owner: Titus-Rex Gièse
Seestrasse 18, 86831 Rheinsberg, Germany
Tel: (033931) 4030, Fax: (033931) 40399
12 Rooms, Double: €110–€125
Open: all year, Credit cards: MC,VS
Region: Sachsen, Michelin Map: 542
www.karenbrown.com/hotelseehof.html

The Schlosshotel Rheinsberg is located north of Berlin in the idyllic Müritz National Park, a splendid, heavily forested region dotted with lakes. Most of the small towns in the area are nice, but not outstanding. However, Rheinsberg is the exception—it is right on the lake with pretty painted houses facing the village green, a dock where you can hop on a boat to explore the lake, and a stunning castle. For many years this cute town was lacking in good accommodations, but that changed instantly when Titus-Rex Gièse purchased two bankrupt hotels in the center of town, renovated them with excellent taste and top-notch quality, and opened both in 2003 as beautiful small hotels. Schlosshotel Rheinsberg is the more lavish in terms of decoration. Sitting on a corner, the pastel yellow building with soft blue-gray trim and red-tile roof is instantly appealing. Inside, the most dramatic room is the large, lavish restaurant with peach-colored walls with white trim, gleaming hardwood floors, a large chandelier, and, highlighted in the middle of the room, a white grand piano. Guests can also dine in another pleasing restaurant that shares the same room as a stunning bar. The guestrooms are spacious and very attractive with traditional style décor and include all the amenities of a fine hotel. The hotel wraps around a central garden courtyard, an inviting area with tables and chairs shaded by umbrellas. *Directions:* In the center of Rheinsberg, one block from the boat dock.

SCHLOSSHOTEL RHEINSBERG   New
Owner: Titus-Rex Gièse
Seestrasse 13, 86831 Rheinsberg, Germany
Tel: (033931) 39059, Fax: (033931) 39063
31 Rooms, Double: €110–€125
Closed: Jan & Feb, Credit cards: MC,VS
Region: Sachsen, Michelin Map: 542
www.karenbrown.com/hotelrheinsberg.html

The Burg Hotel is a winning combination: a lovely hotel with an awesome view in a "must-visit" town. The Burg Hotel peers over Rothenburg's ramparts to a sky-wide vista of the meandering River Tauber and a cluster of timber-framed cottages in a wooded valley. Enjoy this lovely view from the sunny breakfast room. Breakfast is the only meal served but this is not a problem as there are a great many restaurants within easy strolling distance. Guests can relax in the attractive little parlor with its 150-year-old mini-grand piano and lovely grandfather clock. The ground-floor Constantine Suite has a piano in the sitting room, a bedroom, and doors opening to the battlement terrace, which leads to one of the ancient watchtowers along the town's walls. Whether bedrooms face out to "the view" or to the monastery garden towards town, all are absolutely delightful and stylishly decorated by Gabriele Berger. Gabriele grew up at the nearby Markusturm Hotel and being a gracious hôtelier is certainly in her blood. Just steps up the street, the hotel also offers a superb suite—a fabulous value for a family or group. Gabriele has converted the 700-year old dungeons under the hotel into a conference room and soon-to-be spa and wellness area. *Directions:* Rothenburg is located off the A7 between Würzburg and Feuchtwangen. Pass through the Galgen Gate and continue into the old town, or pass under the Klingen Gate and turn right after the church.

BURG HOTEL
Owner: Gabriele Berger-Klatte
Klostergasse 1–3, 91541 Rothenburg, Germany
Tel: (09861) 94890, Fax: (09861) 948940
15 Rooms, Double: €110–€190
Open: all year, Credit cards: all major
Region: Bayern, Michelin Map: 545
www.karenbrown.com/burghotel.html

The Hotel Eisenhut is Rothenburg's most deluxe hotel but with rooms very competitively priced when compared to other hotels in this "must-visit" town. The promise of a special experience is created as you walk into the spacious reception hall which has a hearty, German-castle look; with beamed ceiling, Oriental carpets, massive, wrought-iron chandeliers, weaponry, large oil paintings, and a sweeping wooden staircase. Beyond the stately entrance there are comfortable lounges and several dining rooms opening onto a garden terrace, a wonderful retreat to escape the throng of daytime visitors. The high-ceilinged breakfast room, once a courtyard, is full of lovely, country-style tables and chairs. Throughout the hotel there is a fascinating collection of large, mural-like oil paintings depicting scenes of the Thirty Years' War. Because the Eisenhut was created out of four 15th- to 16th-century patrician mansions, the guestrooms are intriguingly tucked along a maze of corridors. While bedrooms at the front of the hotel are larger, we preferred the smaller back rooms with their peaceful countryside views. The hotel has not changed hands since established four generations ago by the Eisenhut family. Hans J. Pirner, the great grandson of the founder Georg Andreas Eisenhut, continues the tradition. *Directions:* Rothenburg is located off the A7 between Würzburg and Feuchtwangen. The Eisenhut is located in the heart of the old town.

HOTEL EISENHUT
Owner: Dr. Hans J. Pirner
Herrngasse 3–7, 91541 Rothenburg, Germany
Tel: (09861) 7050, Fax: (09861) 70545
79 Rooms, Double: €144–€340*
*Breakfast not included: €15
Closed: Jan 3 to Mar 1, Credit cards: all major
Region: Bayern, Michelin Map: 545
www.karenbrown.com/hoteleisenhut.html

The Gasthof Hotel Kloster-Stüble, dating from 1300, is a perfect little inn, combining reasonable prices with history, charm, and a good location. Just two blocks from the central market square, the Kloster-Stüble is tucked away on a quiet side street behind an old church and has pretty views of the surrounding countryside from many bedroom windows. The comfortable bedrooms, furnished in beautiful, country-pine reproductions, are mostly snug in size, though a couple are larger. A large apartment, set under the eaves, is perfect for families or longer stays. Downstairs, the dining room and stube are cozily rustic. Murals depicting life in days gone by decorate the stube walls and in the evenings regulars gather at the Stammtisch, a special table reserved only for those who come every day. In the adjoining dining room pretty, rose-colored walls and tablecloths set a romantic tone. Tables dressed with gleaming silver, china, and glassware, are topped with fresh flowers. Jutta Hammel, who speaks excellent English, is your energetic young hostess and her husband, Rudolf, is the chef. Enjoy a typical Franconian meal before setting out to join the nightwatchman on his nightly tour of the town. *Directions:* Rothenburg is off the A7 between Würzburg and Feuchtwangen. The hotel is inside the walls—drive through Galgen Gate and pass the next gate, Weisser Turm, to the market square. Turn right at the square and left by the church to the inn.

GASTHOF HOTEL KLOSTER-STÜBLE
Owners: Jutta & Rudolf Hammel
Heringsbronnengassechen 5
91541 Rothenburg, Germany
Tel: (09861) 6774, Fax: (09861) 6474
21 Rooms, Double: €76–€126
Open: all year, Credit cards: MC, VS
Region: Bayern, Michelin Map: 545
www.karenbrown.com/gasthofhotelklosterstuble.html

Rothenburg, a fairy-tale medieval town completely enclosed by ramparts, walls, and turrets, is a popular daytime destination; but don't come just for the day. Plan to overnight here so that you can enjoy the town's cobblestone streets and timbered façades after the throngs have departed. The Markusturm, built in 1264 as a tollhouse, commands one of the town's prime locations on a main street, just a block or two from the main square and Rothenburg's famous clock. Your gracious hosts, Stephan and Lilo, are the fourth generation of the Berger family to run the Markusturm, which has been a hotel since 1488. The charming Lilo Berger personally decorates all of the rooms, and without exception, they show her talent and loving touch: some are delightfully old-fashioned and furnished with antiques, while others have bleached pine furniture and a fresh, very pretty, pastel decor. Stephan, an excellent chef, is in charge of the restaurant—be sure to try his delicious wine soup and sample his wonderful, home-made beer! *Directions:* Rothenburg is located off the A7 between Würzburg and Feuchtwangen. Go through the Galgen Gate, straight along Galgengasse, and immediately after the next tower turn left onto Milchmarkt, then at the end of the road turn left. Unload your luggage at the left side in front of the hotel.

ROMANTIK HOTEL MARKUSTURM
Owners: Lilo & Stephan Berger
Rodergasse 1, 91541 Rothenburg, Germany
Tel: (09861) 94280, Fax: (09861) 9428113
25 Rooms, Double: €125–€190
Open: all year, Credit cards: all major
Region: Bayern, Michelin Map: 545
www.karenbrown.com/romantikhotelmarkusturm.html

This is it—Sleeping Beauty's castle where, deep within the "enchanted" Reinhard forest, Jacob and Wilhelm Grimm set their famous fairy tale. Dating back to 1334, the once-proud fortress is now largely a romantic ruin but, fortunately, part of the castle has been restored as a hotel. The romance of staying in Sleeping Beauty's castle cannot be denied, but be aware that it has a very isolated location. You must also realize that this is not Walt Disney's Sleeping Beauty's castle—he chose the ethereal towers and turrets of Neuschwanstein Castle in Bavaria as his model. Tables in the dining room are assigned by management: the only way to ensure a lovely countryside view is to request a window table as you check in. Traditional bedrooms are found in a new wing. A walk through the ruined castle brings you to the tower, where you find four more romantic bedrooms up the broad spiral staircase. These are the hotel's most expensive rooms with lots of charm and sparkling modern bathrooms. In honor of the Brothers Grimm and their world-famous tales, the German Tourist Office has outlined a fairy-tale route, the Deutsche Marchen Strasse, signposted by a smiling good fairy and accompanied by a picture map. The Dornröschenschloss Sababurg is included on this routing and, as a consequence, is a popular tourist attraction. *Directions:* 23 km north of Kassel. From Kassel take the N7 and then the N83 to Hofgeismar. Travel northeast to Sababurg.

 P ᵞ¶

DORNRÖSCHENSCHLOSS SABABURG
Owners: Sabine, Karl & Gúnther Koseck
34369 Sababurg, Germany
Tel: (05671) 8080, Fax: (05671) 808200
17 Rooms, Double: €150–€210
Closed: Jan, Credit cards: all major
Region: Hessen, Michelin Map: 541
www.karenbrown.com/sababurg.html

Just to the north of Saint Goar, the Hotel Landsknecht has an enchanting location on the bank of the River Rhine, just up from the famous Lorelei. And just as the siren mesmerized sailors and drew them to her rocks, the stenciled façade of the Landsknecht will draw you to its door. There are only 15 guestrooms, most of them overlooking the river traffic, even if only from a side window. Of the top-floor rooms a special favorite is number 8, a small and intimate bedroom with arched windows framing the river. Down one floor, number 5 is definitely the most dramatic—this is an end room that juts out, affording views through windows on three sides of the constant stream of barges. On the floor below the restaurant all the guestrooms are identical, with attractive arched windows at the same level as the river, giving the impression of being on board a ship. On the entry level you find a charming restaurant decorated in pines, which has earned widespread recognition, and next to it a larger, more informal restaurant opening onto a terrace with a spectacular view of the river. Just off the entry, the Vinothek is a room set with one large oval table nestled into the edge of a bay window where you can taste and purchase wine and order food off the restaurant menu. This is a definitely a busy tourist hotel near the (somewhat noisy) train tracks. *Directions:* From Saint Goar, travel north 3 km towards Koblenz and the hotel is on the right after the bridge.

HOTEL LANDSKNECHT
Owner: Nickenig Family
An der Rheinuferstrasse
56329 Saint Goar, Germany
Tel: (06741) 2011, Fax: (06741) 7499
15 Rooms, Double: €80–€160
Open: all year, Credit cards: all major
Region: Rheinland-Pfalz, Michelin Map: 543
www.karenbrown.com/hotellandsknecht.html

The Romantik Hotel Josthof is located less than an hour's drive south of Hamburg in a lovely, peaceful region where spacious fields are dotted with handsome old thatched-roofed farmhouses. These large buildings are often constructed using exposed red brick between the wooden framework, instead of the more commonplace stucco and half-timber combination. This unusual, and very attractive, architectural style is typified by the Romantik Hotel Josthof. Happily, the interior is as charming as the exterior. The first floor houses a gourmet restaurant which is well-known and frequented by diners from far and wide. Decorated in typical German-country style, the several dining rooms of the restaurant are all very cozy; each with its own personality. Ceilings are laced with massive beams and candlelight reflects off mellow and paneled walls. Beautiful, tiled ceramic ovens and cheerful fireplaces warm the rooms on cold evenings. Antiques abound—grandfather clocks, cradles, pewter plates, copper pans—all enhancing the old-fashioned ambiance. Upstairs and in an adjacent building, reflecting the same style of architecture, there are 16 rooms available for overnight guests. These bedrooms, although not decorated with antiques, are modern and pretty and each has a private bathroom. *Directions:* From Hamburg take the A7 south to exit 40 and then travel a few miles east to Salzhausen.

ROMANTIK HOTEL JOSTHOF
Owners: Martina & Jörg Hansen
Am Lindenberg 1, 21376 Salzhausen, Germany
Tel: (04172) 90980, Fax: (04172) 6225
16 Rooms, Double: €100–€129
Restaurant open daily in summer
Open: all year, Credit cards: all major
Region: Niedersachsen, Michelin Map: 541
www.karenbrown.com/josthof.html

In the Black Forest, on a hillside in the town of Schluchsee, stands a delightful, modern hotel. Constructed in 1969 with a new wing added in 1984, Heger's Parkhotel Flora is beautiful in its decor and its views down to the Schluchsee. Each room is pleasant, with modern furniture, built-in headboards, and good lights for reading. Each also has a modern, tiled bathroom. Herr Heger has ambitious plans to add four luxurious new suites and convert the pool area to a very sophisticated facility. Some of the bedrooms overlook the lake: views can be enjoyed from either a private balcony or terrace. The hallways are beamed, spacious, and airy, with floor-to-ceiling windows. Public rooms are attractive, with colorful prints on the walls, wrought-iron fixtures, plants, and pink and green fabrics. Herr Heger is frequently found in the lobby in chef's attire greeting guests and is as eager to make you comfortable as he is to please and tempt your palate. The St. Georgstube and the café-terrace restaurant are delightful—it is especially romantic to eat outside when the weather permits. The entry hall with its open fireplace is a cozy place to settle in inclement weather. In warm summer weather the Schluchsee comes alive with the sails of gaily colored sailing boats and windsurfers. *Directions:* From Freiburg take the B31 southeast to Hinterzarten. Continue for a few kilometers to the B500 towards Lenzkirch and go southeast on the B500 to Schluchsee.

HEGER'S PARKHOTEL FLORA
Owner: Hugo Heger
Sonnhalde 22, 79857 Schluchsee, Germany
Tel: (07656) 97420, Fax: (07656) 1433
36 Rooms, Double: €115–€225
Open: all year, Credit cards: all major
Region: Baden-Württemberg, Michelin Map: 545
www.karenbrown.com/hegersparkhotelflora.html

The Alpenhotel Zechmeisterlehen is the most delightful resort situated in a picturesque Alpine meadow, superbly convenient for Berchtesgaden and the Königssee, but wonderfully removed from the bustle and crowds. Chock-full of amenities (indoor and outdoor pools, health spa, children's playroom, conference rooms, several dining rooms), the hotel is popular with individuals as well as groups. Heidi and Siefried Angerer have maintained an Alpine ambiance, with lots of pine paneling and wooden balconies draped in summer with a profusion of red geraniums, and have embellished the interior decor with lots of knickknacks and artificial flowers. Every bedroom has a view across a vast meadow dotted with picture-postcard chalets to distant towering mountains. Rooms come in all shapes and sizes, including a small double, a spacious junior suite with a low partition dividing the bedroom from the sitting area, non-smoking rooms, and an apartment with separate sitting room and a bedroom for the children. This hotel has them all, and several other types as well. There is a lot to explore locally and if you are drawn to beautiful cities, go to Salzburg, just a 30-minute drive away. *Directions:* From Munich take the A8, exit at Bad Reichenhall, and follow signs for Berchtesgaden. Before the town turn right towards Ramsau, Kö, and Königssee. After 300 meters turn left towards Schönau am Königssee, cross the river, and take the first left to the hotel.

ALPENHOTEL ZECHMEISTERLEHEN
Owners: Heidi & Siefried Angerer
Wahlstrasse 35
83471 Schönau am Königssee, Germany
Tel: (08652) 9450, Fax: (08652) 945299
42 Rooms, Double: €110–€208
Restaurant closed for lunch & Sun dinner
Open: Jan 1 to Nov 6, Credit cards: all major
Region: Bayern, Michelin Map: 546
www.karenbrown.com/zechmeisterlehen.html

The friendly Heim family has been receiving guests into their home for over 45 years and Bettina Willer-Heim continues in the family tradition of offering guests a warm welcome. Many of the guests who came as children now return with their children and grandchildren. It is easy to see why the Pension Heim is such a success: the entire family is warm and genuine and the house spotless and homey. Cheerful houseplants brighten all the rooms and hallways and a rustic feeling pervades the breakfast room. Upstairs, the very comfortable bedrooms are fitted out in light oak, with each room accompanied by a snug shower room. Ask for a room with a balcony and view to the distant towering mountains—you may even catch a glimpse of the famous Zugspitze on a clear day. For those who want extra space there are two commodious suites with large living room and separate bedroom. A delicious breakfast sets you up for a day of exploring the area. It's an ideal base for visiting Ludwig's famous castles Linderhof and Neuschwanstein. The rolling hills and pastures of this region make it perfect for relaxed hiking in the summer and cross-country skiing in the winter. *Directions:* Coming from Füssen, take the first left as you enter the village (Aufmberg). You will find the Pension Heim on the right-hand side.

PENSION HEIM
Owner: Bettina Willer-Heim
Aufmberg 8, 87637 Seeg, Germany
Tel: (08364) 258, Fax: (08364) 1051
16 Rooms, Double: €74–€84
Open: Dec 25 to Nov 1, Credit cards: MC, VS
Region: Bayern, Michelin Map: 546
www.karenbrown.com/pensionheim.html

The Schloss Sommersdorf, conveniently located near the Romantic Road, is a picturesque small castle with all the ingredients of a proper fairy-tale: keep, turrets, tall towers, spiral staircases, stone bridges, ramparts, and even a moat. This is not a standard hotel at all, but rather the private home of Dr. Manfred von Crailsheim, who welcomes guests that come to stay for at least a week. You enter the castle through an outer guardhouse (a pink building topped by a whimsical clock), go over a moat, into a rose-filled courtyard, through a massive door, and up a spiral staircase. All of the guestrooms in the castle have an old-world, homelike ambiance. Most of the rooms are in the main house, but my favorite accommodations by far are the three suites in a beautifully renovated separate building. When making reservations, ask for one of these new apartments — they offer the most luxurious of the accommodations and make a good base to call "home" while exploring the Romantic Road. The presence of your host Manfred von Crailsheim makes this a very special place to stay. He lived in the castle as a boy and loves to share his home with guests. He's a natural host and an absolute delight. *Directions:* Traveling between Nürnberg and Heilbronn, take exit 52 at Ansbach. Drive south on the B13, then turn right towards Wassertrudingern and continue for 8 km to Sommersdorf. The castle is on the right. There is no sign to mark the entrance.

SCHLOSS SOMMERSDORF
Owner: Dr. Manfred von Crailsheim
91595 Sommersdorf, Germany
Tel: (09805) 91920, Fax: (09805) 919293
9 Rooms, Double: €70–€130*
*Breakfast not included: €10
Dinner by special request
Open: all year, Credit cards: none
Region: Bayern, Michelin Map: 546
www.karenbrown.com/schlosssommersdorf.html

Come dream a romantic dream or two at one of our favorite castles, the idyllic Schloss Spangenberg. High atop a hill with the town of Spangenberg spread at its feet far below, this once-proud fortress is now a gem of a castle hotel. All the romantic castle ingredients are here—a deep, grassy moat, a tower keep, and thick fortified walls. After surviving a seven-century history of battles, this fortification was badly damaged by British bombers in the closing days of World War II. The exterior has been painstakingly reconstructed and the interior converted into an inviting hotel. Gleaming polished floors lead you down the long hallways to extremely attractive, individually furnished guestrooms. Everything is meticulously maintained and the decor throughout is comfortable and welcoming—not in the least stiffly formal or hotel-like. Many of the guestrooms have a fabulous bird's-eye view over the dense forest to the charming town of Spangenberg nestled at the foot of the hill. My favorite room (number 16) has a romantic bay window—a perfect niche to sit and dream of knights and their ladies while gazing over the castle walls. If you are traveling with your family, you might wish to stay in the dear little gatekeeper's house with its doll-sized living room, sleeping loft, tiny bedroom, and two bathrooms. *Directions:* From Kassel travel 28 km south on the N83 and then 11 km east on the N487 to Spangenberg.

SCHLOSS SPANGENBERG
Owners: Angela & Wilfried Wichmann
34286 Spangenberg, Germany
Tel: (05663) 98930, Fax: (05663) 7567
26 Rooms, Double: €88–€183
Restaurant closed Sun evenings
Closed: 2 weeks in Jan, Credit cards: all major
Region: Hessen, Michelin Map: 543
www.karenbrown.com/spangenberg.html

At the core of Staufen's pedestrian-only district, the pretty façade of the Krone is sure to draw your attention. Its three stories are painted a pretty, soft, salmon wash and windows are hung with beige shutters and dressed with windowboxes. The front of the building is lavishly painted with a historic mural depicting the revolution of 1848. You can enter off the main street directly into the charming two-room restaurant with richly painted wainscoting, intimate seating, and pretty lace curtains with layers of country fabrics. A side entrance is also available for the convenience of hotel guests. The hotel has nine guestrooms, six of which enjoy their own private terrace. Housed within the old walls of this lovely building, guestrooms are simple yet quite modern in terms of conveniences. Furnishings are in light pine and beds are decked with fresh, plump, white duvets and large pillows. A separate room from the restaurant, found on the first floor, is a charming (non-smoking) breakfast room whose buffet is set with an assortment of mueslis, fruit juices, rolls, jams, and hot beverages. A delightful couple, the Lahns are personally involved with the hotel's operation: Herr Lahn is the chef and Frau Lahn oversees the welcome. *Directions:* Leave the A5 traveling between Freiburg and Basel at the Bad Krozingen exit, which is also signposted Staufen. In Staufen drive into the city center and pedestrian district.

GASTHAUS DIE KRONE
Owner: Kurt Lahn Family
Hauptstrasse 30, 79219 Staufen, Germany
Tel: (07633) 5840, Fax: (07633) 82903
9 Rooms, Double: €75
Open: all year, Credit cards: all major
Region: Baden-Württemberg, Michelin Map: 545
www.karenbrown.com/diekrone.html

As you enter the heart of the pedestrian district of Staufen, on the main street just up from the town square and characterful Rathaus, you find the Gasthof Kreuz Post, a handsome building painted a soft yellow with blue shutters and flowers at the windowboxes. The hotel was built in 1844 and is referred to as the Sixtus Schladerer das Gasthof Kreuz. Later it became an official postal stop as well, hence the addition of "Post" to the name. You cannot help noticing the details, such as the polished brass street sign with its darling little coach insignia. Tables are set at the front of the building under the yellow striped awning. Up a few steps, you enter the Gasthof, pretty with its soft-green wainscoting so typical of the region. On the second floor the Sixtus Schladerer Stube is decorated in subtle, rich tones of blue, and the adorable linen-capped lanterns can be seen at the windows. There are only five guestrooms, all beautifully appointed and decorated with pretty regional fabrics and attractive paintings. Rooms are spacious and thoughtfully equipped with all modern conveniences. This is a luxurious choice for such an enchanting village. Closed Wednesdays—Ruhetag! *Directions:* Leave the A5 traveling between Freiburg and Basel at the Bad Krozingen exit, which is also signposted Staufen. In Staufen drive into the city center and pedestrian district.

GASTHOF KREUZ POST
Owner: Zahn Family
Hauptstrasse 65, 79219 Staufen, Germany
Tel: (07633) 95320, Fax: (07633) 953232
5 Rooms, Double: €95–€100
Closed: 2 weeks in Jan and Wednesdays
Credit cards: MC, VS
Region: Baden-Württemberg, Michelin Map: 545
www.karenbrown.com/gasthofkreuzpost.html

The Romantik Hotel Traube, conveniently located across the expressway from the Stuttgart airport, is a beguiling little inn. Should you be flying into Stuttgart to visit the Mercedes factory and perhaps pick up a car, the Hotel Traube would be an excellent choice for a place to spend the night since the factory is only a short drive from the hotel. The contrast between this small inn and the modern industrial city of Stuttgart, only about a half-hour's drive away, is dramatic. Located on a small cobblestoned square just off a main street that cuts through this modern suburb and contained in a cluster of three timbered buildings, the Hotel Traube offers an escape from the more sterile surroundings. The most famous feature of the hotel is its restaurant, and the staff is understandably quite occupied with meal service at lunch and dinner. The food is exceptional and the decor worthy of multiple stars. Tables laid with soft-pink cloths, flowers, and candles are tucked under beams into cozy corners paneled in rich wood. If you'd prefer less formal dining, consider the neighboring casual restaurant, managed by the gracious son and daughter who maintain the same high standards set by their parents. The guestrooms, located far enough away from the street to be quiet, are attractive with traditional decor and comfortable beds topped with fluffy down comforters. *Directions:* Exit the A8 at the airport (flughaven) and travel 2 km East to Plieningen.

ROMANTIK HOTEL TRAUBE
Owner: Recknagel Family
Brabandgasse 2, Plieningen
70599 Stuttgart, Germany
Tel: (0711) 458920, Fax: (0711) 4589220
19 Rooms, Double: €105–€225
Restaurant closed Sun
Open: all year, Credit cards: MC, VS
Region: Baden-Württemberg, Michelin Map: 545
www.karenbrown.com/romantikhoteltraube.html

The Adler Bärental, a charming, small, family-owned hotel, is well located for sightseeing in the southern part of the Black Forest. The hotel, which is in the tiny hamlet of Bärental, sits directly on the main road between the towns of Titisee-Neustadt and Feldberg. The house, dating back to 1787, reflects its rich heritage both inside and out. The chalet-style exterior is most appealing with wood shingle siding, a hipped roof, and balconies laden with brightly colored flowers. The interior is country cozy with intimate dining rooms enhanced by beamed ceilings, paneled walls, nostalgic antique tile stove, sweet chandeliers, fresh flowers, crisp linens adorning wood dining tables, pretty curtains, and a cute bar. For a simple, modestly priced hotel, the food is amazingly outstanding. The popularity of the kitchen is evident since the tables are filled each night, not only with guests of the hotel, but also with locals. A staircase leads up to the guest rooms. There are three types of rooms: suites with a sitting room and separate bedroom, maisonettes with a balcony above and a sitting room below, and double rooms. Of the three, I prefer the double bedrooms. All of the rooms are named and have floral paintings to identify them. My favorite room, Akelei (room 4), is especially spacious, has a canopy bed, and a very large bathroom. *Directions:* Located 6 kilometers east of Feldberg on the road to Titisee.

HOTEL ADLER BÄRENTAL
Owners: Sabine & Walter Wimmer
Feldbergstrasse 4, Bärental, Feldberg
79868 Titisee, Germany
Tel: (07655) 933933, Fax: (07655) 930521
16 rooms, Double: €105–€130
Open: all year, Credit cards: MC,VS
Region: Baden-Württemberg, Michelin Map: 545
www.karenbrown.com/hoteladler.html

We fell in love at first sight when we discovered the Alemannenhof—a darling, wood-shingled hotel in the Black Forest that is tucked on a wooded hillside directly above the lake Titisee. Thinking the hotel couldn't possibly be as cute inside as out, we went in and were amazed and delighted to find the interior to be a dream—every room decorated to perfection in a charming, cozy, country style. The dining room is especially adorable with polished wood floors, paneled walls and ceiling, tables surrounded by carved wooden chairs, colorful tablecloths, pretty fabric-covered hanging lamps, and white ruffled curtains accenting casement windows. The guestrooms are spacious and nicely decorated with plump, down duvets on comfortable bed. The choice bedrooms are those with balconies that look out directly to the lake. Although the hotel appears to be centuries old, it was built in 1983 by the Drubba family. They still own the property but management is now in the capable hands of their son. The Drubba family also operates the boat concession in Titisee, and the boat that circles the lake stops at the hotel's pier to pick up guests. There is an indoor swimming pool; plus for guests who want prefer to be out of doors, a path leads down through the trees to a secreted wooden sun deck that overlooks the lake. The Alemannenhof truly is a gem, and happily, a great value. *Directions:* On the west side of the lake Titisee.

ALEMANNENHOF
Owner: Drubba Family
Bruderhalde 21, Hinterzarten am Titisee
79815 Titisee, Germany
Tel: (07652) 91180, Fax: (07652) 705
22 rooms, Double: €108–€170
Open: all year, Credit cards: all major
Region: Baden-Württemberg, Michelin Map: 545
www.karenbrown.com/alemannenhof.html

If you are looking for a hotel in the Black Forest offering all the amenities of a deluxe resort, Treschers Schwarzwald Hotel is a real winner. In addition to being in the Black Forest, the hotel has the advantage of sitting directly on the shore of the pretty Titisee. The cute town of Titisee-Neustadt (a popular tourist destination with its lakeside promenade, restaurants, and shops) is just steps away. Although the property has expanded over the years from a simple lakeside chalet into a moderately large, sophisticated hotel, it still retains its old-world charm and genuine warmth of welcome. The appeal of the chalet-style hotel is set from the first moment you approach; the exterior is made of darkened-with-age wood that is accented by windows framed with green shutters. Window boxes filled with colorful flowers add to the happy scene. The décor within continues to reflect the ambiance of a country home with fine furnishings, wood paneling, lovely fabrics, fresh flowers, and antique accents. There is a bright and cheerful breakfast room overlooking the lake; but my favorite place to dine is the romantic, ever so cozy, dining room that is paneled in antique wood. The guestrooms are elegantly furnished and many have balconies that face the lake. The hotel also offers a very attractive spa with many types of beauty treatments available. *Directions:* Located in the heart of town, directly on the lake.

TRESCHERS SCHWARZWALD HOTEL AM SEE
Owner: Hansjörg Trescher Family
Seestrasse 10, 79822 Titisee, Germany
Tel: (07651) 8050, Fax: (07651) 8116
84 Rooms, Double: €130–€310
Open: all year, Credit cards: all major
Region: Baden-Württemberg, Michelin Map: 545
www.karenbrown.com/treschershotel.html

The appeal of the Parkhotel Wehrle, a sentimentally favorite hotel, has always in large part been due to the warmth of welcome, professionalism, and charm. This is one of the friendliest, best-run small hotels in the country, and has, in fact, received recognition for the excellence of its restaurant. You can easily find this appealing, ivy-covered, yellow-stone inn, as it occupies a prime corner position on the main street of Triberg. There are several parts to the hotel. The reception counter, beautifully decorated dining rooms, and antique-filled lounges are in the original inn, as are some of the guestrooms. This main house is my first choice for accommodation because the rooms have such a comfortable, homey ambiance and old-world charm. There are also two additional houses nestled in the garden with comfortable accommodations but more modern in terms of decor and style. Cuckoo clocks and Triberg's location at the heart of the scenic Black Forest trails are the initial draw to this popular town but the Parkhotel Wehrle is the reason to return. *Directions:* 51 km northeast of Freiburg. Traveling the A81 between Stuttgart and Singen, exit at Villingen and drive to Triberg on the B33, in the direction of Offenburg.

PARKHOTEL WEHRLE
Owner: Gerald Henningsen
Gartenstrasse 24, 78094 Triberg, Germany
Tel: (07722) 86020, Fax: (07722) 860290
52 Rooms, Double: €129–€190
Open: all year, Credit cards: all major
Region: Baden-Württemberg, Michelin Map: 545
www.karenbrown.com/parkhotelwehrle.html

Nicknamed the "White Villa in Green" this is a lovely hotel, spotlessly maintained and very professionally managed, set on a hill a good 15-minute walk from the heart of Trier. Although it seemed at first glance to be a fairly standard hotel, once we stayed there we realized that it had a very special charm and the service and welcome were very professional yet warm from the moment we arrived. Rooms, named for cities, are modern in appointments and have standard hotel decor. Our room had excellent lighting, a comfortable work area for myself and a lounge area for my husband, a television with English and American channels, and quiet comfort, even though at breakfast all the tables were taken with both businessmen and families. Monday through Thursday this is a businessman's hotel (this doesn't affect the ambiance as conferences aren't held here) and has a limited but good dinner menu. Breakfast every day is a gourmet repast with orange juice, vitamin juice, an assortment of teas, coffee, yogurt, granolas, meats, fish, cheeses, breads, and a choice of eggs. The hotel also has a wonderful, large, indoor pool and nice sauna rooms for guests' use. Trier is one of Germany's oldest cities, though it appears modern, and makes a wonderful beginning for a tour of the Mosel River Valley. *Directions:* Ask for detailed printed directions when making reservations. The hotel is located within walking distance of town.

HOTEL VILLA HÜGEL
Owner: Schütt Family
Bernhardstrasse 14, 54295 Trier, Germany
Tel: (0651) 937100 or (0651) 33066, Fax: (0651) 37958
35 Rooms, Double: €99–€145
Meals for guests (Mon-Thur)
Open: all year, Credit cards: all major
Region: Mosel, Michelin Map: 543
www.karenbrown.com/villahuegel.html

The exterior of the Romantik Hotel Menzhausen is a 16th-century dazzler with a half-timbered façade and painted decorations. Found on the pedestrian main street of this attractive town, the Hotel Menzhausen has been offering travelers lodging for over 400 years. The hotel has expanded by adding a wing of rooms behind the original building connected to it by a covered walkway over a cobbled lane. The restaurants are full of country charm and are in keeping with the historic core of the hotel. Herr Höfs, the manager, takes special pride is his wine cellar, and he will be happy to show you around. It is great fun to follow him down the low, narrow, dark, brick passage into the cellars lined with neat rows of bottles. The decor of the bedrooms improves as you move from the front of the hotel to the back: rooms in the old building are somewhat dated but behind them you find small, smart bedrooms. In the garden wing, the stylish rooms are larger and have peaceful views of the pretty garden. The garden wing also contains the delightful breakfast room whose arched windows overlook the luxurious indoor swimming pool. Uslar features on the Deutsche Marchen Strasse or Fairy-Tale Route. The hotel has lots of off-street parking and a parking garage. *Directions:* Located 62 km north of Kassel. Traveling south from Hannover, exit the A7 at Nörten-Hardenberg and take the B241 to Uslar.

ROMANTISCHES HOTEL MENZHAUSEN
Manager: Sigfried Höfs
Langestrasse 12, 37170 Uslar, Germany
Tel: (05571) 92230, Fax: (05571) 922330
40 Rooms, Double: €80–€150
Open: all year, Credit cards: all major
Region: Niedersachsen, Michelin Map: 541
www.karenbrown.com/menzhausen.html

The little towns along the River Main, upstream from Würzburg, produce some of Germany's most delightful, dry, white wines. One of the most picturesque towns is Volkach with its medieval walls, colorful town hall, and pretty houses. Almost opposite the town hall on the town's main street, you find the exceptionally charming, 600-year-old Zur Schwane, an inn and winery. Relax in its sheltered, cobbled courtyard and sample their wines and then enjoy dinner in one of the cozy, adorable restaurants with their old-fashioned tables and chairs set beneath low, paneled ceilings. The inn has been extended to the rear and some delightful bedrooms are found in this new wing, which has half-paneled walls and ceilings and wood furniture to replicate the mood of the restaurants. Some of the guestrooms exude a quiet elegance with light wood paneling enhanced by pretty pastel-colored fabrics. An apartment has a sitting room with ceramic stove, tables, and chairs, and a spacious bedroom. The Pfaff family produce their own wine and are happy to take those with an interest in wine production on a tour of their vast cellars. Eva Pfaff-Düker is a winetaster and can arrange for a tasting in the ancient barrel-vaulted cellar filled with oak wine casks (a special cask was made to celebrate the birth of her son Julius in 1992). *Directions:* From Würzburg travel 10 km north on the N1 and after crossing the A7, travel 18 km east to Volkach.

ROMANTIK HOTEL ZUR SCHWANE
Owner: Eva Pfaff-Düker
Hauptstrasse 12, 97332 Volkach, Germany
Tel: (09381) 80660, Fax: (09381) 806666
25 Rooms, Double: €90–€198
Restaurant closed Mon
Closed: Dec 23-31, Credit cards: all major
Region: Bayern, Michelin Map: 546
www.karenbrown.com/zurschwane.html

Schlosshotel Waldeck has a stunning hilltop location overlooking the Edersee. If you arrive at midday, you might be surprised to see so many cars, but most of these belong to the day tourists who have come to visit the museum located in one wing of the castle. (Be sure to visit the museum—especially the foyer where life-size figures depict peasant life 1,000 years ago.) As you enter the hotel, you find a large room with stone walls. The reception counter is to the left and sitting areas are tucked into cozy niches formed by the vaulted ceiling. Look carefully and you will see above the reception desk the chimney for the giant fireplace that warmed the room in days gone by. Although the castle look is dominant, the hotel exudes a sleek, sophisticated air and offers all the amenities of a modern hotel with three dining rooms, conference rooms, banquet facilities, outdoor terraces for dining, and an indoor swimming pool nestled within stone walls with a skylight overhead. Some of the guestrooms are in the castle; others are in an impressive new wing. The rooms, which have a modern-hotel decor, are similar, but my preference is for staying in the old castle. I especially like number 407, a spacious room with large windows that give you a bird's-eye view of the evening sun setting over the lake. *Directions:* 57 km southwest of Kassel. Take the 251 east of Kassel and go 8 km south on the 485 at Sachsenhausen to Waldeck.

SCHLOSSHOTEL WALDECK
Owner: Karel F. Isenberg
34513 Waldeck am Edersee, Germany
Tel: (05623) 5890, Fax: (05623) 589289
40 Rooms, Double: €146–€207
Closed: Jan 5 to mid-Feb, Credit cards: all major
Region: Hessen, Michelin Map: 543
www.karenbrown.com/waldeck.html

The main claim to fame of the Hotel Alte Post is its location in the very heart of Wangen, one of Germany's colorful medieval villages. The Alte Post was built in 1409 as a posting station and is now one of the oldest hotels in Germany. In days gone by horses were stabled below the existing building and exchanged to cover the next postal journey. You can easily spot the hotel (a boxy, three-story building with small gabled windows peeking out from a steeply pitched gray roof) as it sits in the center of town, opening onto a cobblestoned, pedestrian-only square. Rooms on the first level are devoted to the hotel's restaurants. As in many German hotels, the dining rooms have more personality than the guestrooms whose decor varies from comfortable contemporary to traditional. From the third-floor guestrooms (tucked under beamed ceilings) you can hear the peal of the nearby church bells. *Directions:* From Bregenz on the eastern tip of Lake Constance (Bodensee) travel north 15 km on the A96 to exit 5 and then travel 4 km south to Wangen on N32.

ROMANTIK HOTEL ALTE POST
Owner: Gisela Veile
Postplatz 2, 88239 Wangen, Germany
Tel: (07522) 97560, Fax: (07522) 22604
19 Rooms, Double: €95–€140
Restaurant closed for lunch & Sun
Open: all year, Credit cards: all major
Region: Baden-Württemberg, Michelin Maps: 545, 546
www.karenbrown.com/altepost.html

Weimar is a magical city where you can still hear the haunting melodies of Bach and Liszt, who long ago called Weimar home. The town has so many cultural traditions that it prompted Germany's democrats to put Weimar's name on the new republic in 1919. The Hotel Elephant occupies a prize-winning location within the old town. It faces the large market square, which is enclosed by beautifully preserved medieval buildings, including a stunning, timbered, 16th-century Rathaus—one of Germany's finest. Although the hotel has been reconstructed, its history dates back hundreds of years and it lists many famous guests, such as Johann Sebastian Bach, Franz Liszt, Richard Wagner, and Lilly Palmer. The lobby has a modern-hotel look with gray marble floor, black leather sofas, and black accent tables. There are two restaurants, my favorite being the Elephantenkeller, a pub-like restaurant serving regional specialties. A curved stairway with polished brass handrails leads to the floors above. All of the guestrooms have private bathrooms, mini-bars, and televisions. Instead of an old-world ambiance, the mood is modern with a no-frills, masculine style. *Directions:* Weimar is located 6 km to the north of the A4, 132 km west of Chemnitz and 22 km east of Erfurt. The hotel is at the city center on the market place.

HOTEL ELEPHANT
Manager: Paul J. Kernatsch
Markt 19, 99423 Weimar, Germany
Tel: (03643) 8020, Fax: (03643) 802610
99 Rooms, Double: €141–€455*
*Breakfast not included: €18
Open: all year, Credit cards: all major
Region: Thüringen, Michelin Map: 546
www.karenbrown.com/hotelelephant.html

Nestled in a park of beech, oak, chestnut and fruit trees, the Romantik Hotel Dorotheenhof is a jewel. Just 3 kilometers north of Weimar, it is easily accessible by car or bus (a bus stops nearby every 12 minutes). This region of Thüringen is rich in fascinating sights. The property originally supplied fruits and vegetables for Tiefurt Castle. In 1902 Captain von Kalchkreuth built a splendid mansion here naming it for his wife, Dorotheen. In the mid-1990s, the property was lovingly restored by your gracious hosts, Sabine and Matthias Barleben, who have added the amenities and quality of a top-notch hotel. The exterior is painted a pastel butter-yellow with white trim and a red-tiled roof. In front, a lawn slopes gently downward with sitting areas strategically placed to capture the idyllic view. Inside, sunlight streams through the windows, highlighting creamy white walls. A fresh country-style décor is found throughout the cozy lounges, dining rooms, and guestrooms with light wood furniture, attractive fabrics, fresh flowers, and antique accents. In the kitchen, the chef uses freshly picked vegetables and herbs from the hotel's garden. Perhaps most important, the hotel staff is professional yet extremely friendly and attentive. *Directions:* From A4, take West Weimar/Bad Berka exit 48 toward Weimar. At the second stoplight, turn right toward Weimar. Continue straight for 9 km. After the roundabout and the Aral station, there are signs to the hotel.

☕ 🏊 💳 ☎ 🚻 🏋 🍷 P 🍴 🚭 🌸 🖼 ⚓ 🔨 🏃 🐎

ROMANTIK HOTEL DOROTHEENHOF WEIMAR New
Owners: Sabine & Matthias Barleben
Dorotheenhof 1, D-99427 Weimar, Germany
Tel: (03643) 4590, Fax: (03643) 459200
60 Rooms, Double: €102–€150
Open: all year, Credit cards: all major
Region: Thüringen, Michelin Map: 546
www.karenbrown.com/dorotheenhof.html

The Schloss Weitenburg, dating back to the 11th century, is superbly positioned in the rolling, wooded hills south of Stuttgart. The castle has been in the von Rassler family since 1720 and the present Baron von Rassler still lives there. Once within the castle, you are thrust back to days gone by: small windows looking out through more than one-meter-thick walls, massive stone floors, beamed ceilings, hunting trophies, and ancestors watching your every move from portraits on the walls. The dining room was formerly the kitchen, as evidenced by the enormous metal flue in the ceiling where the smoke from the stove escaped. The bedrooms are scattered throughout the maze of hallways. Some are quite mediocre in decor with modern furnishings, but others have a marvelous antique flair. I especially like number 104, a paneled corner room with antique furniture and an exquisite panorama of rolling forest and the meandering Neckar River. Other favorites are numbers 105 and 110, both bright and cheerful rooms overlooking the front courtyard. If twin beds appeal, number 102 stands out for its gorgeous views. An old-fashioned, enclosed swimming pool lies just over a covered footbridge from the castle. Note: Weitenburg is not on most maps, but is easy to find. *Directions:* Driving south from Stuttgart on A81, take the Rottenburg exit then turn right to Ergenzingen. Travel through town and follow the white "Schloss Weitenburg" signs to the castle.

HOTEL SCHLOSS WEITENBURG
Owner: Freiherr von Rassler
72181 Weitenburg, Germany
Tel: (07457) 9330, Fax: (07457) 933100
34 Rooms, Double: €100–€152
Closed: Dec 21 to 25, Credit cards: MC, VS
Region: Baden-Württemberg, Michelin Map: 545
www.karenbrown.com/schlossweitenburg.html

Set at the foot of the Harz Mountains, Wernigerode is a beautiful town of timber-framed houses with an elaborately decorated, twin-spired town hall. On the pedestrian cobbled market square sits the Hotel Weisser Hirsch, where you find a brand-spanking-new hotel behind its ancient, timbered façade. From the marketplace you enter directly into the lovely, old-world dining room all decked out in bleached oak. Center stage sits a large buffet whose tempting breakfast fare is replaced at lunchtime with a splendid array of salads. Reception lies at the back of the hotel, for guests usually arrive here via the elevator from the underground parking garage. All the bedrooms are decorated similarly in a fashionable, modern style with light-wood fitted furniture, soft pastel decor, and matching drapes and chairs. Each room is accompanied by a smart, white-tiled shower room with red accent tiles. If you prefer peace and quiet, request a back room but for views request a room overlooking the Marktplatz where a produce market is held every Tuesday and Friday. Set off on foot to explore the cobbled streets full of very nice shops and delightful cafés. A little tractor-train will take you through the suburbs and up the hill to the castle, which is more a grand, 19th-century home than a fortification. *Directions:* 88 km south of Braunschweig. Take the A395 south from Braunschweig, then exit 15 north of Bad Harzburg and travel 21 km east to Wernigerode.

HOTEL WEISSER HIRSCH
Owner: Jörg Wieland Family
Marktplatz 5, 38855 Wernigerode, Germany
Tel: (03943) 602020, Fax: (03943) 633139
54 Rooms, Double: €112–€145
Open: all year, Credit cards: all major
Region: Sachsen-Anhalt, Michelin Map: 541
www.karenbrown.com/weisserhirsch.html

Just a two-hour drive north of Berlin, the Romantik Hotel Borchard's Rookhus is tucked in the heart of the Müritz National Park, an idyllic region with pristine forests dotted with lakes. When the Borchard family bought the property, it had been abandoned for years after serving as a hostel during the communist regime. Although it was in poor condition, the setting on the edge of the lake was idyllic. The Borcard family poured labor and love into the transformation. Alexander is an excellent chef, his father a builder, his wife an architect, and his mother great with decorating. With this winning team, the Romantik Hotel Borchard's Rookhus became a reality. Though not real fancy, the hotel is charming and exudes warmth. It overlooks a lake, the Grossen Labussee. In front a lawn gently rolls down to the water's edge where there is a small swimming beach and several boats tied up at the dock. The guestrooms are all prettily decorated with a country flair. There are two restaurants: the "Fürst Nikolaus" an outstanding gourmet restaurant with a glassed-in terrace overlooking the lake, and "Storchennest" an adorable casual restaurant with whimsical country accents. There is a third special dining opportunity sometimes in summer, Alexander prepares a romantic gourmet meal for guests on the houseboat as it plies the placid lake. *Directions:* From Berlin, take A24 North and exit A19 at Robel. Turn right on B198 to Wesenberg and follow signs.

ROMANTIK BORCHARD'S ROOKHUS AM SEE New
Owners: Andrea & Alex Borchard
Am Grossen Labussee 12
17255 Wesenberg, Germany
Tel: (039832) 500, Fax: (039832) 50100
45 Rooms, Double: €90–€150
Open: all year, Credit cards: all major
Region: Mecklenburger Seenplatte, Michelin Map: 542
www.karenbrown.com/borchardsrookhus.html

If you get homesick for the beloved pet you left at home, a stay at the Villa Kunterbunt is the perfect solution. This hotel is not only pet-friendly, but almost everyone arrives with pet on leash! This pretty yellow villa with blue trim and steeply pitched red-tile roof, fronts directly on the Grosser Labussee, a pristine lake in the beautiful Müritz National Park. The property is owned by the same Borchard family that operates the lovely Romantik Hotel Borchard's Rookhus, located a few kilometers down the road. This is really a family operation. Alex manages the Rookhus and his mother, Claudia, and sister, Alice, run the much simpler, pensione-like Villa Kunterbunt which has eight sweetly decorated guestrooms. In addition to being a hotel, the Villa also features a wellness center with therapy rooms and a huge indoor swimming pool with a wall of glass looking out to the lake. While training to become a therapist, Alice's instructor suggested that she also learn to treat dogs, which was his specialty. Today, most guests arrive with their canine and can have their massage with the pet sighing with contentment as he or she also enjoys a massage beside them on a mat on the floor. Of course, you do not need to have your pet with you to thoroughly enjoy this sweet small hotel. *Directions:* When you arrive in Wesenberg, follow signs to the Romantik Hotel Borchard's Rookhus. The Villa Kunterbunt is about 2 km further down the road.

VILLA KUNTERBUNT   *New*
Owners: Borchard Family
Am Grossen Labussee, Dorsfstrasse 50
17255 Wesenberg, Germany
Tel: (039832) 28100, Fax: (039832) 281022
8 Rooms, Double: €75–€110
Open: all year, Credit cards: MC,VS
Region: Mecklenburger Seenplatte, Michelin Map: 542
www.karenbrown.com/villakunterbunt.html

There are many restaurants on Germany's lovely Isle of Sylt and among the finest is the well-known Restaurant Jörg Müller. The restaurant, which has earned a coveted Michelin star, also offers—luckily for the gourmet traveler—pretty guestrooms for overnight guests. In keeping with the fairy-tale quality of most of the houses on the island, the Restaurant Jörg Müller is brimming with charm. The appealing, red-brick house with thick thatched roof is made even lovelier by a lacing of climbing roses. A small lawn and garden in front complete the attractive picture. Inside, there is a sitting area for guests waiting for dinner. On the left are two subdued, pastel-colored dining rooms where French cuisine is served. To the right of the reception is the most enchanting dining room, decorated entirely in white, blue, and light-toned woods. The walls are covered in white tiles whose blandness is relieved by interspersing tiles with blue designs, which seem Dutch in origin. The ceiling is paneled in a light wood, and the chairs and floor are also of light wood. In this extraordinarily fresh and pretty room, regional specialties are served. Jörg Müller, the owner, is also the chef and dining at his restaurant is a memorable occasion. *Directions:* Take the train from the mainland to the Island of Sylt. You can drive onto the train and stay in your car during the trip. This restaurant-hotel is located on the road to Rantum.

RESTAURANT JÖRG MÜLLER
Owner: Jörg Müller
Süderstrasse 8, Sylt
25980 Westerland, Germany
Tel: (04651) 27788, Fax: (04651) 201471
22 Rooms, Double: €180–€295
Restaurant closed Mon
Closed: Jan 6 to Feb 15, Credit cards: all major
Region: Schleswig-Holstein, Michelin Map: 541
www.karenbrown.com/joergmueller.html

Sylt, a tiny island in the north of Germany, is connected to the mainland by a narrow thread of land negotiable only by train. Although most of the island embraces a tranquil scene of windswept sand dunes and picture-perfect thatched cottages, the principal town of Westerland bustles with activity. In the midst of this touristy town, the Hotel Stadt Hamburg is an absolute oasis of charm and tranquility. The hotel, in the Hentzschel family for three generations, dates back to 1869. You will be enchanted from the moment you walk into the exquisite lounge where rich-red walls create the perfect background for comfortable sofas and chairs grouped in intimate settings. Fine English antiques abound, including many grandfather clocks, gorgeous tables, and chests whose woods gleam with the patina of age. The lounge is so homelike, so inviting, that guests must almost welcome dreary weather for an excuse to settle into a cozy corner with a good book. The guestrooms, some located in the original hotel and others in a new wing, are exquisitely furnished in an English style. This elegant hotel happily maintains the warmth and hospitality of a small inn, and its richness of beauty and elegance truly impressed me— this is definitely the most beautiful hotel on the island, if not in all of Germany. *Directions:* Take the train from the mainland to the Island of Sylt (160 km northwest of Hamburg). The Stadt Hamburg is east of Westerland's waterfront.

HOTEL STADT HAMBURG
Owner: Harald Hentzschel
Strandstrasse 2, Sylt
25980 Westerland, Germany
Tel: (04651) 8580, Fax: (04651) 858220
72 Rooms, Double: €170–€360
Open: all year, Credit cards: all major
Relais & Chateaux
Region: Schleswig-Holstein, Michelin Map: 541
www.karenbrown.com/stadthamburg.html

Herrmann's Romantik Posthotel, found on the main square of Wirsberg, a village just off the autobahn north of Bayreuth, was once a posting station. Although part of the hotel appears modern, the reception area and hallway are set under heavy beams, and there is a cozy little room tucked back into a corner with leaded-glass windows where breakfast is served. For lunch or evening meals the hotel's Patrizier Salon is an elegantly set restaurant; while the Jagerstube, the oldest part of the old Posthotel, affords an environment for a more casual rendezvous, beer, or supper. For overnight guests, the Herrmann family's wish is to see to all their comforts and create an atmosphere that will tempt them to linger: "Gastlichkeit mit Herz" (hospitality with heart). The comfortable bedrooms range in decor from comfortable modern to an attractive traditional, and a selection of rooms is renovated with each year. Also available to hotel guests is the fitness center. The pool is styled after a Roman bath, and the walls of the sauna, fitness room, solarium, and massage room are covered with faux rock, vines, and a garden mural. Werner and Melitta are the fifth generation of the Herrmann family to welcome guests at the Romantik Posthotel. *Directions:* 100 km north of Nuremberg. Take exit 39 (Himmelkron/Bad Berneck) off the A9 and then the B303 towards Neuenmarkt/ Wirsberg. Turn right into Wirsberg—the hotel is on the main square.

HERRMANN'S ROMANTIK POSTHOTEL
Owner: Herrmann Family
Marktplatz 11, 95339 Wirsberg, Germany
Tel: (09227) 2080, Fax: (09227) 5860
47 Rooms, Double: €120–€230
Open: all year, Credit cards: all major
Region: Bayern, Michelin Map: 541
www.karenbrown.com/herrmannsromantikposthotel.html

It is difficult to pinpoint the best feature of the Gasthof Hecht because you must choose between its country charm; wonderfully gracious, friendly hosts; and extremely reasonable rates. The 300-year-old gasthof is located on the picturesque pedestrian main street of Wolfach, where its half-timbered façade, overflowing with geraniums, has long been a welcome sight for travelers. The ground floor contains two dining rooms with pewter and pottery collections, beamed ceilings, wood-paneled walls, and fresh flower bouquets. When I was visiting, a friendly neighborhood gathering occupied the tables and chairs that spill over into the cobblestoned street. Leave your diet at home, as traditional, home-style meals are served here, including pork and veal dishes, plenty of vegetables, and mouthwatering tortes for dessert. Eberhard Sattler is responsible for the kitchen, and he studied and apprenticed elsewhere before returning with his charming family to home base. Renate, your lovely, gracious hostess, has redecorated all the guestrooms beautifully in an ultra-modern style. I love the traditional and old, yet the clean lines and modern fixtures and appointments of the guestrooms are attractive and luxurious in comfort. *Directions:* 57 km northeast of Freiburg. Take the N294 48 km north from Freiburg to where it jogs east at Haslach. Drive 8 km to Hausach and then 4 km on the N294 to Wolfach. The hotel is at the heart of this small town.

🍷 💳 ☎ P ⑁

GASTHOF HECHT
Owners: Renate & Eberhard Sattler
Hauptstrasse 51, 77709 Wolfach, Germany
Tel: (07834) 538, Fax: (07834) 47223
17 Rooms, Double: €70–€88
Restaurant closed Mon & Tues
Closed: Jan, Credit cards: all major
Region: Baden-Württemberg, Michelin Map: 545
www.karenbrown.com/gasthofhecht.html

Germany is full of appealing walled villages, one of which is the ever-so-tiny village of Wolframs-Eschenbach in the Romantic Road region, tucked off the beaten path and seldom discovered by tourists. There are two entrances to this medieval jewel, both through old watchtowers. The village's perimeter is formed by old stone walls, and the main street is lined with colorful, half-timbered houses. One of the prettiest of these houses is the Alte Vogtei, which was welcoming guests 100 years before Christopher Columbus discovered America. Its picturesque façade features an intricate pattern of timbered wood, white stucco, green shutters, and geraniums spilling from the windowboxes. The claim to fame of this small hotel is its restaurant, attracting guests from near and far. There are several intimate dining rooms, each brimming with charm. The food is excellent and reasonably priced. Upstairs in the old section of the inn is the best room, the Bridal Suite, with pretty painted furniture and a canopy bed. A corridor leads to the newer section of the hotel where the bedrooms are more motel-like and less charming. If the Bridal Suite is not available, ask for number 30, a large room decorated in a pleasant, contemporary style. *Directions:* Take the N14 southwest from Nürnberg to Ansbach for 38 km and travel 10 km southeast on N13 to Leidendorf. Drive east on N445 to Wolframs-Eschenbach.

ALTE VOGTEI
Owners: Monika & Georg Dörr
Hauptstrasse 21
91639 Wolframs-Eschenbach, Germany
Tel: (09875) 97000, Fax: (09875) 970070
18 Rooms, Double: €58–€65
Restaurant closed Mon
Closed: Christmas, Credit cards: MC, VS
Region: Bayern, Michelin Map: 546
www.karenbrown.com/altevogtei.html

Index

L

M

KAREN BROWN wrote her first travel guide in 1976. Her personalized travel series has grown to 17 titles, which Karen and her small staff work diligently to keep updated. Karen, her husband, Rick, and their children, Alexandra and Richard, live in Moss Beach, a small town on the coast south of San Francisco. They settled here in 1991 when they opened Seal Cove Inn. Karen is frequently traveling but when she is home, in her role as innkeeper, enjoys welcoming Karen Brown readers.

CLARE BROWN was a travel consultant for many years, specializing in planning itineraries to Europe using charming small hotels in the countryside. The focus of her job remains unchanged, but now her expertise is available to a larger audience—the readers of her daughter Karen's country inn guides. When Clare and her husband, Bill, are not traveling, they live either in Hillsborough, California, or at their home in Vail, Colorado, where family and friends frequently join them for skiing.

JUNE EVELEIGH BROWN'S love of travel was inspired by the *National Geographic* magazines that she read as a girl in her dentist's office—so far she has visited over 40 countries. June hails from Sheffield, England and lived in Zambia and Canada before moving to northern California where she lives in San Mateo with her husband, Tony, their daughter Clare, their two German Shepherds, and a Siamese cat.

JANN POLLARD, the artist responsible for the beautiful painting on the cover of this guide, has studied art since childhood, and is well known for her outstanding impressionistic-style watercolors, which she has exhibited in numerous juried shows, winning many awards. Jann travels frequently to Europe (using Karen Brown's Guides) where she loves to paint historical buildings. Jann's original paintings are represented through The Gallery, Burlingame, CA, 650-347-9392 or www.thegalleryart.net. Fine-art giclée prints of the cover paintings are also available at www.karenbrown.com.

BARBARA MACLURCAN TAPP, the talented artist who produces all of the hotel sketches and delightful illustrations in this guide, was raised in Sydney, Australia where she studied interior design. Although Barbara continues with architectural rendering and watercolor painting, she devotes much of her time to illustrating the Karen Brown guides. Barbara lives in Kensington, California, with her husband, Richard, and is Mum to Jono, Alex and Georgia.

Karen Brown Presents Her Own Special Hideaways

Karen Brown's Seal Cove Inn

Spectacularly set amongst wildflowers and bordered by cypress trees, Seal Cove Inn (Karen's second home) looks out to the distant ocean. Each room has a fireplace, cozy sitting area, and a view of the sea. Located on the coast, 35 minutes south of San Francisco.

Seal Cove Inn, Moss Beach, California
toll free telephone: (800) 995-9987
www.sealcoveinn.com

Karen Brown's Dolphin Cove Inn

Hugging a steep hillside overlooking the sparkling deep-blue bay of Manzanillo, Dolphin Cove Inn offers guests outstanding value. Each room has either a terrace or a balcony, and a breathtaking view of the sea. Located on the Pacific Coast of Mexico.

Dolphin Cove Inn, Manzanillo, Mexico
toll free telephone: (888) 497-4138
www.dolphincoveinn.com